ANTILLES

(DUTCH CARIBBEAN)

INVESTMENT AND BUSINESS GUIDE

VOLUME 2

BUSINESS, INVESTMENT OPPORTUNITIES AND INCENTIVES

International Business Publications, USA
Washington DC, USA - Antilles

ANTILLES

INVESTMENT AND BUSINESS GUIDE

VOLUME 2 BUSINESS, INVESTMENT OPPORTUNITIES AND INCENTIVES

UPDATED ANNUALLY

Cover Design: International Business Publications, USA

We express our sincere gratitude to all government agencies and international organizations which provided information and other materials for this guide

2016 Edition Updated Reprint International Business Publications, USA
ISBN 1-5775-1881-0

This guide provides basic information for starting or/and conducting business in the country. The extraordinary volume of materials covering the topic, prevents us from placing all these materials in this guide. For more detailed information on issues related to any specific investment and business activity in the country, please contact Global Investment Center, USA

Please acquire the list of our business intelligence and marketing reports and other business publications. We constantly update and expand our business intelligence and marketing materials. Please contact the center for the updated list of reports on over 200 countries.

in the USA: **Global Investment Center, USA.**
P.O.Box 15343, Washington, DC 20003
Phone: (202) 546-2103, Fax: (202) 546-3275, E-mail: rusric@erols.com

For additional analytical, marketing and other information please contact Global Investment Center, USA

Printed in the USA

ANTILLES

(DUTCH CARIBBEAN)

INVESTMENT AND BUSINESS GUIDE

VOLUME 2

BUSINESS, INVESTMENT OPPORTUNITIES AND INCENTIVES

TABLE OF CONTENTS

STRATEGIC AND DEVELOPMENT PROFILES

The **Dutch Caribbean** are the six island countries and municipalities of the Kingdom of the Netherlands that are located in the Caribbean – **Aruba**, **Curaçao** (including the islet of *Klein Curaçao*, "Little Curaçao"), **Sint Maarten** (comprising only the southern half of the island of Saint Martin), **Bonaire** (including the islet of *Klein Bonaire*, "Little Bonaire"), **Sint Eustatius** and **Saba** – regardless of their legal status in Dutch law. The term may sometimes also be used interchangeably with the term Caribbean Netherlands to refer to just three of those islands (Bonaire, Sint Eustatius and Saba) which are special municipalities of the Netherlands proper.

All of the islands in the Dutch Caribbean were, at some point in their history, part of the constituent country of the Netherlands Antilles and its predecessor, the colony of Curaçao and its dependencies. By contrast, the former Dutch colony of Suriname was not considered to be part of Dutch Caribbean, although it was relatively close by on the continent of South America.

ARUBA

Capital and largest city	Oranjestad 12°31′N 70°2′W12.517°N 70.033°W
Official languages	• Dutch • Papiamento
Religion	81% Roman Catholic
Demonym	Aruban
Sovereign state	Kingdom of the Netherlands
Government	Unitary parliamentary representative democracy under constitutional monarchy
• Monarch	Willem-Alexander
• Governor	Fredis Refunjol
• Prime Minister	Mike Eman
Legislature	Estates of Aruba
Autonomy from the Netherlands Antilles	
• Date	18 March 1986
Area	
• Total	178.91 km^2 69.08 sq mi
• Water (%)	negligible
Population	
• 2014 estimate	103,400 (197th)
• Density	575.21/km^2 (22nd) 1,489.79/sq mi
GDP (PPP)	2009 estimate
• Total	US$2.516 billion (182nd)
GDP (nominal)	2013 estimate
• Total	US$2.565 billion (162nd)

• Per capita	US$28,924 (32nd)
HDI (2014)	0.879 very high
Currency	Aruban florin (AWG)
Time zone	AST (UTC−4)
Drives on the	right
Calling code	+297
ISO 3166 code	AW
Internet TLD	.aw

Aruba is a constituent country of the Kingdom of the Netherlands in the southern Caribbean Sea, located about 1,600 kilometres (990 mi) west of the main part of the Lesser Antilles and 29 kilometres (18 mi) north of the coast of Venezuela. It measures 32 kilometres (20 mi) long from its northwestern to its southeastern end and 10 kilometres (6 mi) across at its widest point. Together with Bonaire and Curaçao, Aruba forms a group referred to as the ABC islands. Collectively, Aruba and the other Dutch islands in the Caribbean are often called the Dutch Caribbean.

Discovered and claimed for Spain in 1499, Aruba was acquired by the Dutch in 1636. The island's economy has been dominated by three main industries. A 19th century gold rush was followed by prosperity brought on by the opening in 1924 of an oil refinery. The last decades of the 20th century saw a boom in the tourism industry. Aruba seceded from the Dutch Caribbeanin 1986 and became a separate, autonomous member of the Kingdom of the Netherlands. Movement toward full independence was halted at Aruba's request in 1990.

Aruba is one of the four countries that form the Kingdom of the Netherlands, along with the Netherlands, Curaçao and Sint Maarten. The citizens of these countries all share a single nationality: Dutch. Aruba has no administrative subdivisions, but, for census purposes, is divided into eight regions. Its capital is Oranjestad.

Unlike much of the Caribbean region, Aruba has a dry climate and an arid, cactus-strewn landscape. This climate has helped tourism as visitors to the island can reliably expect warm, sunny weather. It has a land area of 179 km^2 (69.1 sq mi) and is densely populated, with a total of 102,484 inhabitants at the 2010 Census. It lies outside Hurricane Alley.

In August 1947, Aruba presented its first *Staatsreglement* (constitution), for Aruba's *status aparte* as an autonomous state within the Kingdom of the Netherlands. By 1954, the Charter of the Kingdom of the Netherlands was established, providing a framework for relations between Aruba and the rest of the Kingdom.

In 1972, at a conference in Suriname, Betico Croes (MEP), a politician from Aruba, proposed a *sui-generis* Dutch Commonwealth of four states: Aruba, the Netherlands, Suriname and the Netherlands Antilles, each to have its own nationality. C. Yarzagaray, a parliamentary member representing the AVP political party, proposed a referendum so that the people of Aruba could choose whether they wanted total independence or *Status Aparte* as a full autonomous state under the Crown.

Croes worked in Aruba to inform and prepare the people of Aruba for independence. In 1976, he appointed a committee that chose the national flag and anthem, introducing them as symbols of Aruba's sovereignty and independence. He set 1981 as a target date for independence. In March 1977, the first Referendum for Self Determination was held with the support of the United Nations; 82% of the participants voted for independence.

The Island Government of Aruba assigned the Institute of Social Studies in The Hague to prepare a study for independence; it was titled *Aruba en Onafhankelijkheid, achtergronden, modaliteiten en mogelijkheden; een rapport in eerste aanleg* (Aruba and independence, backgrounds, modalities and opportunities; a preliminary report) (1978). At the conference in The Hague in 1981, Aruba's independence was set for the year 1991.

In March 1983, Aruba reached an official agreement within the Kingdom for its independence, to be developed in a series of steps as the Crown granted increasing autonomy. In August 1985 Aruba drafted a constitution that was unanimously approved. On 1 January 1986, after elections were held for its first parliament, Aruba seceded from the Netherlands Antilles; it officially became a country of the Kingdom of the Netherlands. Full independence was projected in 1996.

After his death in 1986, Croes was proclaimed *Libertador di Aruba*. At a convention in The Hague in 1990, at the request of Aruba's Prime Minister, the governments of Aruba, the Netherlands, and the Dutch Caribbeanpostponed indefinitely its transition to full independence. The article scheduling Aruba's complete independence was rescinded in 1995, although the process could be revived after another referendum.

As a constituent country of the Kingdom of the Netherlands, Aruba's politics take place within a framework of a 21-member Parliament and an eight-member Cabinet. The governor of Aruba is appointed for a six-year term by the monarch, and the prime minister and deputy prime minister are elected by the Staten (or "Parlamento") for four-year terms. The Staten is made up of 21 members elected by direct, popular vote to serve a four-year term.[15]

Together with the Netherlands, the countries of Aruba, Curaçao and Sint Maarten form the Kingdom of the Netherlands. As they share the same Dutch citizenship, these four countries still also share the Dutch passport as the Kingdom of the Netherlands passport. As Aruba, Curaçao and Sint Maarten have small populations, the three countries had to limit immigration. To protect their population, they have the right to control the admission and expulsion of people from the Netherlands.

Aruba is designated as a member of the Overseas Countries and Territories (OCT) and is thus officially not a part of the European Union, though Aruba can and does receive support from the European Development Fund

On October 12, 2006, the Netherlands reached an agreement with Saba, Bonaire, and Sint Eustatius; this agreement would make these islands special municipalities. On November 3, 2006, Curaçao and Sint Maarten were granted autonomy in an agreement, but this agreement was rejected by Curaçao on November 28. The Curaçao government was not sufficiently convinced that the agreement would provide enough autonomy for Curaçao. On July 9, 2007 Curaçao approved the agreement it had rejected in November 2006.

On February 12, 2007, an agreement was signed between the Netherlands and every island except Curaçao. This agreement would end the Dutch Caribbeanby December 15, 2008 and make available for the islands 1 billion guilders for debt relief, social development and poverty reduction

Background: Once the center of the Caribbean slave trade, the island of Curacao was hard hit by the abolition of slavery in 1863. Its prosperity (and that of neighboring Aruba) was restored in the early 20th century with the construction of oil refineries to service the newly discovered Venezuelan oil fields. The island of Sint Maarten is shared with France (whose northern portion is named Saint Martin and is part of Guadeloupe).

GEOGRAPHY

Location:
Caribbean, island in the Caribbean Sea, north of Venezuela

Geographic coordinates:
12 30 N, 69 58 W

Map references:
Central America and the Caribbean

Area:
total: 180 sq km
land: 180 sq km
water: 0 sq km
country comparison to the world: 218

Area - comparative:
slightly larger than Washington, DC

Land boundaries:
0 km
Coastline:
68.5 km
Maritime claims:
territorial sea: 12 nm

Climate:
tropical marine; little seasonal temperature variation

Terrain:
flat with a few hills; scant vegetation

Elevation:
elevation extremes: lowest point: Caribbean Sea 0 m
highest point: Ceru Jamanota 188 m

Natural resources:
NEGL; white sandy beaches foster tourism

Land use:
agricultural land: 11.1%
arable land 11.1%; permanent crops 0%; permanent pasture 0%

forest: 2.3%
other: 86.6% (2011 est.)

Natural hazards:
hurricanes; lies outside the Caribbean hurricane belt and is rarely threatened

Environment - current issues:
NA
Geography - note:
a flat, riverless island renowned for its white sand beaches; its tropical climate is moderated by constant trade winds from the Atlantic Ocean; the temperature is almost constant at about 27 degrees Celsius (81 degrees Fahrenheit)

PEOPEL

Nationality:
noun: Aruban(s)
adjective: Aruban; Dutch

Ethnic groups:
Dutch 82.1%, Colombian 6.6%, Venezuelan 2.2%, Dominican 2.2%, Haitian 1.2%, other 5.5%, unspecified 0.1% (2010 est.)

Languages:
Papiamento (official) (a creole language that is a mixture of Portuguese, Spanish, Dutch, English, and, to a lesser extent, French, as well as elements of African languages and the language of the Arawak) 69.4%, Spanish 13.7%, English (widely spoken) 7.1%, Dutch (official) 6.1%, Chinese 1.5%, other 1.7%, unspecified 0.4% (2010 est.)

Religions:
Roman Catholic 75.3%, Protestant 4.9% (includes Methodist .9%, Adventist .9%, Anglican .4%, other Protestant 2.7%), Jehovah's Witness 1.7%, other 12%, none 5.5%,
unspecified 0.5% (2010 est.)

Population:
112,162 (July 2015 est.)
country comparison to the world: 190

Age structure:

0-14 years: 17.69% (male 9,953/female 9,888)
15-24 years: 13.27% (male 7,470/female 7,417)
25-54 years: 42.59% (male 23,015/female 24,750)
55-64 years: 13.73% (male 7,114/female 8,287)
65 years and over: 12.72% (male 5,591/female 8,677) (2015 est.)

Dependency ratios:
total dependency ratio: 44%
youth dependency ratio: 26.4%
elderly dependency ratio: 17.6%
potential support ratio: 5.7% (2015 est.)

Median age:
total: 39 years
male: 37.1 years
female: 40.8 years (2015 est.)
country comparison to the world: 56

Population growth rate:
1.33% (2015 est.)
country comparison to the world: 89

Birth rate:
12.56 births/1,000 population (2015 est.)
country comparison to the world: 157

Death rate:
8.18 deaths/1,000 population (2015 est.)
country comparison to the world: 92

Net migration rate:
8.92 migrant(s)/1,000 population (2015 est.)
country comparison to the world: 12
Urbanization:
urban population: 41.5% of total population (2015)
rate of urbanization: -0.28% annual rate of change (2010-15 est.)

Major urban areas - population:
ORANJESTAD (capital) 29,000

Sex ratio:
at birth: 1.02 male(s)/female
0-14 years: 1.01 male(s)/female
15-24 years: 1.01 male(s)/female
25-54 years: 0.93 male(s)/female
55-64 years: 0.86 male(s)/female
65 years and over: 0.64 male(s)/female

total population: 0.9 male(s)/female (2015 est.)

Infant mortality rate:
total: 11.37 deaths/1,000 live births
male: 14.94 deaths/1,000 live births
female: 7.74 deaths/1,000 live births (2015 est.)
country comparison to the world: 127

Life expectancy at birth:
total population: 76.56 years
male: 73.5 years
female: 79.68 years (2015 est.)
country comparison to the world: 83

Total fertility rate:
1.84 children born/woman (2015 est.)
country comparison to the world: 146

Drinking water source:
improved:
urban: 98.1% of population
rural: 98.1% of population
total: 98.1% of population

unimproved:
urban: 1.9% of population
rural: 1.9% of population
total: 1.9% of population (2015 est.)

Sanitation facility access:
improved:
urban: 97.7% of population
rural: 97.7% of population
total: 97.7% of population
unimproved:
urban: 2.3% of population
rural: 2.3% of population
total: 2.3% of population (2015 est.)

Education expenditures:
6% of GDP
country comparison to the world: 41

Literacy:
definition: age 15 and over can read and write
total population: 97.5%

male: 97.5%
female: 97.5% (2015 est.)

School life expectancy (primary to tertiary education):
total: 13 years
male: 13 years
female: 14 years

Unemployment, youth ages 15-24:
total: 28.9%
male: 29.9%
female: 27.5% (2010 est.)
country comparison to the world: 43

GOVERNMENT

Country name:
conventional long form: none
conventional short form: Aruba
etymology: the origin of the island's name is unclear; according to tradition, the name comes from the Spanish phrase "oro huba" (there was gold), but in fact no gold was ever found on the island; another possibility is the native word "oruba," which means "well situated"

Dependency status:
constituent country of the Kingdom of the Netherlands; full autonomy in internal affairs obtained in 1986 upon separation from the Netherlands Antilles; Dutch Government responsible for defense and foreign affairs

Government type:
parliamentary democracy

Capital:
name: Oranjestad
geographic coordinates: 12 31 N, 70 02 W
time difference: UTC-4 (1 hour ahead of Washington, DC, during Standard Time)

Administrative divisions:
none (part of the Kingdom of the Netherlands)

Independence:
none (part of the Kingdom of the Netherlands)

National holiday:
Flag Day, 18 March (1976)

Constitution:

previous 1947, 1955; latest drafted and approved August 1985, enacted 1 January 1986 (regulates governance of Aruba, but is subordinate to the Charter for the Kingdom of the Netherlands); note - in October 2010, following dissolution of the Netherlands Antilles, Aruba became a constituent country within the Kingdom of the Netherlands (2015)

Legal system:
civil law system based on the Dutch civil code

Citizenship:
see the Netherlands

Suffrage:
18 years of age; universal

Executive branch:

chief of state: King WILLEM-ALEXANDER of the Netherlands (since 30 April 2013); represented by Governor General Fredis REFUNJOL (since 11 May 2004)
head of government: Prime Minister Michiel "Mike" Godfried EMAN (since 30 October 2009)

cabinet: Council of Ministers elected by the Legislature (Staten)
elections/appointments: the monarchy is hereditary; governor general appointed by the monarch for a 6-year term; prime minister and deputy prime minister indirectly elected by the Staten for 4-year tern; election last held on 25 September 2009 (next to be held by September 2013)
election results: Michiel "Mike" Godfried EMAN (AVP) elected prime minister; percent of legislative vote - NA

Legislative branch:

description: unicameral Legislature or Staten (21 seats; members directly elected in a single nationwide constituency by proportional representation vote; members serve 4-year terms)
elections: last held on 27 September 2013 (next to be held in 2017)
election results: percent of vote by party - NA; seats by party - AVP 13, MEP 8

Judicial branch:

highest court(s): Joint Court of Justice of Aruba, Curacao, Sint Maarten, and of Bonaire, Sint Eustatitus and Saba or "Joint Court of Justice" (consists of the presiding judge, NA members, and NA substitutes); final appeals heard by the Supreme Court, in The Hague, Netherlands
note - prior to 2010, the Joint Court of Justice was the Common Court of Justice of the Dutch Caribbeanand Aruba

judge selection and term of office: Joint Court judges appointed by the monarch for life
subordinate courts: Courts in First Instance

Political parties and leaders:
Aruban People's Party or AVP [Michiel "Mike" EMAN]
People's Electoral Movement Party or MEP [Evelyn WEVER-CROES]
Real Democracy or PDR [Andin BIKKER]

Political pressure groups and leaders:
other: environmental groups

International organization participation:
Caricom (observer), FATF, ILO, IMF, Interpol, IOC, ITUC (NGOs), UNESCO (associate), UNWTO (associate), UPU
Diplomatic representation in the US:
none (represented by the Kingdom of the Netherlands); note - there is a Minister Plenipotentiary for Aruba at the Embassy of the Kingdom of the Netherlands

Diplomatic representation from the US:
the US does not have an embassy in Aruba; the Consul General to Curacao is accredited to Aruba

Flag description:
blue, with two narrow, horizontal, yellow stripes across the lower portion and a red, four-pointed star outlined in white in the upper hoist-side corner; the star represents Aruba and its red soil and white beaches, its four points the four major languages (Papiamento, Dutch, Spanish, English) as well as the four points of a compass, to indicate that its inhabitants come from all over the world; the blue symbolizes Caribbean waters and skies; the stripes represent the island's two main "industries": the flow of tourists to the sun-drenched beaches and the flow of minerals from the earth

National symbol(s):
Hooiberg (Haystack) Hill; national colors: blue, yellow, red, white

National anthem:
name: "Aruba Deshi Tera" (Aruba Precious Country)

ECONOMY

Economy - overview:
Tourism, petroleum bunkering, hospitality, and financial and business services are the mainstays of the small open Aruban economy.

Tourist arrivals have rebounded strongly following a dip after the 2008 global financial crisis. Tourism now accounts for a majority of economic activity. Over 1 million tourists per year visit Aruba, with the large majority of those from the US.

The rapid growth of the tourism sector has resulted in a substantial expansion of other activities. Construction continues to boom with hotel capacity five times the 1985 level.

Aruba is heavily dependent on imports and is making efforts to expand exports to achieve a more desirable trade balance. Almost all consumer and capital goods are imported, with the US, the Netherlands, and Panama being the major suppliers.

Aruba weathered two major shocks in recent years: fallout from the global financial crisis, which had its largest impact on tourism, and the closure of its oil refinery in 2009. However, tourism and related industries have continued to grow, and the Aruban government is working to attract more diverse industries. Aruba's banking sector withstood the recession well, and unemployment has significantly decreased.

GDP (purchasing power parity):
$2.516 billion (2009 est.)
$2.258 billion (2005 est.)
$2.205 billion (2004 est.)
country comparison to the world: 191

GDP (official exchange rate):
$2.516 billion (2009 est.)
GDP - real growth rate:
2.4% (2005 est.)
country comparison to the world: 129

GDP - per capita (PPP):
$25,300 (2011 est.)
country comparison to the world: 74

GDP - composition, by end use:
household consumption: 63.3%
government consumption: 28.3%
investment in fixed capital: 22.9%
investment in inventories: 0%
exports of goods and services: 68.1%
imports of goods and services: -82.6%
(2015 est.)

GDP - composition, by sector of origin:
agriculture: 0.4%
industry: 33.3%
services: 66.3%

Agriculture - products:

aloes; livestock; fish

Industries:
tourism, petroleum transshipment facilities, banking

Labor force:
51,610
note: of the 51,610 workers aged 15 and over in the labor force, 32,252 were born in Aruba and 19,353 came from abroad; foreign workers are 38% of the employed population (2007 est.)
country comparison to the world: 192

Labor force - by occupation:
agriculture: NA%
industry: NA%
services: NA%

note: most employment is in wholesale and retail trade, followed by hotels and restaurants

Unemployment rate:
6.9% (2005 est.)
country comparison to the world: 81

Population below poverty line:
NA%
Household income or consumption by percentage share:
lowest 10%: NA%
highest 10%: NA%

Budget:
revenues: $648.1 million
expenditures: $838.3 million (2015 est.)

Taxes and other revenues:
25.8% of GDP (2015 est.)
country comparison to the world: 115

Budget surplus (+) or deficit (-):
-7.6% of GDP (2015 est.)
country comparison to the world: 195

Public debt:
67% of GDP
55% of GDP (2012)
country comparison to the world: 52

Fiscal year:
calendar year

Inflation rate (consumer prices):
1% (2015 est.)
0.4% (2014 est.)
country comparison to the world: 68

Central bank discount rate:
1% (31 December 2010)
3% (31 December 2009)
country comparison to the world: 123

Commercial bank prime lending rate:
9% (31 December 2015 est.)
7.3% (31 December 2014 est.)
country comparison to the world: 95

Stock of narrow money:
$990.2 million (31 December 2014 est.)
$990.2 million (31 December 2014 est.)
country comparison to the world: 154

Stock of broad money:
$1.942 billion (31 December 2014 est.)
$1.838 billion (31 December 2013 est.)
country comparison to the world: 158

Stock of domestic credit:
$1.754 billion (31 December 2014 est.)
$1.754 billion (31 December 2014 est.)
country comparison to the world: 142

Exports:
$189.2 million (2015 est.)
$236.5 million (2014 est.)
country comparison to the world: 188

Exports - commodities:
live animals and animal products, art and collectibles, machinery and electrical equipment, transport equipment

Exports - partners:
Colombia 31.2%, Dutch Caribbean21.7%, US 15.7%, Venezuela 12.4%, Netherlands 6.1% (2014)

Imports:

$1.329 billion (2015 est.)
$1.35 billion (2014 est.)
country comparison to the world: 172

Imports - commodities:
machinery and electrical equipment, refined oil for bunkering and reexport, chemicals; foodstuffs

Imports - partners:
US 56%, Netherlands 11.3% (2014)

Debt - external:
$693.2 million (31 December 2014 est.)
$666.4 million (31 December 2013 est.)
country comparison to the world: 172

Exchange rates:
Aruban guilders/florins per US dollar -
1.79 (2015 est.)
1.79 (2014 est.)
1.79 (2013 est.)
1.79 (2012 est.)
1.79 (2011 est.)

ENERGY

Electricity - production:
990 million kWh (2012 est.)
country comparison to the world: 149

Electricity - consumption:
920.7 million kWh (2012 est.)
country comparison to the world: 157
Electricity - exports:
0 kWh (2013 est.)
country comparison to the world: 95

Electricity - imports:
0 kWh (2013 est.)
country comparison to the world: 112

Electricity - installed generating capacity:
320,000 kW (2012 est.)
country comparison to the world: 148

Electricity - from fossil fuels:
90.6% of total installed capacity (2012 est.)
country comparison to the world: 73

Electricity - from nuclear fuels:
0% of total installed capacity (2012 est.)
country comparison to the world: 34

Electricity - from hydroelectric plants:
0% of total installed capacity (2012 est.)
country comparison to the world: 154

Electricity - from other renewable sources:
9.4% of total installed capacity (2012 est.)
country comparison to the world: 39

Crude oil - production:
0 bbl/day (2014 est.)
country comparison to the world: 102

Crude oil - exports:
0 bbl/day (2012 est.)
country comparison to the world: 92

Crude oil - imports:
229,000 bbl/day
country comparison to the world: 32

Crude oil - proved reserves:
0 bbl (1 January 2015 est.)
country comparison to the world: 102

Refined petroleum products - production:
234,600 bbl/day (2012 est.)
country comparison to the world: 48

Refined petroleum products - consumption:
6,400 bbl/day (2013 est.)
country comparison to the world: 163

Refined petroleum products - exports:
234,600 bbl/day (2012 est.)
country comparison to the world: 30

Refined petroleum products - imports:
6,341 bbl/day (2012 est.)
country comparison to the world: 150
Natural gas - production:
1 cu m (2013 est.)
country comparison to the world: 96

Natural gas - consumption:
1 cu m (2013 est.)
country comparison to the world: 114

Natural gas - exports:
1 cu m (2013 est.)
country comparison to the world: 52

Natural gas - imports:
1 cu m (2013 est.)
country comparison to the world: 75

Natural gas - proved reserves:
0 cu m (1 January 2014 est.)
country comparison to the world: 107

Carbon dioxide emissions from consumption of energy:
876,400 Mt (2012 est.)
country comparison to the world: 168

COMMUNICATION

Telephones - fixed lines:
total subscriptions: 35,000
subscriptions per 100 inhabitants: 32 (2014 est.)

country comparison to the world: 169

Telephones - mobile cellular:
total: 139,700
subscriptions per 100 inhabitants: 126 (2014 est.)
country comparison to the world: 185

Telephone system:
general assessment: modern fully automatic telecommunications system
domestic: increased competition through privatization; 3 mobile-cellular service providers are now licensed
international: country code - 297; landing site for the PAN-AM submarine telecommunications cable system that extends from the US Virgin Islands through Aruba to Venezuela, Colombia, Panama, and the west coast of South America; extensive interisland microwave radio relay links

Broadcast media:
2 commercial TV stations; cable TV subscription service provides access to foreign channels; about 20 commercial radio stations broadcast

Radio broadcast stations:

AM 2, FM 16, shortwave 0

Television broadcast stations:
1 (1997)
Internet country code:
.aw
Internet hosts:
40,560
country comparison to the world: 101

Internet users:
total: 87,700
percent of population: 79.2% (2014 est.)
country comparison to the world: 172

TRANSPORTATION

Airports: 1
country comparison to the world: 210

Airports - with paved runways: total: 1
2,438 to 3,047 m: 1

Ports and terminals:
major seaport(s): Barcadera, Oranjestad
oil terminal(s): Sint Nicolaas
cruise port(s): Oranjestad

MILITARY AND SECURITY

Military branches:
no regular military forces

Military - note:
defense is the responsibility of the Netherlands; the Aruba security services focus on organized crime and terrorism

Disputes - international:
none

Illicit drugs:
transit point for US- and Europe-bound narcotics with some accompanying money-laundering activity; relatively high percentage of population consumes cocaine

CURAÇAO

Capital	Willemstad

and largest city	12°7′N 68°56′W12.117°N 68.933°W
Official languages	• Dutch • Papiamentu • English
Demonym	Antillian Dutch
Sovereign state	Kingdom of the Netherlands
Government	Unitary parliamentary representative democracy under constitutional monarchy
• Monarch	Willem-Alexander
• Governor	Lucille George-Wout
• Prime Minister	Ben Whiteman
Legislature	Estates of Curaçao
Autonomy within the Kingdom of the Netherlands	
• Established	10 October 2010 (dissolution of the Netherlands Antilles)
Area	
• Total	444 km^2 171.4 sq mi
Population	
• 2014 estimate	154,843 (179)
• Density	344/km^2 (38th) 881/sq mi
GDP (PPP)	estimate
• Total	US$3.1 billion (149th)
• Per capita	US$22,619 (46th)
GDP (nominal)	estimate
• Total	US$5.6 billion (149th)
• Per capita	US$36,800 (27th)
HDI (2012)	0.811 very high
Currency	Netherlands Antillean guilder (ANG)
Time zone	AST (UTC−4)
Drives on the	right
Calling code	+599 9
ISO 3166 code	CW
Internet TLD	.cw, .an [a]

Curaçao is an island country in the southern Caribbean Sea, approximately 65 kilometres (40 mi) north of the Venezuelan coast, that is a constituent country (Dutch: *land*) of the Kingdom of the Netherlands. Formally called the **Country of Curaçao**, (Dutch: *Land Curaçao*; Papiamento: *Pais Kòrsou*), it includes the main island and the uninhabited island of Klein Curaçao ("Little Curaçao"). It has a population of over 150,000 on an area of 444 km^2 (171 sq mi) and its capital is Willemstad.

The government of Curaçao takes place in a framework of a parliamentary representative democratic country. The Prime Minister is the head of government. Executive power is exercised by the government. Legislative power is vested in both the government and parliament.

Originally settled by Arawak Indians, Curacao was seized by the Dutch in 1634 along with the neighboring island of Bonaire. Once the center of the Caribbean slave trade, Curacao was hard hit economically by the abolition of slavery in 1863. Its prosperity (and that of neighboring Aruba) was restored in the early 20th century with the construction of the Isla Refineria to service the newly discovered Venezuelan oil fields. In 1954, Curacao and several other Dutch Caribbean possessions were reorganized as the Netherlands Antilles, part of the Kingdom of the Netherlands. In referenda in 2005 and 2009, the citizens of Curacao voted to become a self-governing country within the Kingdom of the Netherlands. The change in status became effective in October 2010 with the dissolution of the Netherlands Antilles.

The judiciary is independent of the executive and the legislature.

Convicted felons are held at the Curaçao Centre for Detention and Correction prison.

Curaçao has full autonomy on most matters, with the exceptions summed up in the Charter for the Kingdom of the Netherlands under the title "Kingdom affairs".

Before the dissolution of the Netherlands Antilles on 10 October 2010, Curaçao was administered as the "Island Territory of Curaçao" (Dutch: *Eilandgebied Curaçao*, Papiamentu: *Teritorio Insular di Kòrsou*), one of five island territories of the former Netherlands Antilles.

GEOGRAPHY

Location:
Caribbean, an island in the Caribbean Sea, 30 nm off the coast of Venezuela

Geographic coordinates:
12 10 N, 69 00 W

Map references:
Central America and the Caribbean

Area:
total: 444 sq km
land: 444 sq km
water: 0 sq km
country comparison to the world: 200

Area - comparative:
more than twice the size of Washington, DC

Land boundaries:
0 km
Coastline:

364 km

Maritime claims:
territorial sea: 12 nm
exclusive fishing zone: 12 nm

Climate:
tropical marine climate, ameliorated by northeast trade winds, results in mild temperatures; semiarid with average rainfall of 60 cm/year

Terrain:
generally low, hilly terrain

Elevation:
mean elevation: NA
elevation extremes: lowest point: Caribbean Sea 0 m
highest point: Mt. Christoffel 372 m

Natural resources:
calcium phosphates, aloes, sorghum, peanuts, vegetables, tropical fruit

Land use:
agricultural land: 10%
arable land 10%; permanent crops 0%; permanent pasture 0%
forest: 0%
other: 90%

Natural hazards:
Curacao is south of the Caribbean hurricane belt and is rarely threatened

Geography - note:
Curacao is a part of the Windward Islands (southern) group

PEOPLE

Nationality:
noun: Curacaoan
adjective: Curacaoan; Dutch

Ethnic groups:
Afro-Caribbean majority; Dutch, French, Latin American, East Asian, South Asian, Jewish minorities

Languages:
Papiamento (official) (a creole language that is a mixture of Portuguese, Spanish, Dutch, English, and, to a lesser extent, French, as well as elements of African languages and the language of the Arawak) 81.2%, Dutch (official) 8%, Spanish 4%, English (official) 2.9%, other 3.9% (2001 census)

Religions:
Roman Catholic 72.8%, Pentecostal 6.6%, Protestant 3.2%, Adventist 3%, Jehovah's Witness 2%, Evangelical 1.9%, other 3.8%, none 6%, unspecified 0.6%

Population:
148,406 (July 2015 est.)
country comparison to the world: 189

Age structure:
0-14 years: 20.3% (male 15,334/female 14,739)
15-24 years: 14.7% (male 11,356/female 10,448)
25-54 years: 37.6% (male 27,125/female 28,716)
55-64 years: 13.2% (male 8,545/female 11,150)
65 years and over: 14.2% (male 8,698/female 12,340) (2015 est.)

population pyramid:
Dependency ratios:
total dependency ratio: 51.1%
youth dependency ratio: 28.7%
elderly dependency ratio: 22.4%
potential support ratio: 4.5% (2015 est.)

Median age:
total: 36.1 years
male: 33 years
female: 39.9 years (2015 est.)

country comparison to the world: 69

Population growth rate:
0.43% (2015 est.)
Birth rate:
NA 13.8 births/1,000 population (2015 est.)
Death rate:
8.2 deaths/1,000 population (2015 est.)
country comparison to the world: 98

Net migration rate:
-1.4 migrant(s)/1,000 population (2015 est.)
country comparison to the world: 59

Urbanization:
urban population: 89.3% of total population (2015)
rate of urbanization: 2.04% annual rate of change (2010-15 est.)

Major urban areas - population:

WILLEMSTAD (capital) 145,000 (2014)

Sex ratio:
at birth: 1.05 male(s)/female
0-14 years: 1.04 male(s)/female
15-24 years: 1.09 male(s)/female
25-54 years: 0.94 male(s)/female
55-64 years: 0.77 male(s)/female
65 years and over: 0.7 male(s)/female
total population: 0.92 male(s)/female (2015 est.)

Infant mortality rate:
total: 7.9 deaths/1,000 live births
male: 8.5 deaths/1,000 live births
female: 7.3 deaths/1,000 live births (2015 est.)

Life expectancy at birth:
total population: 78.2 years
male: 75.9 years
female: 80.6 years (2015 est.)
country comparison to the world: 62

Total fertility rate:
2.07 children born/woman (2015 est.)
country comparison to the world: 107

GOVERNMENT

Country name:
Dutch long form: Land Curacao
Dutch short form: Curacao
Papiamentu long form: Pais Korsou
Papiamentu short form: Korsou
former: Netherlands Antilles; Curacao and Dependencies

Dependency status:
constituent country within the Kingdom of the Netherlands; full autonomy in internal affairs granted in 2010; Dutch Government responsible for defense and foreign affairs

Government type:
parliamentary

Capital:
name: Willemstad
geographic coordinates: 12 06 N, 68 55 W
time difference: UTC-4 (1 hour ahead of Washington, DC, during Standard Time)

Administrative divisions:
none (part of the Kingdom of the Netherlands)

Independence:
none (part of the Kingdom of the Netherlands)

National holiday:
King's Day, 27 April 1967

Constitution:
previous 1947, 1955; latest adopted 5 September 2010, entered into force 10 October 2010 (regulates governance of Curacao but is subordinate to the Charter for the Kingdom of the Netherlands); note - in October 2010, with the dissolution of the Netherlands Antilles, Curacao became a constituent country within the Kingdom of the Netherlands

Legal system:

based on Dutch civil law system with some English common law influence

Citizenship:
see the Netherlands

Suffrage:
18 years of age; universal

Executive branch:

chief of state: King WILLEM-ALEXANDER of the Netherlands (since 30 April 2013); represented by Governor Lucille A. GEORGE-WOUT (since 4 November 2013)
head of government: Prime Minister Bernard WHITEMAN (1 September 2015); Prime Minister Ivar ASJES resigned 31 August 2015
cabinet: Cabinet appointed by the governor
elections: the monarch is hereditary; governor general appointed by the monarch; following legislative elections, the leader of the majority party is usually elected prime minister by the parliament; next election is scheduled for 2016

Legislative branch:

description: unicameral Estates of Curacao or Staten van Curacao (21 seats; members directly elected by proportional representation vote to serve 4-year terms)
elections: last held 19 October 2012 (next to be held in 2016)
election results: percent of vote by party - PS 22.6%, MFK 21.2%, PAR 19.7%, PAIS 17.7%, MAN 9.5%, PNP 5.9%, other 3.4%; seats by party - PS 5, MFK 5, PAR 4, PAIS 4, MAN 2, PNP 1

Judicial branch:
highest court(s): Common Court of Justice of Aruba, Curacao, Sint Maarten, Bonaire, Sint Eustatius and Saba (consists of judges from the subordinate courts)
judge selection and terms of office: NA
subordinate courts: first instance courts, appeals court; specialized courts

Political parties and leaders:
Movementu Futuro Korsou or MFK [Gerrit SCHOTTE]
Movishon Antia Nobo or MAN [Hensley KOEIMAN]
Partido Antia Restruktura or PAR [Zita JESUS-LEITO]
Partido pa Adelanto I Inovashon Soshal or PAIS [Alex ROSARIA]
Partido Nashonal di Pueblo or PNP [Humphrey DAVELAAR]
Pueblo Soberano or PS [Ivar ASJES]

Diplomatic representation in the US:
none (represented by the Kingdom of the Netherlands)

Diplomatic representation from the US:
chief of mission: Consul General James R. Moore (since June 2013); note - also accredited to Aruba and Sint Martin

consulate(s) general: J. B. Gorsiraweg
mailing address: P. O. Box 158, Willemstad, Curacao
telephone: [599] (9) 4613066
FAX: [599] (9) 4616489

Flag description:
on a blue field a horizontal yellow band somewhat below the center divides the flag into proportions of 5:1:2; two five-pointed white stars - the smaller above and to the left of the larger - appear in the canton; the blue of the upper and lower sections symbolizes the sky and sea respectively; yellow represents the sun; the stars symbolize Curacao and its uninhabited smaller sister island of Klein Curacao; the five star points signify the five continents from which Curacao's people derive

National symbol(s):

laraha (citrus tree); national colors: blue, yellow, white

National anthem:
name: Himmo di Korsou (Anthem of Curacao)
lyrics/music: Guillermo ROSARIO, Mae HENRIQUEZ, Enrique MULLER, Betty DORAN/Frater Candidus NOWENS, Errol "El Toro" COLINA
note: adapted 1978; the lyrics, originally written in 1899, were rewritten in 1978 to make them less colonial in nature

ECONOMY AND BUSINESS POTENTIAL

Currency	Netherlands Antillean guilder (ANG)
Fiscal year	Calendar Year
Trade organisations	Trade Union Centre of Curaçao
	Statistics
GDP	$3 billion
GDP growth	3.5%
GDP per capita	$22,619
GDP by sector	agriculture: 1%; industry: 15%; services: 84% (est.)
Inflation (CPI)	1.7%
Labour force	63,000
Labour force by occupation	agriculture: 1.2%; industry: 16.9%; services: 81.8%
Unemployment	10.3%
Main industries	Tourism, Petroleum Refining, Petroleum Transshipment Facilities, Light Manufacturing, Financial Services
	External
Exports	$876 million
Export goods	Petroleum products
Main export partners	United States 13.1% Guatemala 10.8% Singapore 10.7% Dominican Republic 9.6% Haiti 7.6% The Bahamas 6.1% Honduras 4.5% Mexico 4.2% (est.)
Imports	$1.34 billion
Import goods	Food and Crude Petroleum
Main import partners	Venezuela 57.3% United States 19.2% Brazil 8.1% (est.)
	Public finances
Public debt	$1.0 billion

Curaçao has one of the highest standards of living in the Caribbean, ranking 46th in the world in terms of GDP (PPP) per capita and 28th in the world in terms of nominal GDP per capita. It possesses a high income economy, as defined by the World Bank. The island has a well-developed infrastructure with strong tourism and financial services sectors. Shipping, international trade, oil refining, and other activities related to the port of Willemstad (like the Free Trade Zone) also make a significant contribution to the economy. To achieve the government's aim to make its economy more diverse, efforts are being made to attract more foreign investment. This policy, called the 'Open Arms' policy, features a heavy focus on information technology companie

TOURISM

Curaçao is a popular tourism destination for the Eastern United States, South America and Holland. It currently leads the Caribbean in cruise tourism growth with 610,186 cruise passengers in 2013, a 41.4% increase over the prior year. Hato International Airport received 1,772,501 passengers in 2013 and recently announced $48 million in capital investments aimed at transforming the airport into a regional hub by 2018. Beginning in early 2014, the Lynx rocketplane is expected to be flying suborbital space tourism flights and scientific research missions from a new spaceport on Curaçao. The island lies outside of the Hurricane belt and has a well-developed tourism infrastructure.

Curaçao's coast has a sharp drop-off known as the "Blue Edge" which makes it a popular scuba diving destination. Coral reefs for snorkeling and scuba diving can be reached without a boat. The southern coast has calm waters as well as many small beaches, such as Jan Thiel and Cas Abou. The coastline of Curaçao features numerous bays and inlets which serve as popular mooring locations for boats.

Some of the coral reefs are affected by tourism. Porto Marie Beach is experimenting with artificial coral reefs in order to improve the reef's condition. Hundreds of artificial coral blocks that have been placed are now home to a large array of tropical fish.

OIL REFINING

The discovery of oil in the Maracaibo Basin of Venezuela in the early 20th century forced the Venezuelan government to search for ideal locations for large scale refining. Curaçao's proximity to the country, naturally deep harbors, and stable government led Royal Dutch Shell to construct the **Isla Refinery**, the largest refinery in the world at the time. The refinery is located in Willemstad harbour and began operating in 1918.

Presently Venezuela's state oil company, Petróleos de Venezuela (PDVSA) operates the Isla refinery, which has a 320,000 barrel per day capacity .

FINANCIAL SERVICES

Curaçao's history in financial services dates from World War I with the conversion of the financial arms of local merchant houses into commercial banks. As the economy grew, these banks began assuming additional functions eventually becoming full-fledged financial institutions. The Dutch Caribbean Securities Exchange is located in the capital of Willemstad, as is the Central Bank of Curaçao and Sint Maarten; the latter of which dates to 1828 making it the oldest central bank in the Western Hemisphere. The island's legal system supports a wide variety of corporate structures and is a popular corporate haven. Curaçao is considered a tax haven yet it adheres to the EU Code of Conduct against harmful tax practices. It holds a qualified intermediary status from the United States I.R.S. and is an accepted jurisdiction of the OECD and Caribbean Financial Action Task Force on Money Laundering. The country strongly enforces Anti-Money Laundering and Counter-Terrorism funding compliance.

SPACEPORT

Starting in 2014 the Lynx rocketplane will launch from the Curaçao spaceport. The rocketplane will be used for space tourism and scientific research. The spaceport differs from traditional ones in that it will serve primarily the personal spaceflight market and will be more commercialized. The spaceport is not expected to be fully operational until 2013 at the earliest

ENERGY

Electricity - production:

1.785 billion kWh (2012 est.)
country comparison to the world: 142

Electricity - consumption:
968 million kWh (2008 est.)
country comparison to the world: 153

Electricity - exports:
0 kWh (est.)
country comparison to the world: 116

Electricity - imports:
0 kWh (est.)
country comparison to the world: 127

Crude oil - proved reserves:
0 bbl (1 January 2011 est.)
country comparison to the world: 115

Refined petroleum products - production:
531 bbl/day (est.)
country comparison to the world: 110

Refined petroleum products - consumption:
72,000 bbl/day (est.)
country comparison to the world: 87

Refined petroleum products - exports:
211,100 bbl/day (est.)
country comparison to the world: 33

Refined petroleum products - imports:

291,700 bbl/day (est.)
country comparison to the world: 25

Natural gas - production:
0 cu m (est.)
country comparison to the world: 167

Natural gas - consumption:
0 cu m (est.)
country comparison to the world: 126

Natural gas - exports:
0 cu m (est.)
country comparison to the world: 74

Natural gas - imports:
0 cu m (est.)
country comparison to the world: 173

Natural gas - proved reserves:
0 cu m (1 January 2011 est.)
country comparison to the world: 121

COMMUNICATION

Telephone system:
international: country code - 599

Broadcast media:
government-run Telecuracao operates a TV station and a radio station; several privately owned radio stations

Internet country code:
.cw

TRANSPORTATION

Roadways:
total: 550 km
country comparison to the world: 193

Ports and terminals:
major seaport(s): Willemstad
oil terminal(s): Bullen Baai (Curacao Terminal)
bulk cargo port(s): Fuik Bay (phosphate rock)

CARIBBEAN NETHERLANDS

Country	Netherlands
Special municipalities	• Bonaire • Sint Eustatius • Saba
Incorporated into the Netherlands	10 October 2010 (dissolution of the Netherlands Antilles)
Government (see Politics of the Netherlands)	
• National Rep.	Gilbert Isabella
• Lt. Governors	• Edison Rijna (Bonaire) • Gerald Berkel (Sint Eustatius) • Jonathan Johnson (Saba)
Area	
• Total	328 km^2 (127 sq mi) (0.8% of the Netherlands)
Highest elevation (Mount Scenery)	887 m (2,910 ft)
Population (2010)	
• Total	21,133
• Density	64/km^2 (170/sq mi) (0.1% of the Netherlands)
Languages	
• Official	Dutch
• Recognised regional	• English (Saba, St. Eustatius) • Papiamentu (Bonaire)
Time zone	AST (UTC−4)
Calling code	+599
ISO 3166 code	BQ, NL-BQ1, NL-BQ2, NL-BQ3
Currency	United States dollar (USD)
Internet TLD	.nl, .an,[a] .bq

The **Caribbean Netherlands** (Dutch: *Caribisch Nederland*) are the three special municipalities of the Netherlands that are located in the Caribbean Sea. They consist of the islands of **Bonaire**, **Sint Eustatius**, and **Saba**, although the term "Caribbean Netherlands" is sometimes used to refer to all of the islands in the Dutch Caribbean. In legislation, the three islands are also known as the **BES islands** (a more traditional acronym of their names). The islands are currently classified as *public bodies* in the Netherlands and as overseas countries and territories of the European Union; thus, EU law does not automatically apply.

Bonaire (including the islet of Klein Bonaire) is one of the Leeward Antilles and is located close to the coast of Venezuela. Sint Eustatius and Saba are in the main Lesser Antilles group and are located south of Sint Maarten and northwest of Saint Kitts and Nevis.

LEGAL STATUS

The three islands gained their current status following the dissolution of the Netherlands Antilles on 10 October 2010. At the same time, the islands of Curaçao and Sint Maarten became autonomous countries (Dutch: *landen*) within the Kingdom of the Netherlands. The island of Aruba is also a country of the Kingdom located in the Caribbean. The term "Dutch Caribbean" may refer to the three special municipalities (e.g. for stamps), but may also refer to all of the Caribbean islands within the Kingdom of the Netherlands. The population of the BES islands is 21,000. Their total area is 328 square kilometres (127 sq mi).

ADMINISTRATION

The **special municipalities** (Dutch: *bijzondere gemeenten*) carry many of the functions normally performed by Dutch municipalities. The executive power rests with the Governing Council headed by a Lieutenant governor. The main democratic body is the island council. Dutch citizens of these three islands are entitled to vote in Dutch national and (as all Dutch nationals) in European elections.

Officially the islands are classed in Dutch law as being *openbare lichamen* (literally translated as "public bodies") and not *gemeenten* (municipalities). Unlike normal municipalities, they do not form part of a Dutch province and the powers normally exercised by provincial councils within municipalities are divided between the island governments themselves and the central government by means of the National Office for the Caribbean Netherlands. For this reason, they are called "special" municipalities.

For many Dutch laws there is a special BES version. For example, social security is not on the same level as it is in the European Netherlands

NATIONAL OFFICE

The **National Office for the Caribbean Netherlands** (Dutch: *Rijksdienst Caribisch Nederland*) is responsible for taxation, policing, immigration, transport infrastructure, health, education, and social security in the islands and provides these services on behalf of the Government of the Netherlands.

This agency was established as the Regional Service Center in 2008 and became the National Office for the Caribbean Netherlands on 1 September 2010. The current director is Sybren van Dam. The *Representative for the public bodies of Bonaire, Sint Eustatius and Saba* represents the Government of the Netherlands on the islands and also performs tasks similar to a King's Commissioner.[] The current representative is Wilbert Stolte.

RELATIONSHIP WITH THE EUROPEAN UNION

The islands do not form part of the European Union and instead constitute "overseas countries and territories" (OCT status) of the Union, to which special provisions apply. The Lisbon Treaty introduced a procedure where the European Council may change the status of an overseas territory of Denmark, France, or the Netherlands regarding the application of the EU treaties to that territory. In June 2008, the Dutch government published a survey of the legal and economic impacts by a switched status from OCT to OMR.

The position of the islands will be reviewed after a five-year transitional period, which began with the dissolution of the Netherlands Antilles in October 2010. The review will be conducted as part of the planned review of the Dutch "Act for the Public bodies Bonaire, Sint Eustatius and Saba" (Dutch: *"Wet openbare lichamen Bonaire, Sint Eustatius en Saba"*), where the islands have been granted the option to become an Outermost region – and thus a direct part of the European Union

CURRENCY

Until 1 January 2011, the three islands used the Netherlands Antillean guilder; after that all three switched to the US dollar, rather than the euro (which is used in the European Netherlands) or the Caribbean guilder (which is being adopted by the other two former Antillean islands of Curaçao and Sint Maarten). The decision to introduce the US dollar on the three islands was taken in November 2008.

COMMUNICATIONS

The telephone country code remains 599, that of the former Netherlands Antilles, and is shared with Curaçao. The International Organization for Standardization has assigned the ISO 3166-1 alpha-2 country code ISO 3166-2:BQ for these islands. The IANA has not established a root zone for the .bq Internet ccTLD and whether it will be used is unknown

BONAIRE

Country	Netherlands
Incorporated into the Netherlands	10 October 2010 (dissolution of the Netherlands Antilles)
Capital (and largest city)	Kralendijk
Government (see Politics of the Netherlands)	
• Lt. Governor	Edison Rijna
Area	
• Total	294 km^2 (114 sq mi)
Population (2013)	
• Total	17,408
• Density	59/km^2 (150/sq mi)
Languages	
• Official	Dutch
• Recognised regional	Papiamentu
Time zone	AST (UTC−4)
Calling code	+599-7
ISO 3166 code	BQ-BO, NL-BQ1
Currency	US dollar (USD)

Internet TLD	.an, .bq, .nl

Bonaire is an island in the Leeward Antilles in the Caribbean Sea. Together with Aruba and Curaçao, it forms the group known as the ABC islands, located less than a hundred miles off the north coast of South America near the western part of Venezuela. Unlike much of the Caribbean region, the ABCs lie outside the hurricane belt and have an arid climate. This helps tourism as visitors to the islands can reliably expect warm, sunny weather. Bonaire is a popular destination for scuba divers, and well known for easy access to its various reefs from the shore.

Bonaire's capital is Kralendijk. The island has a permanent population of 17,408 and an area of 294 km^2 (together with nearby uninhabited Klein Bonaire). Bonaire was part of the Netherlands Antilles until the country's dissolution in 2010, when the island became a special municipality within the country of the Netherlands. It is one of the three BES islands located in the Caribbean, the other two being Sint Eustatius and Saba

REFERENDUM 2010

Prior to the 2010 referendum, the Dutch Caribbeancomprising the islands of Curaçao, Bonaire, St. Eustatius, St. Maarten and Saba, were governed as a parliamentary democracy based on the Dutch system of government with free elections held every four years. Dissension about the political future resulted in four of the five islands advocating for separation from the Netherlands Antilles. Some of the island residents wanted autonomy while others wanted more integration.

In 2005 a conference was held by the governments of the Netherlands, Aruba, and the Dutch Caribbeanto discuss future constitutional reform and dissolution of the Netherlands Antilles. In 2006, Saint Maarten and Curaçao chose autonomy, and Bonaire, St. Eustatius and Saba opted for a closer relationship with the Netherlands. Constitutional referendums and dismantlement of the Dutch Caribbeanwas scheduled to take place in 2010.

Bonaire's announced referendum scheduled for 26 March 2010 was cancelled in February 2010. The Governor of the Dutch Antilles, Frits Goedgedrag, decided to cancel it because it probably contravened international law, since part of the population is barred from voting. European Dutch nationals are only allowed to vote if they arrived on the island before 1 January 2007. The referendum was postponed to September and then October 2010. Eventually the referendum was held on 17 December 2010, with 84% voting in favour of becoming part of the Netherlands. However, as the 35% voter turnout rate was below the required 51%, the results of the referendum were declared invalid.

DISSOLUTION OF THE NETHERLANDS ANTILLES

On 10 October 2010, the Netherlands Antilles was dissolved. As a result, the government of the Netherlands assumed the task of public administration of the Caribbean Netherlands or BES Islands comprising Bonaire, St Eustatius and Saba. The three islands acquired new status as "special municipalities", making them part of the Netherlands itself (bijzondere gemeenten), a form of "public body" (openbaar lichaam) as outlined in article 134 of the Dutch Constitution. Special municipalities do not constitute part of a province.

As a special municipality, Bonaire is very much like ordinary Dutch municipalities in that it has a mayor, aldermen and a municipal council, and is governed according to most Dutch law. Antillean legislation remained in force after 10 October 2010, with the exception of those cases where Antillean law was replaced by Bonaire's municipal law. It was believed best for the island to not introduce the entire body of Dutch legislation at one time as it would cause confusion. Therefore, Dutch legislation is being introduced in stages. Bonaire retained its own unique culture while residents enjoy the same rights as Dutch citizens, including the right to vote in Dutch parliamentary elections in the Netherlands. Residents also have access to new or improved facilities and government benefits including, but not limited to, universal health care; improved health care facilities; better educational facilities with additional training for teachers, new teaching methods, and new school buildings; social housing for low-income individuals and families; a centrally dispatched single police force, fire department and ambulance service.

While the three islands are considered to be land of the Netherlands, they are not a part of the European Union, therefore not subject to European Union Law. They are considered to be an overseas country and territory and will remain as such until at least 2015.

Bonaire's non-governmental organization, "Nos Ke Boneiru Bèk" (We Want Bonaire Back), is against the current constitutional relationship with the Netherlands. With reference to Bonaire's 2004 referendum, the organization is of the opinion that such an arrangement was never the choice of the people. The Dutch Minister of Home Affairs and Kingdom Relations, Ronald Plasterk, replied to the organization confirming that only the "Island Councils in the Caribbean Netherlands have the authority to decide on holding a constitutional referendum, not the Dutch government." In response, the organization gathered more than 3,500 signatures in 2013 favoring a new referendum. In a letter to minister Plasterk, James Finies, chairman of Nos Ke Boneiru Bèk, requested a "new referendum under the right of self-determination". Plasterk responded by advising Finies that preparations for the evaluation of the public entity structure have begun for 2015, but a "possible change of the constitutional relations is not part of that evaluation." The new referendum took place on 18 December 2015. 65% of the turnout voted that they were *not* happy with the current relationship between Bonaire and the Netherlands.

CURRENCY

In 2011 the BES Islands replaced their currency, the Netherlands Antillean guilder (ANG), with the US dollar rather than replacing it with the euro which is used in the European Netherlands. The decision was based primarily on the islands' needs in relation to tourism and trade. Most countries and territories in the Caribbean use the dollar as their currency or have a currency linked to the dollar as legal tender. The guilder (ANG) has been linked to the dollar for decades with an exchange rate of ANG 1.79 = USD 1.00. Adopting the dollar put an end to the dual-currency payment system, and foreign exchange charges.

TAXES

The separate tax regimes for Bonaire, St Eustatius and Saba presents a greater risk of double taxation or double exemption from taxes. In an effort to remove the risk, two plans were introduced. One plan prevents double taxation between the Netherlands (Europe) and the BES Islands while the other prevents double taxation between the BES Islands and third countries. The new regime will generate a total annual tax revenue estimated at $52 million which is equal to the current tax revenues on the three islands. The combined population of the three Islands is approximately 20,000 with about half that many being income-taxpayers

ECONOMY

TOURISM

Bonaire's economy is mainly based on tourism, taking advantage of its warm, dry climate and natural environment. The island caters to scuba divers and snorkelers, as the surrounding coral reefs are well preserved and easily accessible from the shore. Bonaire has been widely recognized for many years in the diving community as one of the world's best shore diving destinations.

Bonaire's Marine Park offers a total of 86 named dive sites, and is home to over 57 species of soft and stony coral and more than 350 recorded fish species. Most resorts and hotels have an on-site dive shop, and other accommodations are affiliated with a dive operation.The license plates carry the logo *Divers Paradise* (in English).

Lac Bay, in the southeastern part of the island, attracts wind surfers from around the world to Bonaire. The shallow Bay is on the windward side of the island, so trade winds are strong and constant. A barrier reef across the mouth of the bay allows windsurfers of all skill levels to select wave conditions they like. Lac Bay is one of the stops in the PWA Windsurfing Freestyle World Cup and has hosted the Prokids IFCA Championship. Five of the PWA's ten highest ranked freestyle windsurfers are from Bonaire: Kiri Thode, Amado Vrieswijk, Bjorn Saragoza, Tonky Frans, and Taty Frans. In the northern end of Lac Bay is one of the best preserved mangrove forests in the Caribbean, which is popular for kayaking and snorkeling.

Bonaire is also a port of call for more than fifteen cruise lines who make more than eighty calls per season at the island. The total passenger capacity for cruise ships in Bonaire is about 185,000

Tourism infrastructure in Bonaire is contemporary and offers a variety of types of accommodations including hotels, full-service resorts, a few small bed and breakfasts, and self-catering vacation rentals of all kinds. Other tourist activities include kite-boarding, mountain-biking, hiking, sailing, charter fishing, boating, and bird-watching. All-in-all tourist expenditures in Bonaire are estimated at $125 million per year.

OTHER INDUSTRY

Salt production – Utilizing the naturally low-lying geography and traditional Dutch dyke design, much of Bonaire's southern half has been made into a giant system of ponds and pools which evaporate seawater to produce salt. Presently operated by Cargill, Bonaire's solar salt works produces 400,000 tons of industrial grade salt per year. After collection, the salt is then washed and stored in large piles. The salt facility operates its own pier where ships are loaded with salt destined for North American, European and Western Pacific markets. Bonaire's salt is used mostly in industrial roles.

The large condensing ponds which ring the crystallizer basins, called the Pekelmeer, are a natural habitat for numerous species of brine shrimp which in turn feed flocks of hundreds of pink flamingoes and other migratory birds. This is the location of Bonaire's flamingo sanctuary.

Oil storage and shipment – The Bonaire Petroleum Corporation (BOPEC) is a fuel oil storage and transhipment terminal on Bonaire. BOPEC is wholly owned by Venezuelan oil company PDVSA, and functions primarily as a storage facility for multiple grades of refined and non-refined oils from Venezuela and refineries on Curaçao and Aruba. BOPEC also has mixing and blending capabilities for its stored fuels. BOPEC's #1 pier can receive tankers up to 500,000DWT, which means there are only seven ships in the world that are too big for the BOPEC terminal. A fire at the BOPEC terminal in 2010 is believed to have had a significant impact on Goto Lake and at least one other nearby lagoon.

TRANSPORTATION

Bonaire's first airport was located near Tra'i Montaña Subi Blanku and walked across the current path of Kralendijk to Rincon and was built in 1936. The airport proved to be too small when American soldiers arrived on Bonaire in the second half of 1943. The commander stated that a new airport had to be built. Construction began in December 1943, with the new "Flamingo Airport" opening in 1945. A small terminal was built that was suitable for the number of passengers at the time. This building was used until mid-1976. The airport had received many extensions of both the runway and the terminal itself.

Today the airport is known as Flamingo International Airport and is served by a variety of both domestic and international airlines. Services from the US include Delta Air Lines and United Airlines. Airlines providing European service include Arkefly and KLM. Consistent air service from Curaçao is available through Divi Divi Air, EZAir, and Insel Air, also direct service from Aruba to Bonaire is provided by Insel Air.

The airport is equipped with a fire station, control tower, and hangar. Plans are underway for modifications to the current airport facilities, runway and the fire station

SINT EUSTATIUS

Country	Netherlands
Incorporated into the Netherlands	10 October 2010 (dissolution of the Netherlands Antilles)
Capital (and largest city)	Oranjestad
Government (see Politics of the Netherlands)	
• Lt. Governor	Gerald Berkel
Area	
• Total	21 km^2 (8 sq mi)
Population (December 2013)	
• Total	4,020
• Density	190/km^2 (500/sq mi)
Demonym(s)	St. Eustatian
Languages	
• Official	Dutch
• Recognised regional	English
Time zone	AST (UTC−4)
Calling code	+599-3
ISO 3166 code	BQ-SE, NL-BQ3
Currency	US dollar (USD)

Internet TLD	.an, .nl

Sint Eustatius, also known affectionately to the locals as **Statia** (/ˈsteɪʃə/), is part of the Caribbean Netherlands: i.e. it is a Caribbean island and a special municipality (officially "public body") of the Netherlands.

The island lies in the northern Leeward Islands portion of the West Indies, southeast of the Virgin Islands. Sint Eustatius is immediately to the northwest of Saint Kitts, and to the southeast of Saba. The regional capital is Oranjestad.

The island has an area of 21 square kilometres (8.1 sq mi). In the 2001 census, the population was recorded as 3,543 inhabitants, with a population density of 169 inhabitants per square kilometre. The official language is Dutch, but English is the "language of everyday life" on the island and education is solely in English. A local English-based creole is also spoken informally. Travellers to the island by air arrive through F.D. Roosevelt Airport.

Formerly part of the Netherlands Antilles, Sint Eustatius became a special municipality within The Netherlands on 10 October 2010.

The name of the island, "Sint Eustatius", is the Dutch name for Saint Eustace (also spelled Eustachius or Eustathius), a legendary Christian martyr, known in Spanish as *San Eustaquio* and in Portuguese as *Santo Eustáquio* or *Santo Eustácio.*

Unlike the other member islands of the Netherlands Antilles, the people of St Eustatius did not vote to leave. In a referendum on 8 April 2005, 77% of voters voted to remain within the Netherlands Antilles, compared to 21% who voted for closer ties with the Netherlands.

However, once the other islands decided to leave, meaning that the Dutch Caribbeanwould become defunct, the island council opted to become a special municipality of the Netherlands, like Saba and Bonaire.

ECONOMY

In the 18th century, "Statia" was the most important Dutch island in the Caribbean and was a center of great wealth from trading. At this time it was known as the "Golden Rock" because of its immense wealth. A very large number of warehouses lined the road that runs along Oranje Bay; most (but not all) of these warehouses are now ruined and many of the ruins are partially underwater.

A French occupation in 1795 was the beginning of the end of great prosperity for Sint Eustatius.

According to the Sint Eustatius government website, "Statia's economy is stable and well placed to grow in the near future. With practically no unemployment and a skilled workforce, we have a infrastructure in place to ensure sustained growth." In reference to this statement, one should understand that the government itself is the largest employer on the island, and the oil terminal owned by "NuStar" is the largest private employer on the island

SABA

Country	Netherlands
Incorporated into the Netherlands	10 October 2010 (dissolution of the Netherlands Antilles)
Capital (and largest city)	The Bottom
Government (see Politics of the Netherlands)	
• Lt. Governor	Jonathan Johnson
Area	
• Total	13 km^2 (5 sq mi)
Population (2013)	
• Total	1,991
• Density	150/km^2 (400/sq mi)
Languages	
• Official	Dutch
• Recognised regional	English
Time zone	AST (UTC−4)
Calling code	+599-4
ISO 3166 code	BQ-SA, NL-BQ2
Currency	U.S. dollar (USD)
Internet TLD	.an, .nl

Saba is a Caribbean island and the smallest special municipality (officially *public body*) of the Netherlands. It consists largely of the potentially active volcano Mount Scenery, at 887 metres (2,910 ft) the highest point of the entire Netherlands.

Saba has a land area of 13 square kilometres (5.0 sq mi). The population was 1,991 inhabitants, with a population density of 150 inhabitants per square kilometre (390/sq mi). Its towns and major settlements are The Bottom (the capital), Windwardside, Hell's Gate and St. Johns.

Saba became a special municipality within the country of the Netherlands after the dissolution of the Netherlands Antilles on 10 October 2010.

As Saba is now part of the Netherlands (after becoming a Netherlands public body), the island recognises and performs same-sex marriage. The first gay marriage was performed in 2012

The population of Saba (the *Sabans*) consists of 1,991 people who come from all over the world. Saba's small size has led to a fairly small number of island families, who can trace their last names back to around a half-dozen families. This means that many last names are shared around the island, the most numerous being Hassell and Johnson.

Most families are an intermixing of Dutch, English, Scottish, and African heritage. The population is also descended from the Irish who were exiled from that country after the accession of King Charles I of England in 1625. Charles exiled these Irish to the Caribbean in an effort to quell rebellion after he had forcibly procured their lands for his Scottish noble supporters.

Historically, Saba was traded among the many European nations that fought for power in the region. Slaves were also imported to work on Saba. In recent years Saba has become home to a large group of expatriates, and around 250 immigrants who are either students or teachers at the Saba University School of Medicine.

ECONOMY

The **economy of Saba**, smallest island of the Netherlands, has always been limited by its small land mass (five square miles) and low population (currently about 1500 people). Because Saba is a dormant volcano with rocky shores and only one beach, tourism was slow to develop. However, the island has become known for its eco-tourist opportunities, such as scuba diving, rock climbing, and hiking. The tourism industry now contributes more to the island's economy than any other sector.

Possibly, Saba's first settlers were a group of Englishmen who shipwrecked on its coast in 1632. However, it is unknown if they remained on the island throughout this decade. Around 1640 Saba was settled by Dutch colonists from nearby St. Eustatius. As the century progressed, Saba became a regional haven for illicit trade. Agriculture, including sugar cane, cotton, tobacco, and indigo were important first industries, as well as fishing. The first enslaved Africans arrived on Saba by at least the 1650s, together with sugar production.

Because many of Saba's men were gone at sea for extended periods, the island's women took up lace making in the late 19th century. When international mail service became available in 1884, women began selling Saba Lace to American consumers by mail order. Saba Lace exports grew in importance over the subsequent decades, reaching sales of $15,000 (US) per year by 1928.

In the latter part of the 20th century, Saba began developing the infrastructure necessary to support tourism. Juancho Yrausquin Airport, built in 1963, made travel between Saba and other islands more accessible. Likewise, the 1972 construction of a pier in Fort Bay has enabled ferry service between Saba and Saint Martin, as well as docking of small cruise ships.

In 1987, Saba's coastline and surrounding waters were designated as the Saba National Marine Park. Because of regulations to help conserve the marine park's reefs and other aquatic life, it has remained a healthy, thriving ecosystem. Scuba divers became increasingly attracted to Saba, since its reefs have been spared the damage suffered by many reefs throughout the world.

Tourism has been steadily increasing in recent years. According to Saba's official tourist bureau, in the first quarter of 2005 tourist arrivals to Saba totaled 7358. Current estimates place the number of yearly tourists at around 11,000. The largest number of tourists come from the United States, but more and more Dutch and other European travelers are making Saba a destination. Agriculture still contributes to the economy, primarily livestock and vegetables, especially potatoes. Saba Lace continues to be sold at shops on the island. The Saba University School of Medicine has grown in importance as it has expanded, contributing about 200 jobs (directly and indirectly) and $4.8 million (US) to the GDP.

STATISTICS

All the statistics in this section come from the Census Bureau of Statistics Netherlands Antilles.

Gross Domestic Product by sector, Saba (mln ANG)

Year	Government	Enterprises	GDP
1996	11.8	15.2	27.0
1997	16.4	15.4	31.8
1998	11.1	21.4	32.6
1999	11.2	22.0	33.2
2000	10.5	21.5	31.5
2001	9.5	22.6	32.1
2002	9.0	23.2	32.2
2003	8.8	24.8	33.6

Businesses per Industry

This information is according to the Business Census. Due to the CSB's criteria for defining a business during this census, very small businesses were not counted. Certain other groups were excluded, such as small independent farmers and fishermen, market vendors, and independent taxi drivers.

The census also does not include government departments and services or foundations completely subsidized by the government.
Agriculture and mining: 1
Manufacturing: 2
Electricity, gas and water: 1
Construction: 3
Trade: 24
Hotels and restaurants: 20
Transport and communication: 5
Financial services: 5
Business services: 2
Education: 1
Health and social work: 0
Other services: 5
Total: 69

PRACTICAL AND LEGAL INFORMATION FOR CONDUCTING BUSINESS

OFFSHORE INFORMATION

Traditionally used in conjunction with The Netherlands for tax efficient routing of dividends from highly taxed countries to an offshore jurisdiction.

ADVANTAGES	Low tax jurisdiction forming a part of The Kingdom of the Netherlands. No withholding taxes. Advance tax rulings. Good professional infrastructure
DISADVANTAGES	No tax exempt companies
CORPORATE LEGISLATION SOURCE	Book 1 Part 2 of the Commercial Code of Dutch Caribbeans(No 37 of 1959 – last amended in 1992)
COMPANY STATUS	NV (Naamloze Venootschap) – a limited liability company
USUAL MINIMUM CAPITAL	US$30,000 at least 20% of which must be issued and of the 20%, 10% of each share must be paid up
COMPANY NAME	Prior approval and reservation required
TIME TAKEN TO INCORPORATE	1 week
ARE SHELF COMPANIES AVAILABLE	Yes
CAPITAL DUTY	None, but US$135 Stamp Duty paid on incorporation
MINIMUM NUMBER OF SHAREHOLDERS	One
ARE BEARER SHARES / SHARES OF NO PAR VALUE POSSIBLE?	Yes, provided they are held by a custodian such as Fiduciary Trust Limited / No
DIRECTORS: MINIMUM NUMBER / CORPORATE DIRECTORS ALLOWED / LOCATION	One / No, unless a trust company / One must be resident
SECRETARY: MANDATORY / CORPORATE SECRETARY ALLOWED / LOCATION	Not recognised under Dutch Caribbeanscorporate law
IS THERE A REQUIREMENT FOR A REGISTERED OFFICE / REGISTERED AGENT	Yes / No
IS THERE A REQUIREMENT BY THE AUTHORITIES PRIOR TO INCORPORATION OR PRIOR TO TAX STATUS BEING GRANTED	'Declaration of No Objection' and foreign exchange licence to be obtained from Ministry of Justice. Granted as a matter of course
INFORMATION AVAILABLE ON PUBLIC FILE	Articles / Managing Director / Members of supervisory board / Capital Structure

DOCUMENTS TO BE KEPT AT REGISTERED OFFICE	Share register, minutes and resolutions, share transfer documents, administrative and book keeping records
CORPORATE BOOKS AND SEAL	See above – concept of seal is unknown
ACCOUNTS REQUIRED / FILED	Yes but not audited / No
ANNUAL RETURN REQUIRED	Annual profits tax return
WHERE ARE MEETINGS TO BE HELD	Shareholders meetings to be in the Antilles. No restriction for board meetings
ANNUAL FEES PAYABLE TO THE GOVERNMENT: TAX / ANNUAL RETURN FILING FEE	3-6% depending on activities and profits / Nil
ARE THERE ANY EXCHANGE CONTROLS	Yes, but Central Bank automatically grants a foreign exchange licence
DOUBLE TAX TREATIES	Netherlands

OFFSHORE COMPANIES REGULATIONS

Under the legislation which applied until 1999, in order to qualify for offshore status a Dutch Caribbeanentity had to be wholly owned by non-residents, and its income had to arise outside the jurisdiction. However, various business sectors have specially favourable taxation regimes which reflect their international nature. These special regimes are described in this section along with the tax treatment of offshore corporations as such.

In December 1999 the Dutch Caribbeanadopted new legislation under the heading of The New Fiscal Framework (NFF). This legislation was intended to avert inclusion on the OECD's threatened 'black-list' of errant offshore jurisdictions in 2000. The NFF involves the abolition of the distinction between offshore and onshore companies, at least for new formations, the introduction of a new company form named NABV (Nederlands Antilliaanse Besloten Vennootschap) which can be tax-exempt but which does not benefit from tax treaties, the introduction of a 10% withholding tax on dividends (not in fact being put into effect), and the reduction of the profits tax rate to 30%. See Forms of Company for details of the conditions under which an NABV can request exemption from profits tax and withholding tax.

Provisions under the NFF and a revised 'BRK' (tax treaty with the Netherlands) came into effect from January 1, 2002. They include:

- for an intial period the proposed Dutch Caribbeandividend withholding tax of 10% will not enter into force
- dividends from a Dutch corporation to Dutch Caribbeancorporate shareholders, who own at least 25% of the shares in the Dutch corporation, will be exempted from Dutch dividend withholding tax, provided that the dividend is subject to Dutch Caribbeantax at a rate of at least 8.3%.
- the Dutch corporation will have to withhold 8.3% dividend withholding tax from the gross dividend. The 8.3% which has been withheld upon the dividend

distribution in the Netherlands can be credited against tax in the Netherlands Antilles

- dividends and capital gains derived from shareholdings in a Netherlands corporation will be exempted from additional profit tax in the Dutch Caribbeanprovided that the shareholding amounts to at least 25% and that 8.3% Dutch Caribbeantax is paid on the gross amount of dividends received

- dividends paid by Dutch corporations to Dutch Caribbeancorporations unable to take advantage of the participation exemption will be subject to 15% Dutch dividend withholding tax. Existing Dutch Caribbeanoffshore corporations may elect for the new dividend treatment.

- the activities of an exempted company (NABV) will be restricted to investments in debt instruments, securities and deposits

- for Dutch Caribbeancoporations incorporated before June 30, 1999, subject to profit tax and having a book year which ends before 1st January 2002, the grandfathering rules with respect to the offshore regime will remain applicable until 2019 as long as the company continues to have substantial business.

In December 2000 the OECD announced the Netherlands Antilles' commitment to eliminate harmful tax practices by 31 December 2005 which has secured the jurisdiction's deletion from the OECD list of countries deemed to possess "harmful" tax practices.

LEGAL REGIME FOR OFFSHORE COMPANIES

Most offshore operations in the Dutch Caribbeanhave hitherto taken the form of a limited liability company (Naamloze Venootschap, or NV). See Types of Company for the basic legal consititution of an NV.

The formation process for an offshore NV follows the normal pattern. Beneficial ownership does not have to be disclosed, but the professional firms involved apply a 'know-your-customer' rule. Opening a bank account will require references of some type. A registered office must be maintained in the jurisdiction.
Offshore companies do not have to be audited, other than financial institutions, which are regulated by the central bank

TAX FOR OFFSHORE OPERATIONS

Domestic Corporate Taxes for the general principles of Dutch Caribbeancorporate taxation, also apply to offshore entities. The taxation of Dutch Caribbeancompanies is governed by the National Ordinance on Profit Tax 1940; special taxation regimes have been introduced for companies falling under articles 8A, 8B, 14 and 14A of the Ordinance, as follows (NB the special regimes normally apply only to non-treaty-related income - also note that these articles have been repealed under the New Fiscal Framework and will only continue to apply to existing companies under the grandfathering provisions of the NFF - see above):

- **Investment and Holding companies** Income is taxed at 2.4% on the first NAf 100,000 of net income and 3% on the balance. Municipal surtax is not applied. Capital gains are not taxed; but capital losses are not deductible.
- **Mutual Funds** These are exempt from profits tax if they have either minimum net assets of $50m, at least fifty shareholders, and four local employees, or if they have minimum net assets of $300m and two local employees; otherwise the fund will be taxed on its net assets, giving a minimum charge to tax of $1,000 rising to a maximum charge of $10,000.
- **Trading companies** The normal applicable rates of tax are 24% on the first NAf 100,000 of net income and 30% thereafter; however it is usually possible to obtain a ruling from the Inspector of Taxes exempting 90% of income, which has the effect of reducing the rates to the usual offshore levels of 2.4% and 3%.
- **Banks** Investment and interest income (which qualifies under Article 14) is taxed on the usual offshore basis at 2.4% and 3%; commission and fee income will suffer 24% and 30% unless a tax ruling can be obtained (normally possible).
- **Intellectual Property Holding companies** If a tax ruling can be obtained, the effective tax rate for income from royalties, licenses, patents, copyrights, trademarks etc will be 1%.
- **Insurance companies** Foreign-owned captive and reinsurance companies not in receipt of treaty-related income benefit from a concession that deems their income to be NAf 100,000, giving them a fixed tax rate of NAf 2,400 annually.
- **Real Estate Holding companies** These companies are not taxed on income derived from real estate (or subsidiaries wholly or predominantly engaged in owning real estate) outside the Netherlands Antilles.
- **Ocean Shipping and Aviation companies** These companies are taxed at 7.73% on the first NAf 100,000 of net income, and 9.66% thereafter (including the 15% municipal surcharge). They have the option of paying tax at the rate of NAf 0.40 per gross registered tonne (minimum tax NAf 1,000 per vessel).

Businesses organised as Stichtings (Foundations) will be treated as if they are companies from a tax point of view. Partnerships are treated as fiscally transparent, so that the individual partners pay taxes, not the partnership

E-COMMERCE TAXATION REGIME

As of April 1, 2001, special tax legislation for international Internet companies on Curacao came into force to act as an incentive to persuade e-commerce companies to relocate their activities to the island. The new law replaces the old Free Zone law and governs 'E-Zones', which are areas within the Dutch Caribbeanwhere international trade and supporting services may be carried out by electronic communication and electronic commerce.

Only companies with capital divided into shares may perform activities in the e-zones including trading or providing services to companies located outside the Netherlands Antilles.

A company may be allowed to conduct business with other firms located in an e-zone but the company has to apply to the local authority before doing so. If approved, the company must meet a certain set of conditions relating to price setting, quality of the goods and services on offer and the distribution of goods. The turnover generated through local business may not exceed 25% of the total turnover.

In terms of profit tax, the profit of companies within the e-zones will be taxed at 2% - including surtax - until January 1, 2026. This rate is not applicable on the profit of an e-zone company if it is generated by the sale of goods or services to companies located in the Dutch Caribbeanor generated through the rendering of services to affiliated companies located in the country. In addition there is no import duty or turnover tax charged on goods entering the e-zones.

Finally, employees who have lived in excess of five years outside the Dutch Caribbeanbefore starting work in an e-zone can qualify for expatriate status, with certain tax-free benefits - providing certain conditions are met. An e-zone company can calculate the wage tax on the net salary of the employee without being required to 'gross up' the salary.

TAXATION OF FOREIGN EMPLOYEES OF OFFSHORE OPERATIONS

Since 1987 there has been a special tax regime in the Dutch Caribbeanfor 'specialist expatriate employees in the financial services (offshore) sector or another important economic business sector generating hard currency and of significance to the community'. As will be seen above, this definition has to be interpreted in the context of each particular business sector. Any individual business or employee therefore needs to take professional advice regarding their 'expatriate' status and the availability of the special tax regime.

Resident expatriates with access to the special regime are allowed 35% tax exemption on fringe benefits up to 40% of their salary, with a maximum of NAf 40,000; in addition, the following benefits are exempt from tax altogether:

- foreign social security contributions towards retirement provision;
- educational costs at the international or Dutch school in Curacao, or an equivalent school abroad, to a maximum of NAf 25,000 per child per year;
- relocation costs including hotel rooms for two months on arrival;
- settling-in and moving-out allowances being the lower of two months' salary or NAf 12,000.working in Cyprus are taxed at 50% of the normal rates and are entitled to personal allowances; remuneration during any period of overseas absence is exempt from tax.

Non-residents (residential status depends on location of permanent home, habitual residence, and 'centre of economic and social interest') are taxed only on certain types of Dutch Caribbeanincome

EXCHANGE CONTROL

Dutch Caribbeancompanies owned by non-residents that do not carry on business on the islands may obtain a license from the Bank of Dutch Caribbean(the central bank) which exempts them from all exchange control regulations.
Many transactions involving foreign exchange in the Dutch Caribbeanattract a 1% 'license' tax which is payable by the bank concerned to the central bank. The rules are complex, and professional advice is needed if this tax is likely to be a significant factor.
The repatriation of income or capital from the Dutch Caribbeanrequires a license, but these are granted automatically on application.

EMPLOYMENT AND RESIDENCE

A stay in the Dutch Caribbeanfor work or residence requires residence and/or work permits, unless you are Antillean, or already a long-time resident (more than 10 years). Residence permits have to be applied for in person at the Governor's offices; a good deal of personal, medical and financial information and documentation is required. Work permits have to be applied for by employers, after advertising a position in local newspapers and failing to fill it.

IMPORTANT FINANCIAL ACTIVITY REGULATIONS

DESCRIPTION OF MONEY MARKET INSTRUMENTS

Effective November 1, 2000, the Bank will discontinue the publication of the discount rate, as the discount window has been replaced by the possibility for commercial banks to borrow against the reserve requirement.

The Bank will use money market instruments whenever the liquidity position of the banking system warrants the use of these instruments. The money market instruments the Bank has at its disposal are the CD- and the REPO-facilities.

Certificates of Deposit

The Bank offers the local commercial banks Certificates of Deposit (CD's) with a nominal amount of NAf. 100,000 and a fixed interest payment, which is linked to the 'Targeted Fed Funds rate'. The spread between the 'Targeted Fed Funds rate' and the interest offered is 137.5 basispoints.

The interest rate offered on the CD's is published each month on the CD-subscription form. This form will be send to you at least two working days before the start of a reserve requirement period, i.e. together with the announcement of the reserve requirement percentage and the size of the reserve requirement. On this form, you can fill out the total nominal amount of CD's you want to buy. The CD-subscription form has to be returned (either by fax or by mail) to the Bank's Treasury Department before 12.00 AM on the first day of the reserve requirement period. The same day, the amount listed on your form will be transferred from your clearing account to a CD-account, which the Bank will open for your institution. Every change on this account will result in a statement.

Interest is calculated using the actual number of days and a year consisting of 365 days. Interest payments will take place at the end of the maturity period. The interest will be deposited on your clearing account, together with the repayment of the principal.

The CD's are negotiable among domestic commercial banks. Whenever commercial banks reach an agreement on the sale and purchase of CD's, they both have to notify the Bank before 2.30 PM to assure same day settlement. The Bank will only act as a counterpart in the transaction if the liquidity position of the banking sector justifies such action.

The CD's qualify as part of the required reserves. This implies increased flexibility for the commercial banks and allows them to earn some interest on the reserve requirement.

REPURCHASE AGREEMENT (REPO)

The REPO-facility covers maturities from 2 weeks up to two months, and provides the commercial banks with an investment opportunity in Antillean Guilders. Under this facility, the Bank is prepared to sell, out of its own portfolio, securities to the local commercial banks under the condition of a repurchase of these securities after a specified period of time. In contrast with the previous policy, these securities not only include Netherlands Antillean government securities but also the Bank's CD's and foreign exchange.

The Bank will offer a yield on these transactions, which will be irrespective of the coupon rate or the market yield of the underlying security and will only depend on the length of the period during which the commercial bank is the holder of the securities. The Bank will not sell securities, which fall due or have their coupon date during a repurchase period.

Securities of the Central Government and the Island Government of Curaçao bought under this REPO-facility have to be reported under the Chart of Account items 1301 and 1302, respectively. The securities bought under the REPO-facility will increase domestic credit extension to the government sector by your institution. To counteract this development, your limit for domestic credit to the government will be temporarily increased during the repurchase period, in case a month-end lies within this period. Commercial banks will be notified of the increase on their monthly Monetary Cash Reserve Table.

POLICY ON FOREIGN POSITIONS

Commercial banks are required to submit their weekly B-9 reporting form stating their positions on Friday on each Monday. This reporting requirement is based on the 'Aanwijzing no. 5 van de Bekendmaking inzake het Deviezenverkeer AW/2000-1' and section 14 of the National Ordinance on the Supervision of Banking and Credit Institutions (P.B. 1994, no. 4).

Under the policy, it is not allowed to have a negative Net Foreign Assets position, but the Net Foreign Assets position is not bound to a maximum. When your institution has a negative Net Foreign Assets position, the Bank will charge an administration fee equal to the amount of the negative position multiplied by 7% (the Bank's pledging rate or "beleningsrente") and again by (7/360) [1]. This formula to calculate the fee is subject to change by the Bank without prior notice. The fee is calculated weekly and billed on a monthly basis.

In view of the urgency for accurate and timely information, the Bank has introduced a penalty for late reporting of the B-9. The Bank will issue a warning in case your B-9 reporting is submitted after Monday more then once. If late reporting continues after this warning, the Bank will impose a penalty of NAf. 1,000 for each day of late reporting, starting 7 days after the issue of the warning (please refer to the national decree of September 23, 1994 (P.B. 1994, no. 110)).

REGULATIONS FOR SPECIALIZED CREDIT INSTITUTIONS AND SAVINGS BANKS IN THE DUTCH CARIBBEAN

ADMISSION POLICY

In principle, specialized credit institutions and savings banks are only admitted as long as the banking market provides sufficient opportunities for a sound development in the banking sector.

MANAGEMENT / SUPERVISION OF MANAGEMENT

- A secondary financial institution must have a Board of Managing Directors with at least two members and a Board of Supervisory Directors with at least three members.
- The members of the Board of Managing Directors and the Board of Supervisory Directors must possess sufficient experience in banking, have a thorough knowledge of banking activities and be of high personal integrity.
- At all times at least two members of the Board of Managing Directors must be in function and be a resident of the Netherlands Antilles.
- At least one member of the Board of Supervisory Directors must be a resident of the Netherlands Antilles.
- All members of the Board of Managing Directors and the Board of Supervisory Directors must be natural persons.
- Members of the Board of Managing Directors shall not be members of the Board of Supervisory Directors and vice versa.
- The objectives or antecedents of aforementioned persons must not endanger the interest of the depositors or future depositors and any other liability holder or future liability holders.
- The appointment of the members Board of Managing Directors and the Board of Supervisory Directors is subject to written approval of the Bank.

Capital

- A secondary financial institution being a mortgage bank in the legal form of a limited liability company must have a free and unencumbered minimum equity capital of at least NAf. 3 million. All other secondary financial institutions being limited liability companies must have a free and unencumbered equity capital of at least NAf 1 million.
- A secondary financial institution being a branch must pro-vide the Bank with a guarantee of its head office stating that the head office shall guarantee all liabilities of the branch.

Shareholders

- The persons exercising a considerable influence on the affairs of the secondary financial institution by means of voting rights derived from shares, or in any comparable manner, must be of high personal integrity. The objectives or antecedents of these persons must not influence the institution in an undesirable way.
- The ultimate beneficial owners must be known to the Bank.

Shares

- In the articles of incorporation a "repurchase of own shares" clause shall not be included.
- All shares of the secondary financial institution must be registered.

Share Holding by Individuals

- A natural person, shall not, without the approval of the Bank, directly or indirectly, control or hold more than 5% of the institution's capital.
- The total of individual shareholding by natural persons shall not, without the approval of the Bank, exceed 25% of total share capital.

FINANCIAL POSITION PARENT COMPANY / HEAD OFFICE

The financial statements of the last three years of the parent company or, in case of a branch, the head office, should reflect an unqualified opinion.

Business Plan and System of Internal Controls
A secondary financial institution must submit a business plan together with its financial forecasts reflecting a sound and realistic projection of the activities the institution will undertake to accomplish its statutory objectives.
The intended system of internal controls must reflect adequate controls, including accounting controls, to safeguard the assets of the institution and the operations against any undue risks. Moreover, the intended system of internal controls should reflect adequate segregation of duties at least within the critical areas of operations of the institution.

Scope of Activities
The articles of incorporation shall not enable the secondary financial institution to develop activities which are outside the scope of their normal business and that might pose a danger to sound policy.

Legal Form
The legal form is that of a limited liability company ("naamloze vennootschap") or a branch of a foreign credit institution with a legal form comparable to that of a limited liability company, or a form acceptable to the Bank.

Name
The name of the institution must clearly indicate the identity of its parent institution or head office.
When applying the following procedures must be adhered to:

1. The Bank must obtain an application for a license under the terms of article 3 of the National Ordinance on the Supervision of Banking and Credit Institutions 1994 (P.B. 1994 no. 4). For all applications an application form must be submitted by registered mail to the Bank. This form can be obtained at the Bank.
2. The application is considered to have been filed when the following correct and complete information has been received by the Bank:
    1. The application form.
    2. A duly signed statement of a Certified Public Accountant certifying that the applicant has free and unencumbered equity capital of at least NAf. 5 million. Taking into consideration the nature of the activities of the institution, the Bank may in its final decision require that the institution has capital in excess of NAf. 5 million.

3. It is advisable to commence business with an amount of capital well in excess of the minimum required by the Bank. In case of a branch office, the head office should issue a guarantee for all the liabilities of the secondary financial institution.
4. A statement from the supervisory authority of the head office or parent company, stating that there are no legal impediments to the establishment in the Dutch Caribbeanand indicating to the Bank how, and to what extent supervision will be exercised upon the applicant institution.
5. A list of the correspondent banks.
6. Personal Questionnaires and resumes of experience of all intended Managing Directors, the Board of Supervisory Directors and of all individual shareholders being natural persons.
7. Certified personal financial statements of each individual shareholder, being a natural person.
8. A Declaration of good conduct ("verklaring van goed gedrag") of the prospective managing and supervisory directors. Such declaration may be obtained from the police/judicial authority and certified by the Embassy or Consulate of the Kingdom of the Netherlands in the home country.
9. Proof of the place of residence of the members of the Board of Managing Directors and the Board of Supervisory Directors and all their addresses of the last five years.
10. A copy of the shareholders register.

Additional information may be requested if necessary during the analysis of the information submitted.
Within six (6) months of the issuance of the license subject bank must commence its activities, otherwise the license will be withdrawn pursuant to article 9, paragraph 1b of the National Ordinance on the Supervision of Banking and Credit Institutions 1994 (PB 1994 no. 4).

REGULATIONS FOR LOCAL GENERAL BANKS

Admission Policy
In principle, general banks are only admitted as long as the banking market provides sufficient opportunities for a sound development in the banking sector.

Management / Supervision of Management

- A local general bank must have a Board of Managing Directors with at least two members and a Board of Supervisory Directors with at least three members.
- The members of the Board of Managing Directors and the Board of Supervisory Directors must possess sufficient experience in banking, have a thorough knowledge of banking activities and be of high personal integrity.
- At all times at least two members of the Board of Managing Directors must be in function and be a resident of the Netherlands Antilles. At least one member of

the Board of Supervisory Directors must be a resident of the Netherlands Antilles.

- All members of the Board of Managing Directors and the Board of Supervisory Directors must be natural persons.
- Members of the Board of Managing Directors shall not be members of the Board of Supervisory Directors and vice versa.
- The objectives or antecedents of aforementioned persons must not endanger the interests of the depositors or future depositors and any other liability holder or future liability holders.
- The appointment of the members of the Board of Managing Directors and the Board of Supervisory Directors is subject to the prior written approval of the Bank.

Capital

A local general bank must have a minimum equity capital of at least NAf. 5 million, free and unencumbered.

Shareholders

- The persons exercising a considerable influence on the affairs of the local general bank by means of voting rights derived from shares, or in any comparable manner, must be of high personal integrity. The objectives or antecedents of these persons must not influence the bank in an undesirable way.
- The ultimate beneficial owners must be known to the Bank.

Shares

- In the articles of incorporation a "repurchase of own shares" clause shall not be included.
- All shares of the local general bank must be registered.

Share Holding by Individuals

- A natural person, shall not, without the approval of the Bank, directly or indirectly, control or hold more than 5% of the bank's capital.
- The total of individual shareholding by natural persons shall not, without the approval of the Bank, exceed 25% of total share capital.

Financial Position Parent Companies / Affiliated Companies

The financial statements of the last three years of the parent or affiliated companies should reflect an unqualified opinion.

Business Plan and System of Internal Controls

A local general bank must submit a business plan together with its financial forecasts reflecting a sound and realistic projection of the activities the bank will undertake to accomplish its statutory objectives. The intended system of internal controls must reflect adequate controls, including accounting controls, to safeguard the assets of the institution and the operations against any undue risks.

Moreover, the intended system of internal controls should reflect adequate segregation of duties at least within the critical areas of operations of the institution.

Scope of Activities

The articles of incorporation shall not enable the bank to develop activities which are outside the scope of normal banking business and that might pose a danger to sound banking policy.

Legal Form

The legal form is that of a limited liability company (see definition)

When applying the following procedures must be adhered to:

1. The Bank must obtain an application for a license under the terms of article 3 of the National Ordinance on the Supervision of Banking and Credit Institutions 1994 (P.B. 1994 no. 4). For all applications an application form must be submitted by registered mail to the Bank. This form can be obtained at the Bank.
2. The application is considered to have been filed when the following correct and complete information has been received by the Bank:
    1. The application form.
    2. A duly signed statement of a Certified Public Accountant certifying that the applicant has at its disposal equity capital of at least NAf. 5 million. Taking into consideration the nature of the activities of the institution the Bank may, in its final decision, require that the institution's capital be in excess of NAf. 5 million. It is advisable to commence business with an amount of capital well in excess of the minimum required by the Bank.
    3. A statement from the supervisory authority of the parent or affiliated bank, stating that there are no legal impediments to the establishment in the Dutch Caribbeanand indicating to the Bank how, and to what extent, supervision will be exercised upon the applicant bank. >

TRANSFER INTERRUPTED!

list of the correspondent banks of the prospective bank.

4. Personal Questionnaires and resumes of experience of all intended Managing Directors, the Board of Supervisory Directors and of all individual shareholders, being natural persons.
5. Certified personal financial statements of each individual shareholder, being a natural person.
6. A Declaration of good conduct ("Verklaring van goed gedrag") of the prospective managing and supervisory directors. Such declaration may be obtained from the police/judicial authority and certified by the Embassy or Consulate of the Kingdom of the Netherlands in the home country.
7. Proof of the place of residence of the members of the Board of Managing Directors and the Board of Supervisory Directors and all their addresses of the last five years.
8. A copy of the shareholders register.

Additional information may be requested if necessary during the analysis of the information submitted.

Within six (6) months of the issuance of the license subject bank must commence its activities, otherwise the license will be with-drawn pursuant to article 9, paragraph 1b of the National Ordinance on the Supervision of Banking and Credit Institutions 1994 (PB 1994 no. 4).

For Subsidiaries of Foreign General Banks

Admission Policy

In principle, general banks are only admitted as long as the banking market provides sufficient opportunities for a sound development in the banking sector.

Management / Supervision of Management

- A subsidiary of a foreign general bank must have a Board of Managing Directors with at least two members and a Board of Supervisory Directors with at least three members.
- The members of the Board of Managing Directors and the Board of Supervisory Directors must possess sufficient experience in banking, have a thorough knowledge of banking activities and be of high personal integrity.
- At all times at least two members of the Board of Managing Directors must be in function and be a resident of the Netherlands Antilles. At least one member of the Board of Supervisory Directors must be a resident of the Netherlands Antilles.
- All members of the Board of Managing Directors and the Board of Supervisory Directors must be natural persons.
- Members of the Board of Managing Directors shall not be members of the Board of Supervisory Directors and vice versa.
- The objectives or antecedents of aforementioned persons must not endanger the interests of the depositors or future depositors and any other liability holder or future liability holders.
- **Management**; The appointment of the members of the Board of Managing Directors and the Board of Supervisory Directors is subject to the prior written approval of the Bank.

Capital

A subsidiary of a foreign general bank must have a minimum equity capital of at least NAf. 5 million, free and unencumbered.

Shareholders

- The persons exercising a considerable influence on the affairs of the subsidiary of a foreign general bank by means of voting rights derived from shares, or in any comparable manner, must be of high personal integrity. The objectives or antecedents of these persons must not influence the bank in an undesirable way.
- The ultimate beneficial owners must be known to the Bank.

Shares

- In the articles of incorporation a "repurchase of own shares" clause shall not be included.

All shares of the subsidiary of a foreign general bank must be registered.

Share Holding by Individuals

- A natural person, shall not, without the approval of the Bank, directly or indirectly, control or hold more than 5% of the bank's capital.
- The total of individual shareholding by natural persons shall not, without the approval of the Bank, exceed 25% of total share capital.

Financial Position Parent Company

The financial statements of the last three years of the parent company should reflect an unqualified opinion.

Business Plan and System of Internal Controls

A subsidiary of a foreign general bank must submit a business plan together with its financial forecasts reflecting a sound and realistic projection of the activities the bank will undertake to accomplish its statutory objectives. The intended system of internal controls must reflect adequate controls, including accounting controls, to safeguard the assets of the institution and the operations against any undue risks. Moreover, the intended system of internal controls should reflect adequate segregation of duties at least within the critical areas of operations of the institution.

Scope of Activities

The articles of incorporation shall not enable the subsidiary of a foreign general bank to develop activities which are outside the scope of normal banking business and that might pose a danger to sound banking policy.

Legal Form

The legal form is that of a limited liability company (see definition).

When applying the following procedures must be adhered to:

1. The Bank must obtain an application for a licence under the terms of article 3 of the National Ordinance on the Supervision of Banking and Credit Institutions 1994 (P.B. 1994 no. 4). For all applications an application form must be submitted by registered mail to the Bank. This form can be obtained at the Bank.
2. The application is considered to have been filed when the following correct and complete information has been received by the Bank:
    1. The application form.
    2. A duly signed statement of a Certified Public Accountant certifying that the applicant has at its disposal equity capital of at least NAf.5 million. Taking into consideration the nature of the activities of the institution the Bank may in its final decision require that the institution's capital be in excess of NAf. 5 million. It is advisable to commence business with an amount of capital well in excess of the minimum required by the Bank.

3. A statement from the supervisory authority of the affiliated or parent bank, stating that there are no legal impediments to the establishment in the Dutch Caribbeanand indicating to the Bank how, and to what extent supervision will be exercised upon the applicant bank.
4. A list of the correspondent banks of the prospective bank.
5. Personal Questionnaires and resumes of experience of all intended Managing Directors, the Board of Supervisory Directors and of all individual shareholders, being natural persons.
6. Certified personal financial statements of each individual shareholder, being a natural person.
7. A Declaration of good conduct ("verklaring van goed gedrag") of the prospective managing and supervisory directors. Such declaration may be obtained from the police/judicial authority and certified by the Embassy or Consulate of the Kingdom of the Netherlands in the home country.
8. Proof of the place of residence of the members of the Board of Managing Directors and the Board of Supervisory Directors and all their addresses of the last five years.
9. A copy of the shareholders register.

Additional information may be requested if necessary during the analysis of the information submitted.

Within six (6) months of the issuance of the licence subject bank must commence its activities, otherwise the licence will be withdrawn pursuant to article 9, paragraph 1b of the National Ordinance on the Supervision of Banking and Credit Institutions 1994 (PB 1994 no. 4).

For Branches of Foreign General Banks

Admission Policy

In principle, general banks are only admitted as long as the banking market provides sufficient opportunities for a sound development in the banking sector.

Management / Supervision of Management

- A branch must have at least two managers. The head office of the branch must have a Board of Supervisory Directors with at least three members.
- The managers must possess sufficient experience in banking, have a thorough knowledge of banking activities and be of high personal integrity.
- At all times the managers must be in function and be a resident of the Netherlands Antilles.
- All managers must be natural persons.
- The objectives or antecedents of aforementioned persons must not endanger the interests of the depositors or future depositors and any other liability holder or future liability holders.
- The appointment of the managers is subject to the prior written approval of the Bank.

Capital

- A branch must provide the Bank with a guarantee of its head office stating that the head office shall guarantee all liabilities of the branch. A sample of the guarantee letter is available at the Bank.

Financial Position Head Office

The financial statements of the last three years of the head office should reflect an unqualified opinion.

Business Plan and System of Internal Controls

A branch must submit a business plan together with its financial forecasts reflecting a sound and realistic projection of the activities the bank will undertake to accomplish the statutory objectives of its head office. The intended system of internal controls must reflect adequate controls, including accounting controls, to safeguard the assets of the institution and the operations against any undue risks. Moreover, the intended system of internal controls should reflect adequate segregation of duties at least within the critical areas of operations of the institution.

Scope of Activities

The articles of incorporation of the head office shall not enable the branch to develop activities which are outside the scope of normal banking business and that might pose a danger to sound banking policy.

Legal Form

The legal form is that of a branch of a foreign general bank which has a legal form comparable to that of a limited liability company.

Name

The name of the institution must clearly indicate the identity of its head office.

When applying the following procedures must be adhered to:

1. The Bank must obtain an application for a license under the terms of article 3 of the National Ordinance on the Supervision of Banking and Credit Institutions 1994 (P.B. 1994 no. 4). For all applications an application form must be submitted by registered mail to the Bank. This form can be obtained at the Bank.
2. The application is considered to have been filed when the following correct and complete information has been received by the Bank:
    1. The application form.
    2. A guarantee issued by the head office for all the liabilities of the branch.
    3. A statement from the supervisory authority of the head office, stating that there are no legal impediments to the establishment in the Dutch Caribbeanand indicating to the Bank how, and to what extent supervision will be exercised upon the applicant bank.
    4. A list of the correspondent banks of the bank.
    5. Personal Questionnaires and resumes of experience of all managers.
    6. A Declaration of good conduct ("Verklaring van goed gedrag") of the prospective managers. Such declaration may be obtained from the police/judicial authority and certified by the Embassy or Consulate of the Kingdom of the Netherlands in the home country.
    7. Proof of the place of residence of the managers.

Additional information may be requested if necessary during the analysis of the information submitted.

Within six (6) months of the issuance of the license subject bank must commence its activities, otherwise the license will be withdrawn pursuant to article 9, paragraph 1b of the National Ordinance on the Supervision of Banking and Credit Institutions 1994 (PB 1994 no. 4).

For Specialized Credit Institutions and Savings Banks in the Dutch Caribbean

Admission Policy

In principle, specialized credit institutions and savings banks are only admitted as long as the banking market provides sufficient opportunities for a sound development in the banking sector.

Management / Supervision of Management

- A secondary financial institution must have a Board of Managing Directors with at least two members and a Board of Supervisory Directors with at least three members.
- The members of the Board of Managing Directors and the Board of Supervisory Directors must possess sufficient experience in banking, have a thorough knowledge of banking activities and be of high personal integrity.
- At all times at least two members of the Board of Managing Directors must be in function and be a resident of the Netherlands Antilles.
- At least one member of the Board of Supervisory Directors must be a resident of the Netherlands Antilles.
- All members of the Board of Managing Directors and the Board of Supervisory Directors must be natural persons.
- Members of the Board of Managing Directors shall not be members of the Board of Supervisory Directors and vice versa.
- The objectives or antecedents of aforementioned persons must not endanger the interest of the depositors or future depositors and any other liability holder or future liability holders.
- The appointment of the members Board of Managing Directors and the Board of Supervisory Directors is subject to written approval of the Bank.

Capital

- A secondary financial institution being a mortgage bank in the legal form of a limited liability company must have a free and unencumbered minimum equity capital of at least NAf. 3 million. All other secondary financial institutions being limited liability companies must have a free and unencumbered equity capital of at least NAf 1 million.
- A secondary financial institution being a branch must pro-vide the Bank with a guarantee of its head office stating that the head office shall guarantee all liabilities of the branch.

Shareholders

- The persons exercising a considerable influence on the affairs of the secondary financial institution by means of voting rights derived from shares, or in any comparable manner, must be of high personal integrity. The objectives or antecedents of these persons must not influence the institution in an undesirable way.
- The ultimate beneficial owners must be known to the Bank.

Shares

- In the articles of incorporation a "repurchase of own shares" clause shall not be included.
- All shares of the secondary financial institution must be registered.

Share Holding by Individuals

- A natural person, shall not, without the approval of the Bank, directly or indirectly, control or hold more than 5% of the institution's capital.
- The total of individual shareholding by natural persons shall not, without the approval of the Bank, exceed 25% of total share capital.

Financial Position Parent Company / Head Office

The financial statements of the last three years of the parent company or, in case of a branch, the head office, should reflect an unqualified opinion.

Business Plan and System of Internal Controls

A secondary financial institution must submit a business plan together with its financial forecasts reflecting a sound and realistic projection of the activities the institution will undertake to accomplish its statutory objectives.

The intended system of internal controls must reflect adequate controls, including accounting controls, to safeguard the assets of the institution and the operations against any undue risks. Moreover, the intended system of internal controls should reflect adequate segregation of duties at least within the critical areas of operations of the institution.

Scope of Activities

The articles of incorporation shall not enable the secondary financial institution to develop activities which are outside the scope of their normal business and that might pose a danger to sound policy.

Legal Form

The legal form is that of a limited liability company ("naamloze vennootschap") or a branch of a foreign credit institution with a legal form comparable to that of a limited liability company, or a form acceptable to the Bank.

Name

The name of the institution must clearly indicate the identity of its parent institution or head office.

When applying the following procedures must be adhered to:

1. The Bank must obtain an application for a license under the terms of article 3 of the National Ordinance on the Supervision of Banking and Credit Institutions 1994 (P.B. 1994 no. 4). For all applications an application form must be submitted by registered mail to the Bank. This form can be obtained at the Bank.

2. The application is considered to have been filed when the following correct and complete information has been received by the Bank:
   1. The application form.
   2. A duly signed statement of a Certified Public Accountant certifying that the applicant has free and unencumbered equity capital of at least NAf. 5 million. Taking into consideration the nature of the activities of the institution, the Bank may in its final decision require that the institution has capital in excess of NAf. 5 million.
   3. It is advisable to commence business with an amount of capital well in excess of the minimum required by the Bank. In case of a branch office, the head office should issue a guarantee for all the liabilities of the secondary financial institution.
   4. A statement from the supervisory authority of the head office or parent company, stating that there are no legal impediments to the establishment in the Dutch Caribbeanand indicating to the Bank how, and to what extent supervision will be exercised upon the applicant institution.
   5. A list of the correspondent banks.
   6. Personal Questionnaires and resumes of experience of all intended Managing Directors, the Board of Supervisory Directors and of all individual shareholders being natural persons.
   7. Certified personal financial statements of each individual shareholder, being a natural person.
   8. A Declaration of good conduct ("verklaring van goed gedrag") of the prospective managing and supervisory directors. Such declaration may be obtained from the police/judicial authority and certified by the Embassy or Consulate of the Kingdom of the Netherlands in the home country.
   9. Proof of the place of residence of the members of the Board of Managing Directors and the Board of Supervisory Directors and all their addresses of the last five years.
   10. A copy of the shareholders register.

Additional information may be requested if necessary during the analysis of the information submitted.
Within six (6) months of the issuance of the license subject bank must commence its activities, otherwise the license will be withdrawn pursuant to article 9, paragraph 1b of the National Ordinance on the Supervision of Banking and Credit Institutions 1994 (PB 1994 no. 4).

For Consolidated International Banks in the Dutch Caribbean

Top 1000 Policy
In principle, only credit institutions belonging to the world Top 1000, based on total assets, are considered for admittance as a consolidated international bank. The Bank may, in exceptional cases deviate from this policy.

Management / Supervision of Management

- The consolidated international bank must have a Board of Managing Directors with at least two members being natural persons and a Board of Supervisory Directors with at least three members being natural persons.
- The members of the Board of Managing Directors and the Board of Supervisory Directors must possess sufficient experience in banking, have a thorough knowledge of banking activities and be of high personal integrity.
- At all times at least two members of the Board of Managing Directors must be in function and at least one of them must be a resident of the Netherlands Antilles.
- At least one member of the Board of Supervisory Directors must be a resident of the Netherlands Antilles.
- A legal entity may act as a Managing Director, in addition to the Managing Directors being natural persons.
- Members of the Board of Managing Directors shall not be members of the Board of Supervisory Directors and vice versa.
- The objectives or antecedents of aforementioned persons must not endanger the interests of the depositors or future depositors and any other liability holder or future liability holders.
- The appointment of the members of the Board of Managing Directors and the Board of Supervisory Directors is subject to the prior written approval of the Bank.

Capital

- consolidated international bank being a limited liability company must have a minimum equity capital of at least NAf. 5 million, free and unencumbered.
- A consolidated international bank being a branch must provide the Bank with a guarantee of its head office stating that the head office shall guarantee all liabilities of the branch.
- In view of the nature of the activities of the consolidated international bank, the Bank may in its final decision, require that the institution has capital in excess of NAf. 5 million.

Shareholders

- The persons exercising a considerable influence on the affairs of the consolidated international bank by means of voting rights derived from shares, or in any comparable manner, must be of high personal integrity. The objectives or antecedents of these persons must not influence the consolidated international bank in an undesirable way.
- The ultimate beneficial owners must be known to the Bank.

Shares

- In the articles of incorporation a "repurchase of own shares" clause shall not be included.
- All shares of the consolidated international bank must be registered.

Share Holding by Individuals

- A natural person, shall not, without the approval of the Bank, directly or indirectly, control or hold more than 5% of the bank's capital.
- The total of individual shareholding by natural persons shall not, without the approval of the Bank, exceed 25% of total share capital.

Financial Position Parent Company / Head Office
The financial statements of the last three years of the parent company or, in case of a branch, the head office, should reflect an unqualified opinion.

Business Plan and System of Internal Controls
A consolidated international bank must submit a business plan together with its financial forecasts reflecting a sound and realistic projection of the activities the institution will undertake to accomplish its statutory objectives.
The intended system of internal controls must reflect adequate controls, including accounting controls, to safeguard the assets of the institution and the operations against any undue risks. Moreover, the intended system of internal controls should reflect adequate segregation of duties at least within the critical areas of operations of the institution.

Scope of Activities
The articles of incorporation shall not enable the consolidated international bank to develop activities which are outside the scope of normal banking business and that might pose a danger to sound banking policy.

Legal Form
The legal form is that of a limited liability company ("naamloze vennootschap") or a branch of a foreign credit institution with a legal form comparable to that of a limited liability company.

Name
The name of the institution must clearly indicate the identity of its parent institution or head office.
When applying the following procedures must be adhered to:

1. The Bank must obtain an application for a license under the terms of article 3 of the National Ordinance on the Supervision of Banking and Credit Institutions 1994 (P.B. 1994 no. 4). For all applications a application form must be submitted by registered mail to the Bank. This form can be obtained at the Bank.
2. The application is considered to have been filed when the following correct and complete information has been received by the Bank:
    1. The application form.
    2. A duly signed statement of a Certified Public Accountant certifying that the applicant has at its disposal equity capital of at least NAf. 5 million. Taking into consideration the nature of the activities of the institution, the Bank may in its final decision require that the institution's capital be in excess of NAf. 5 million.
    3. It is advisable to commence business with an amount of capital well in excess of the minimum required by the Bank. In case of a branch office, the head office should issue a guarantee for all the liabilities of the consolidated international bank.

4. A statement from the supervisory authority of the head office or parent company, stating that there are no legal impediments to the establishment in the Dutch Caribbeanand indicating to the Bank how, and to what extent super- vision will be exercised upon the applicant institution.
5. A list of the correspondent banks.
6. Personal Questionnaires and resumes of experience of all intended Managing Directors, the Board of Supervisory Directors and of all individual shareholders, being natural persons.
7. Certified personal financial statements of each individual shareholder, being a natural person.
8. A Declaration of good conduct ("verklaring van goed gedrag") of the prospective managing and supervisory directors. Such declaration may be obtained from the police/judicial authority and certified by the Embassy or Consulate of the Kingdom of the Netherlands in the home country.
9. Proof of the place of residence of the members of the Board of Managing Directors and the Board of Supervisory Directors and all their addresses of the last five years.
10. A copy of the shareholders register.

Additional information may be requested if necessary during the analysis of the information submitted.

Within six (6) months of the issuance of the license subject bank must commence its activities, otherwise the license will be withdrawn pursuant to article 9, paragraph 1b of the National Ordinance on the Supervision of the Banking and Credit Institutions 1994 (PB 1994 no. 4). Within one year of the date of the license the consolidated international bank must establish a permanent office in the Netherlands Antilles.

For Non-consolidated International Banks in the Dutch Caribbean

Top 1000 Policy

In principle, only credit institutions belonging to the world Top 1000 based on total assets are considered for admittance as a non-consolidated international bank. The Bank may, in exceptional cases deviate from this policy.

Management / Supervision of Management

- The foreign international bank must have a Board of Managing Directors with at least two members being natural persons and a Board of Supervisory Directors with at least three members being natural persons.
- The members of the Board of Managing Directors and the Board of Supervisory Directors must possess sufficient experience in banking, have a thorough knowledge of banking activities and be of high personal integrity.
- At all times at least two members of the Board of Managing Directors must be in function and at least one of them must be a resident of the Netherlands Antilles.
- At least one member of the Board of Supervisory Directors must be a resident of the Netherlands Antilles.

- A legal entity may act as a Managing Director, in addition to the Managing Directors being natural persons.
- Members of the Board of Managing Directors shall not be members of the Board of Supervisory Directors and vice versa.
- The objectives or antecedents of aforementioned persons must not endanger the interests of the depositors or future depositors and any other liability holder or future liability holders.
- The appointment of the members of the Board of Managing Directors and the Board of Supervisory Directors is subject to the prior written approval of the Bank.

Capital
A non-consolidated international bank must have a minimum equity capital of at least NAf. 5 million, free and unencumbered.
Shareholders

- The persons exercising a considerable influence on the affairs of the foreign international bank by means of voting rights derived from shares, or in any comparable manner, must be of high personal integrity. The objectives or antecedents of these persons must not influence the bank in an undesirable way.
- The ultimate beneficial shareholders must be known to the Bank.

Shares

- In the articles of incorporation a "repurchase of own shares" clause shall not be included.
- All shares of the foreign international bank must be registered.

Share Holding by Individuals

- A natural person, shall not, without the approval of the Bank, directly or indirectly, control or hold more than 5% of the bank's capital.
- The total of individual shareholding by natural persons shall not, without the approval of the Bank, exceed 25% of total share capital.

Financial Position Parent Company
The financial statements of the last three years of the parent company or, affiliated company, should reflect an unqualified opinion.
Business Plan and System of Internal Controls
A foreign international bank must submit a business plan together with its financial forecasts reflecting a sound and realistic projection of the activities the institution will undertake to accomplish its statutory objectives.
The intended system of internal controls must reflect adequate controls, including accounting controls, to safeguard the assets of the institution and the operations against any undue risks. Moreover, the intended system of internal controls should reflect adequate segregation of duties at least within the critical areas of operations of the institution.

Scope of Activities
The articles of incorporation shall not enable the foreign international bank to develop activities which are outside the scope of normal banking business and that might pose a danger to sound banking policy.
Legal Form
The legal form is that of a limited liability company ("naamloze vennootschap").
When applying the following procedures must be adhered to:

1. The Bank must obtain an application for a license under the terms of article 3 of the National Ordinance on the Supervision of Banking and Credit Institutions 1994 (P.B. 1994 no. 4). For all applications an application form must be submitted by registered mail to the Bank. This form can be obtained at the Bank.
2. The application is considered to have been filed when the following correct and complete information has been received by the Bank:
    1. The application form.
    2. A duly signed statement of a Certified Public Accountant certifying that the applicant has at its disposal equity capital of at least NAf.5 million. Taking into consideration the nature of the activities of the institution, the Bank may, in its final decision, require that the institution's capital be in excess of NAf. 5 million. It is advisable to commence business with an amount of capital well in excess of the minimum required by the Bank.
    3. A statement from the supervisory authority of the parent or related company, stating that there are no legal impediments to the establishment in the Dutch Caribbeanand indicating to the Bank how, and to what extent supervision will be exercised upon the applicant institution.
    4. A list of the correspondent banks.
    5. Personal Questionnaires and resumes of experience of all intended Managing Directors, the Board of Supervisory Directors and of all individual shareholders being natural persons.
    6. Certified personal financial statements of each individual shareholder, being a natural person.
    7. A Declaration of good conduct ("verklaring van goed gedrag") of the prospective managing and supervisory directors. Such declaration may be obtained from the police/judicial authority and certified by the Embassy or Consulate of the Kingdom of the Netherlands in the home country.
    8. Proof of the place of residence of the members of the Board of Managing Directors and the Board of Supervisory Directors and all their addresses of the last five years.
    9. A copy of the shareholders register.

Additional information may be requested if necessary during the analysis of the information submitted.
Within six (6) months of the issuance of the license subject bank must commence its activities, otherwise the license will be withdrawn pursuant to article 9, paragraph 1b of the National Ordinance on the Supervision of Banking and Credit Institutions 1994 (PB 1994 no. 4).
Within one year of the date of the license the bank must establish a permanent office in the Netherlands Antilles.

POLICY MEMORANDUM
On the change of external auditors of a credit institution

INTRODUCTION

The purpose of this Policy Memorandum is to provide information on the process of changing external auditors by banking institutions and to ensure an orderly course of action during this process.

I. ACCEPTANCE OF THE ENGAGEMENT TO CONDUCT AN AUDIT ON THE ANNUAL FINANCIAL STATEMENTS OF A CREDIT INSTITUTION.

The following procedures are of importance from a supervisory point of view when appointing a new external auditor for the audit of the financial statements.

I.1. Notice of change

Pursuant to section 24 of the National Ordinance on the Supervision of Banking and Credit Institutions of 1994, any intended change in external auditor should be reported to the Bank, and can only be affected upon approval of the new auditor by the Bank.

I.2. Documentation on transfer of audit responsibility

The newly engaged external auditor should seek to obtain information about the institution from the former auditor, prior to accepting the engagement. Minutes of meetings in this regard should be kept, containing all important points of discussion, in order to avoid any misunderstandings in the transfer of audit responsibilities. A copy of subject minutes should be available to the Bank prior to the authorization of the new auditor.

I.3. Provision of information by auditors and consequences for the engagement letter

The provision of information to the Bank by the external auditors of credit institutions is covered in section 15, paragraph 3 of the National Ordinance on the Supervision of Banking and Credit Institutions of 1994.

Pursuant to section15, the supervised institution must provide written instructions to the external auditor to audit its financial statements. The audit engagement letter should provide for the external auditor to be authorized to:

a. submit to the Bank a copy of the auditor's report, the management letter, as well as all correspondence with regard to the auditor's opinion on the annual reports and the Chart of Accounts;
b. inform the Bank, of any circumstantial facts that would inhibit the issuance of an unqualified opinion on the annual statements and/or Chart of Accounts; and elaborate in a meeting, if deemed necessary by the Bank, on the documents mentioned under a. and b. above.

Furthermore, viewing the importance of the EDP system for banking operations, the engagement letter should also indicate that the external auditor should reach, within the scope of the audit of the financial statements, an opinion on the continuity and reliability of the EDP system in so far the system is critical for the institution's daily operations. Finally, the Bank will usually not request the correspondence as indicated under a. above in the case of an unqualified audit opinion on the set of financial statements.

II. EXIT MEETING
The Bank will inquire from the credit institution and the resigning auditor about the reasons for the change of external auditors during an exit meeting. If on the basis of the information received prior to such meeting, in combination with the known facts, an exit meeting is not deemed meaningful or necessary for supervisory purposes, then the Bank may elect to disregard such a meeting. The Bank will inform the institution of this decision.
If, on the other hand, the Bank does find an exit meeting meaningful, the resigning auditor will be invited for a meeting. The institution will again be informed of and allowed to be present at the meeting. In this meeting the question will be raised as to the reasons for termination of the engagement and whether there are other issues of significance for the Bank's supervision. Also, the Bank will review the applicable rules and regulations governing the activities of the institution with the new auditor.
III. REPORTING AND APPROVAL
The Bank evaluates the procedures which are relevant to the Bank in the change of external auditor and prepares an audit transfer memorandum. The current and coming auditors will cooperate as much as possible in the review of the transfer of audit responsibility.
After the memorandum has been finalized, the Bank will issue a declaration of no objection to the institution concerning the approval of the new external auditor

MEMORANDUM FOR CREDIT INSTITUTIONS

I. INTRODUCTION

The "Year 2000" problem requires our immediate and full attention. The consequences for institutions which fail to make timely preparations may, in view of possible systematic risks, be far-reaching.

Failure to address this issue in a timely manner could cause financial institutions to experience operational problems or even bankruptcy which may result in disruption of financial markets. As a result, financial institutions must take the necessary steps to ensure that problems and disruptions are minimized.

The major computer system overhauls financial institutions are confronting is caused by the fact that many computers still indicate years by their last two digits, without a century-designation. The turn of the century could cause errors in calculations, which are based on a comparison of dates.

For example:

a. many calculations will either indicate that transactions have been opened for nearly a hundred years or produce negative numbers;
b. new files may not be recognized as the most recent data, causing files to be erased or archived as old data.

Additional complications may arise, due to the fact that the "Year 2000" is a leap year. It appears that software programmers have not taken this fact sufficiently into account. A further problem is that the date designation '99' was frequently used in the past to refer to data with special characteristic. This means that problems could already start in 1999. The outlined problems may occur in all automated systems, hardware operating systems and application software, databases, internal and external communications network, etc. They may further occur in numerous embedded systems which rely on computer technology, such as telephone systems, elevators, access security systems, vaults etc. etc.

In this memorandum, you will find an overview of some relevant issues that have to be addressed in order to adequately approach the "Year 2000" problem. Individual institutions are given the necessary freedom to develop an adequate tailor-made-project. The time paths included in this memorandum are binding.

II. NATURE OF THE PROBLEM

The magnitude and complexity of the problem and the impact it may have on the business as a whole makes it imperative not to dismiss it as just a technical computer problem. In our modern society and at financial institutions in particular, information systems play an increasingly important role.

A large-scale disturbance in the functioning of these systems may have serious consequences, due particularly to the multiple interconnections between systems, both internally and externally. Relevant points of attention are decentralization of the information supply, external links with clients and suppliers and payment systems. The magnitude of the problem, combined with its far-reaching consequences, means that a timely and adequate plan of action is impossible without a sustained close involvement of management. Top management needs to recognize the strategic importance of the issue and also monitor plans and progress actively across the institution.

Institutions run an additional risk if clients fail to make timely preparations for the "Year 2000". This may result, for example, in a substantial increase in the number of bad debts.

Considering this, it is of great importance that credit officers and relationship officers understand the "Year 2000" risks faced by their customers, and the progress made in handling this issue. Developing appropriate contingency plans should also be part of this assessment.

III. AWARENESS

An adequate approach to the millennium problem requires the commitment of the entire organization. The organization must be convinced of the strategic importance of a sound and thorough approach to the problem. The following relevant points can be distinguished in this respect.

III.1 Making the problem visible within the organization

Assessing all adjustments required of the system(s) is only possible if the strategic importance of solving the "Year 2000" problem is understood and appreciated throughout the whole organization.

III.2 The strategic importance of a timely preparation

The certainty of 1999 becoming 2000 makes postponement impossible and makes full implementation of corrective actions a necessity. The turn of the century requires a large degree of involvement of management. In this case, there should be adequate supervision on the progress made by and on behalf of management. This can be done by means of an adequate project organization, resulting in clear target dates, a clear division of responsibilities, and progress reports.

III.3 Allocation of human resources and materials

Allocation of human resources and materials in an early stage is required. Budgets should be adapted to that end. Institutions should recognize that the "Year 2000" problem has to be given a high priority, and that the test phase should be the most extensive and complex phase of the project.

III.4 Subsidiaries or Branches

As far as subsidiaries or financial institutions which do not have their registered office in the Dutch Caribbean(branches) are concerned , there is a separate responsibility next to that of the parent. It is very much possible that some used applications or systems which are not "Year 2000" compliant, will not be converted by your head-office because they are only used locally.

These institutions are expected to take their own measures, or to see to it, that timely preparations and adjustments are made by their parent company or head-office.
Furthermore, we recommend that an individual inventory of computer systems, applications and other systems that are dependent on microchips are done in order to assess whether or not these are included in the program of the head-office.

IV. STRATEGY

Defining, devising and managing the strategy to be followed regarding the "Year 2000" problem is the final responsibility of management.

IV.1 This strategy should in any case focus on:

- centralized and decentralized systems;
- hardware, operating systems and applications;
- office automation, front- and back office systems;
- systems, which partially make use of computer technology
- (embedded systems) such as elevators, vaults, access security systems;
- payment systems, settlement systems, internal communications network and public carriers.

IV.2 The contents of the strategy should also be aimed at:

- minimizing the risks, making use of a risk analysis resulting in a clear set of priorities;
- defining clear time paths;
- creating adequate control mechanisms, resulting in the timely recognition and
- reporting of bottlenecks.

IV.3 Adequate project organization
This strategy is translated into an adequate project organization, with clear-cut phases and division of responsibilities.
IV.4 Proper coordination
From the perspective of control, it is advisable to separate the millennium project from other projects. The "Year 2000" project should be properly coordinated with current projects, thus ruling out any delay.
The current lack of sufficient capacity and human resources must force institutions to carefully weigh the risk involved and to set priorities. It might be necessary to temporarily hold off other major projects, acquisitions, etc. The required (recruitment of) capacity and human resources should at this stage already be secured. Failing to make timely arrangements entails several risks, particularly as a result of the large claim that will be laid on the available capacity, the timely availability of the required resources and their quality. Management should make available the financial means required for that purpose.
IV.5 Assessing credits
The promptness with which the clients of the institution tackle the millenium problem, also plays an important role from the strategic point of view. Clients which have failed to take timely measures, may after all become a potential credit risk to the institution. Attention should be paid to this aspect when assessing credits. Clients should be actively approached in order to encourage them to take the necessary measures.

V. ASSESSMENT

Institutions should assess all required adjustments by means of detailed inventories covering both centralized and decentralized systems, software, hardware, operating systems, network, interfaces and all other applications where computer technology plays a role. Another objective of this assessment is to arrive at a risk analysis, resulting in quantification of these risks and a set of priorities.

V. 1 End-users and EDP-organization

Internal partnership should be created between end-users on one hand, and the EDP organization on the other hand, with a clear division of responsibilities. Agreement should be reached on time schedules, at the same time creating a framework for monitoring the observance of deadlines and, related to these, progress reports for the purpose of accountability to the management.

V.2 Suppliers and service providers

Suppliers and service providers should be consulted about their approach and how it is progressing. However, the institution's own responsibility, both with respect to the monitoring of time paths, to be observed by third parties, and the testing of adapted software, to be supplied by third parties, within the institution's own environment should not be neglected. It is important for the institution to ascertain that it has the most recent versions of software and operating systems, to avoid complications as a result of incompatibility. Furthermore, it is important to determine whether the rights and obligations vis-à-vis third parties are sufficiently covered by contracts.

V.3 Project plans

This phase results in elaborated and detailed plans. Besides the required adjustments, these plans also specify the time paths to be observed, the responsibilities and the procedure for submitting progress reports. These plans comprise both internally developed applications and packages and pertain to both the internal organization and relationships with third parties.

VI. RENOVATION

In this phase, which is primarily of a technical nature, the actual adjustment of the eligible systems are carried out. In so far as it has been decided to replace existing systems, it is done in this phase. It includes negotiating with software vendors, outsource suppliers and solution implementers and creating legal protection for the enterprise especially when adjustments will be made by third parties. It also includes revising not only the systems, but also the supporting documentation, end-user procedures, manuals, screen images, archiving and all other related activities.

Contingency plans

An important aspect is drawing up and working out contingency plans. The contingency plans are aimed at determining alternative approaches if renovations lag or fail, if critical delivery dates are not met or if vendors or service providers are not able to deliver in time.

These contingency plans should be geared towards the critical time path incorporated in the project structure. Again, attention should be paid to centralized and decentralized systems, internal and external organization, contracts with third parties and interfaces with clients or suppliers. The details of these emergency plans are based on the risk analyses performed.

VII. TESTING

The most extensive phase in the "Year 2000" project is the test phase. Prior to this phase, detailed plans have to be developed, where special attention is paid to the interrelations and interdependence of the various (sub) systems. Relevant in this respect is, that adequate testing is only possible if all elements involved are 2000-proof.

VII.1 What to test?

The test should focus on the institution's own systems, but also on links with third party systems such as payment and clearing systems, electronic banking facilities, etc. This means that the institution's own plans must be carefully coordinated with those of the service providers and clients. Only then will it be possible to obtain the required certainty.

Year 2000 critical dates that should also be included in your test are:

Cycle	Reason for testing
31 December 1998 to 1 January 1999	First day in 1999
8 September 1999 to 9 September 1999	Date comprised of all 9' (9/9/99)
30 December 1999 to 3 January 2000	• Last business day and rollover to first day in 2000 • First business day in 2000
28 February 2000 to 1 March 2000	2000 is a leap year
28 February 2001 to 1 March 2001	No leap year
31 January 2000 to 1 February 2000	First month end in 2000
31 December 2000 to 1 January 2001	First year end of the century.

VII.1 Compliance of systems

It should be noted that certification is an important part in the "Year 2000" exercise. However, some vendors may indicate that their product is compliant when in fact it is not. Even if compliant, the product should still be tested by the institution to make sure that it runs properly within the institution's own environment and interfaces properly with other applications. The user manual should be updated in time.

VIII. IMPLEMENTATION

The implementation of the adjusted systems requires careful planning, where particular attention should be paid to any interconnections and interaction between the (sub) systems. Systems should be certified compliant by an independent control function.

IX. CONDITIONS FOR AN ADEQUATE APPROACH

In order to effectively tackle the millennium problem, institutions have to make sure that a number of constraints are met:

- a large degree of management involvement;
- sufficient supervision by or on behalf of the management on the progress made; a clear definition of the scope of the project, where attention is also paid to decentralized developments and embedded systems;
- an adequate project organization, resulting in a clear division of responsibilities;
- the chosen project structure should provide latitude for clearly set time paths and targets dates. The institution should formulate a policy which is aimed at timely recognizing which credit clients are insufficiently prepared for the "Year 2000";
- the institution is further expected to develop a policy, which is also aimed at determining in time whether adequate millennium measures have been taken for national and international payment systems, clearing and settlement systems.

X. TIME SCHEDULE

Considering that it is imperative that this problem is solved in time and the fact that the deadline is not adjustable, the Bank has drawn up a binding time schedule, which must be observed in order to address the problem in time.

Phases	Completion deadline
Awareness	Should have been completed by now
Strategy	Should have been completed by now
Assessment	Should have been completed by now
Renovation	Mid 1998
Testing	End 1998 for the main systems
	Mid 1999 for all systems
Implementation	Mid 1999

XI. ROLE OF THE EXTERNAL AUDITOR

Given the fact that an institution's continuity depends to a large extent on a proper functioning of its computer systems, the Bank wishes to underscore the importance of having the institution's external auditor form an opinion about the control measures taken by your institution with regard to the millennium problem. We request you to have the external auditor report his findings in the management letter.

Considering its supervisory task and the magnitude of this problem, the Bank will continue to monitor the progress made in this area.

MEMORANDUM FOR INSTITUTIONAL INVESTORS

I. INTRODUCTION

The "Year 2000" problem requires our immediate and full attention. The consequences for institutions which fail to make timely preparations may, in view of possible systematic risks, be far-reaching.

Failure to address this issue in a timely manner could cause institutional investors to experience operational problems or even bankruptcy which may result in disruption of financial markets. As a result, institutional investors must take the necessary steps to ensure that problems and disruptions are minimized.

The major computer system overhauls institutional investors are confronting is caused by the fact that many computers still indicate years by their last two digits, without a century-designation. The turn of the century could cause errors in calculations, which are based on a comparison of dates.

For example:

a. many calculations will either indicate that transactions have been opened for nearly a hundred years or produce negative numbers;
b. new files may not be recognized as the most recent data, causing files to be erased or archived as old data.

Additional complications may arise, due to the fact that the "Year 2000" is a leap year. It appears that software programmers have not taken this fact sufficiently into account. A further problem is that the date designation '99' was frequently used in the past to refer to data with special characteristic. This means that problems could already start in 1999.

The outlined problems may occur in all automated systems, hardware operating systems and application software, databases, internal and external communications network, etc. They may further occur in numerous embedded systems which rely on computer technology, such as telephone systems, elevators, access security systems, vaults etc. etc.

In addition insurers must be made aware that this unique situation could result in increased and unexpected claims.

In this memorandum, you will find an overview of some relevant issues that have to be addressed in order to adequately approach the "Year 2000" problem. Individual institutions are given the necessary freedom to develop an adequate tailor-made-project. The time paths included in this memorandum are binding.

II. IMPLICATION OF THE PROBLEM

For insurance companies the "Year 2000" could result in higher than anticipated claims on insurance policies. For example:

- Professional Liability Exposure for technology procedures, designers, consultants etc. who may be sued for errors, omissions or failure to complete contracts;
- Directors and Officers Exposure for managers and directors failing to take adequate measures to address the problem;
- losses caused indirectly by a "Year 2000" failure – e.g., fire due to computer breakdown or malfunctioning, fire causes loss of inventory, etc. ;
- Loss of Profit Exposure for policies written on a "all risks" form, or from material
- Liability Exposure third party losses because insureds' computers or products containing an embedded computer chip are not "Year 2000" compliant;
- Property Damage Exposure – fire or water damage cause by failure of peripheral computer-based services (alarm systems, elevators, sprinkler systems, etc.);
- Marine or Aviation Exposure – from non compliant guidance or traffic control systems;
- Automobile Exposure – from non compliant traffic or street lighting systems.

Insurance companies need to assess their potential liability for the "Year 2000" problems and take measures to mitigate potential claim. This will involve:

- Identifying situations in which date-related computer system problems may result in claims for loss or damage to property or to bodily injury or loss of business income;
- Determining which policies may be affected by such claims;
- Analyzing the possible impacts on the reinsurance plan of the company;
- Assessing the extent to which applicants or insureds are exposed to such losses; and
- if required, amending wordings on policies or endorsements or reassessing premiums to reduce loss exposure.

The nature of claims arising from problems associated with the "Year 2000" cannot be fully anticipated. In certain cases it may not be clear whether claims are eligible for insurance coverage. As a result, insurers may suffer significant legal costs.
All institutional investors must be individually pro-active in preparing for the "Year 2000" in order to ensure that critical business functions work properly and that the company is not adversely affected.

III. NATURE OF THE PROBLEM
The magnitude and complexity of the problem and the impact it may have on the business as a whole makes it imperative not to dismiss it as just a technical computer problem. In our modern society and at institutional investors in particular, information systems play an increasingly important role.
A large-scale disturbance in the functioning of these systems may have serious consequences, due particularly to the multiple interconnections between systems, both internally and externally. Relevant points of attention are decentralization of the information supply, external links with clients and suppliers and payment systems. The magnitude of the problem, combined with its far-reaching consequences, means that a timely and adequate plan of action is impossible without a sustained close involvement of management. Top management needs to recognize the strategic importance of the issue and also monitor plans and progress actively across the institution. Institutions run an additional risk if clients and/ or insured or brokers fail to make timely preparations for the "Year 2000". Considering this, it is of great importance that all personnel understand the "Year 2000" risks faced by their customers, and the progress made in handling this issue. Developing appropriate contingency plans should also be part of this assessment.

IV. AWARENESS
An adequate approach to the millennium problem requires the commitment of the entire organization. The organization must be convinced of the strategic importance of a sound and thorough approach to the problem. The following relevant points can be distinguished in this respect.
IV.1 Making the problem visible within the organization
Assessing all adjustments required of the system(s) is only possible if the strategic importance of solving the "Year 2000" problem is understood and appreciated throughout the whole organization.
IV.2 The strategic importance of a timely preparation.
The certainty of 1999 becoming 2000 makes postponement impossible and full implementation of corrective actions a necessity. The turn of the century requires a large degree of involvement of management. In this case, there should be adequate supervision on the progress made by and on behalf of management.
This can be done by means of an adequate project organization, resulting in clear target dates, a clear division of responsibilities, and progress reports.
IV.3 Allocation of human resources and materials
Allocation of human resources and materials in an early stage is required. Budgets should be adapted to that end. Institutions should recognize that the "Year 2000" problem has to be given a high priority, and that the test phase should be the most extensive and complex phase of the project.
IV.4 Subsidiaries or Branches
As far as subsidiaries or insurance companies which do not have their registered office in the Dutch Caribbean(branches), there is a separate responsibility next to that of the parent. It is very much possible that some used applications or systems which are not "Year 2000" compliant, will not be converted by your head-office because they are only used locally.

These institutions are expected to take their own measures, or to see to it, that timely preparations and adjustments are made by their parent company or head-office.
Furthermore, we recommend that an individual inventory of computer systems, applications and other systems that are dependent on microchips are done in order to assess whether or not these are included in the program of the head-office.

V. STRATEGY
Defining, devising and managing the strategy to be followed regarding the "Year 2000" problem is the final responsibility of management.
V.l This strategy should in any case focus on:

- centralized and decentralized systems;
- hardware, operating systems and applications;
- office automation, front- and back office systems;
- systems, which partially make use of computer technology
- (embedded systems) such as elevators, vaults, access security systems;
- benefit payment systems, premium income systems, internal communications network and public carriers.

V.2 The contents of the strategy should also be aimed at:

- minimizing the risks, making use of a risk analysis resulting in a clear set of priorities;
- defining clear time paths;
- creating adequate control mechanisms, resulting in the timely recognition and
- reporting of bottlenecks.

V.3 Adequate project organization
This strategy is translated into an adequate project organization, with clear-cut phases and division of responsibilities.
V.4 Proper coordination
From the perspective of control, it is advisable to separate the millennium project from other projects. The "Year 2000" project should be properly coordinated with current projects, thus ruling out any delay.
The current lack of sufficient capacity and human resources must force institutions to carefully weigh the risk involved and to set priorities. It might be necessary to temporarily hold off other major projects, acquisitions, etc. The required (recruitment of) capacity and human resources should at this stage already be secured. Failing to make timely arrangements entails several risks, particularly as a result of the large claim that will be laid on the available capacity, the timely availability of the required resources and their quality. Management should make available the financial means required for that purpose.
V.5 Assessing clients preparation
The promptness with which the major clients and/or insiders or brokers of the institution tackle the millenium problem, also plays an important role from the strategic point of view. Clients and/or insureds or brokers which have failed to take timely measures, may after all become a potential credit risk to the institution. Attention should be paid to this aspect when assessing their readiness. Major clients and/or insureds or brokers should be actively approached in order to encourage them to take the necessary measures.

VI. ASSESSMENT

Institutions should assess all required adjustments by means of detailed inventories covering both centralized and decentralized systems, software, hardware, operating systems, network, interfaces and all other applications where computer technology plays a role. Another objective of this assessment is to arrive at a risk analysis, resulting in quantification of these risks and a set of priorities.

VI.1 End-users and EDP-organization

Internal partnership should be created between end-users on one hand, and the EDP organization on the other hand, with a clear division of responsibilities. Agreement should be reached on time schedules, at the same time creating a framework for monitoring the observance of deadlines and, related to these, progress reports for the purpose of accountability to the management.

VI.2 Suppliers and service providers

Suppliers and service providers should be consulted about their approach and how it is progressing. However, the institution's own responsibility, both with respect to the monitoring of time paths, to be observed by third parties, and the testing of adapted software, to be supplied by third parties, within the institution's own environment should not be neglected. It is important for the institution to ascertain that it has the most recent versions of software and operating systems, to avoid complications as a result of incompatibility. Furthermore, it is important to determine whether the rights and obligations vis-à-vis third parties are sufficiently covered by contracts.

VI.3 Project plans

This phase results in elaborated and detailed plans. Besides the required adjustments, these plans also specify the time paths to be observed, the responsibilities and the procedure for submitting progress reports. These plans comprise both internally developed applications and packages and pertain to both the internal organization and relationships with third parties.

VII. RENOVATION

In this phase, which is primarily of a technical nature, the actual adjustment of the eligible systems are carried out. In so far as it has been decided to replace existing systems, it is done in this phase. It includes negotiating with software vendors, outsourced suppliers and solution implementers and creating legal protection for the enterprise especially when adjustments will be made by third parties. It also includes revising not only the systems, but also the supporting documentation, end-user procedures, manuals, screen images, archiving and all other related activities.

Contingency plans

An important aspect is drawing up and working out contingency plans. The contingency plans are aimed at determining alternative approaches if renovations lag or fail, if critical delivery dates are not met or if vendors or service providers are not able to deliver in time.

These contingency plans should be geared towards the critical time path incorporated in the project structure. Again, attention should be paid to centralized and decentralized systems, internal and external organization, contracts with third parties and interfaces with clients, brokers, insureds or suppliers. The details of these emergency plans are based on the risk analyses performed.

VIII. TESTING

The most extensive phase in the "Year 2000" project is the test phase. Prior to this phase, detailed plans have to be developed, where special attention is paid to the interrelations and interdependence of the various (sub) systems. Relevant in this respect is, that adequate testing is only possible if all elements involved are 2000-proof.

VIII.1 What to test? The test should focus on the institution's own systems, but also on links with third party systems such as benefit payment systems, re-insurers and regulatory reporting. This means that the institution's own plans must be carefully coordinated with those of the service providers and clients. Only then will it be possible to obtain the required certainty.

Year 2000 critical dates that should also be included in your test are:

Cycle	Reason for testing
31 December 1998 to 1 January 1999	First day in 1999
8 September 1999 to 9 September 1999	Date comprised of all 9' (9/9/99)
30 December 1999 to 3 January 2000	• Last business day and rollover to first day in 2000 • First business day in 2000
28 February 2000 to 1 March 2000	2000 is a leap year
28 February 2001 to 1 March 2001	No leap year
31 January 2000 to 1 February 2000	First month end in 2000
31 December 2000 to 1 January 2001	First year end of the century.

VIII.2 Compliance of systemsIt should be noted that certification is an important part in the "Year 2000" exercise. However, some vendors may indicate that their product is compliant when in fact it is not. Even if compliant, the product should still be tested by the institution to make sure that it runs properly within the institution's own environment and interfaces properly with other applications. The user manual should be updated in time.

IX. IMPLEMENTATION

The implementation of the adjusted systems requires careful planning, where particular attention should be paid to any interconnections and interaction between the (sub) systems. Systems should be certified compliant by an independent control function.

X. CONDITIONS FOR AN ADEQUATE APPROACH

In order to effectively tackle the millennium problem, institutions have to make sure that a number of constraints are met:

- a large degree of management involvement;
- sufficient supervision by or on behalf of the management on the progress made;
- a clear definition of the scope of the project, where attention is also paid to
- decentralized developments and embedded systems;
- an adequate project organization, resulting in a clear division of responsibilities;
- the chosen project structure should provide latitude for clearly set time paths and
- targets dates. The institution should formulate a policy which is aimed at timely
- recognizing which credit clients are insufficiently prepared for the "Year 2000";
- the institution is further expected to develop a policy, which is also aimed at
- recognizing in time which major clients and/or insureds or brokers are insufficiently prepared for the "Year 2000".

XI. TIME SCHEDULE

Considering that it is imperative that this problem is solved in time and the fact that the dead-line is not adjustable, the Bank has drawn up a binding time schedule, which must be observed in order to address the problem in time.

Phases	Completion deadline
Awareness	Should have been completed by now
Strategy	Should have been completed by now
Assessment	Should have been completed by now
Renovation	Mid 1998
Testing	End 1998 for the main systems
	Mid 1999 for all systems
Implementation	Mid 1999

XII. ROLE OF THE EXTERNAL AUDITOR

Given the fact that an institution's continuity depends to a large extent on a proper functioning of its computer systems, the Bank wishes to underscore the importance of having the institution's external auditor form an opinion about the control measures taken by your institution with regard to the millennium problem. We request you to have the external auditor report his findings in the management letter.
Considering its supervisory task and the magnitude of this problem, the Bank will continue to monitor the progress made in this area.

GUIDE TO CONTINGENCY PLANNING AND BUSINESS CONTINUITY

INTRODUCTION

Over the past year, financial institutions in the Dutch Caribbeanhave undertaken extensive efforts in preparing for one of the largest business challenges ever: the Year 2000 (Y2K) problem.

While many preparations are taking place, it is clear, that not all Year 2000 issues will be resolved before the Year 2000 deadline. Despite the efforts of each financial institution to assess, renovate and validate their critical systems, their organization still remains vulnerable to the disruption of business processes. In fact, it is even likely, that systems that have been renovated and tested may face unanticipated Year 2000 problems.

The risk of Year 2000 failure is not only limited to an organization's internal information system, but also dependent on the interrelationship with third parties, such as clients, vendors, other service providers and public entities (for instance, utility and telecommunication companies).

In this context, it is essential to the Year 2000 program that institutions develop effective contingency planning to reduce any risks of business failure and guarantee business continuity.

The business continuity plan, in short, is the result of an extensive business analysis process that consists of different individual contingency plans. Each individual plan assesses the risks faced by the institution in each core business process. For each core business process, a contingency plan should be developed, describing how the institution will resume normal business operations if the system does not perform as expected. Also the risks posed by third parties such as vendors is assessed and contingency plans developed.

At the same time, the readiness of each public infrastructure process such as utility and telecommunications is assessed against the institution's core business processes.

To complement this process, the alternate measures are then evaluated based on the available resources, time and costs to mitigate those risks.

To this end, the Bank van de Nederlandse Antillen (the Bank) in cooperation with the Association of International Bankers in the Dutch Caribbean(IBNA), the Curaçao Bankers Association (CBA) and the Nederlandse Antilliaanse Vereniging van Verzekeraars (NAVV) have instituted a "Working Group" to prepare a guide to Contingency Planning and Business Continuity for the Financial Sector in the Netherlands Antilles.

The purpose of this guide is to further assist management of financial institutions and their Y2K responsible staff or their installed Y2K Project Team in the preparation of a contingency plan. The "Contingency Working Group" believes, that by taking an active approach the group can provide guidance and recommendations to Management in developing their Year 2000 Contingency Plan. This guide is however not intended to be an all inclusive Y2K contingency planning solution, the responsibility to develop an effective and comprehensive plan remains with each institution.

The group also believes, that each organization is unique and operates within its own structure and confines. Consequently, there is no ideal or simple solution to contingency planning and contingency plans should therefore be tailored to the individual situation of each institution

Management of each institution is therefore responsible for developing an adequate plan for its institution in order to ensure the continuation of its operations well beyond January 1, 2000.

Finally, the Bank wants to remind you that contingency planning needs to be addressed since it will help each institution to prepare for potential crisis and facilitate the restoration of normal business at the earliest possible time and in the most cost-effective manner.

1. **Project Initiation**

The commitment of management and the establishment of a contingency planning committee are crucial to the success of a business continuity plan.

a. **Request Commitment of Senior Management**

The development and implementation of an effective and cost-efficient contingency plan is highly dependent on the senior management of the institution.

i Management should be fully aware of the potential risks faced by the organization in case of critical systems failures.

ii Senior management's support can be demonstrated through active participation and monitoring of the plan's implementation. Briefings and status reports to management must take place on a regular basis.

b. **Establish a Business Continuity Committee**

- i To adequately coordinate and control the process, Management should establish a Business Continuity Committee. The main responsibility of the committee is the preparation of the Business Continuity Plan.
- ii There should be a close-working relationship between the committee and the Year 2000 project coordinators and/or staff, since access to information on the status of the institutions' Year 2000 program is critical.
- iii The composition of the committee is highly dependent on the size and complexity of the institution. The committee could consist of representatives of all major business units, business continuity experts, information experts and analysts with overall planning ability. The committee should also have access to legal staff when necessary.
- iv The committee should establish a plan of action with the assigning of specific responsibilities to each committee member. Individual members could be appointed for the preparation of contingency plans for each core business process.
- v The committee should also prepare a time schedule for the finalization of plans for each business process and the validation thereof.

II. Business Risk Analysis Process

The main purpose of the business risk analysis process is to assess the effects of potential failures and disruptions on the operations and viability of the institution's core business processes.

The results of the business risk analysis process will form the basis for the contingency plan.

a. Establish a planning strategy

The institution should define the techniques, methods and information requirements it will use in developing the business continuity plan. An assessment of the information systems environment should be performed and the strengths and weaknesses of the institution should be identified.

The following categories of information requirements may be distinguished:

- i The main Year 2000 business risk areas and the scope of their impact.
- ii The business process composition.
- iii The main operational and service levels, interrelationships and dependencies.
- iv The costs and benefits of the business continuity strategies.

b Define the institution's Year 2000 risk scenarios

Each institution should assess the potential risk of disruption of business and services as a result of failures or delays in renovation, testing and implementation by performing a risk assessment of the different areas of risks for its business.

The following risks scenarios for Year 2000 failure may be addressed:

i Risks to the financial institution's own internal system.

ii Risks to the financial institution's external system such as clients, business-partners and vendors; and public infrastructure such as utilities, telecommunications and government.

c. **Perform a risk analysis of each core business process**

i Evaluate the status of the Year 2000 program for each core business and define the risks for all critical systems which will be replaced or renovated.

ii Determine the impact of internal and external system failures on each core business process. Analyze both manual and automated system support requirements.

iii If a core business process is dependent on an external organization, it is recommended to contact the organization on its Year 2000 status.

d. **Assess public infrastructure risks**

Institutions should determine the readiness of each individual public infrastructure entity such as utility and telecommunication companies. The risk should be assessed taking into consideration its impact on the institution's core business processes.

e. **Prioritize core business processes**

i When reviewing business processes, risks should be considered based on their importance to the institution's continuity. Critical systems must be ranked based on operational loss or potential financial loss to the institution if the application is not available. Besides, it is also important to determine the minimum level of service and output required for each business process.

ii Business processes may be prioritized as follows:

Group 1: Business processes which must be run on schedule;

Group 2: Business processes which can be run as resources become available;

Group 3: Business processes which may be delayed.

Within each group the systems may be ranked from most critical to least critical.

III. **Contingency Planning**

Contingency planning is the process by which plans are developed for each core business process. The costs and benefits of each alternative is evaluated and the best contingency strategy is selected.

Included in the plan should be the procedures, description of resources and the trigger dates for its implementation.

a. Select a contingency strategy for each core business process

Institutions should assess the benefits, risks and costs of contingency strategies and select the best possible contingency strategy for each core business process.

The most important factors to be considered in the selection process are:

i Functionality : to what extend does each alternative provide for a minimum level of output for a given core business process.

ii Cost: the cost of each alternative, their testing and training.

iii Deployment: the time necessary for selecting, testing and implementing the contingency.

b. Identify, and document contingency plans and implementation strategies

Institutions should maintain adequate written documentation supporting every stage of the contingency plan progress. The documentation provides an audit trail which may facilitate corrections or adaptations of the program if necessary.

It is also important to include in the contingency plan for each business process strategies that can meet the minimum acceptable output requirements. Institutions may consider partial replacement, full replacement or outsourcing.

As part of the contingency planning process, it is recommended that each institution prepares a contact list with the names of all organizations with which they are interrelated. The list should contain names of their clients, vendors, bank, insurance company, and government agencies.

c. Establish trigger dates to activate contingency plans

i After the best contingency plans have been selected for each core business process, trigger dates need to be set for the implementation of the contingency plan.

ii The trigger dates may be set, based on the Year 2000 program (schedule of implementation of renovated or replaced systems) or on the deployment date stipulated in the schedule of each contingency plan.

d. Establish a plan for the "Rollover"

Plans should be made by each institution for the actual rollover, December 31, 1999 – January 3, 2000. Critical to the planning process is that January 1, 2000 is a Saturday, thus not a work day for most financial institutions.

Consequently, institutions must consider if it is important to have computer and information specialists available during the rollover period to check for system failures. Another option for financial institutions may be to shut down all their systems on December 31, 1999 and power-up on Saturday, January 1, 2000.

e. **Establish an Emergency Response Team**
Each institution can establish an Emergency Response Team. The emergency response team is responsible for the implementation of contingency plans. Within the emergency response team responsibility should be divided for each core business process.

IV. **Testing**

The main purpose of testing is to evaluate if the individual contingency plans can provide the desired objective.

An independent review of the plan and a legal review are important since they may validate the effectiveness of the plan and provide assurance that the plan complies with the applicable requirements.

A full scenario of disruption must be created to test business continuity plans. Management may use internal auditors, external auditors or other qualified sources to evaluate tests.

a. **Validation of the business contingency plan**
The institution should state the objective of the test, the scope of the test and develop the test scenario.

b. **Document the testing process**
Test plans should include the test objectives, type of test, test approach, equipment and resources needed, personnel to participate in the test, procedures and expected results.

V. **Maintenance and Updating of the Plan**

After testing has taken place the contingency plan should be updated with the necessary changes. The plan must be modified continually due to changes in applications, software and operations.

i It is important to ensure that all changes and up-dates are incorporated in the plan. Some information which should be incorporated are: new safety requirements, new applications, configuration changes and vendor agreements.

ii Institutions should develop a schedule for the independent review of all parts of the Business Continuity Plan. All review actions should be performed on a timely basis.

VI. **Crisis Coordination and Public Relations**

The main goal of public relations is to reassure the public through the

media that the institution is in control and that the Year 2000 issue is being handled in a timely and organized manner.

a. Each institution should prepare plans to handle the public, especially clients and media, if necessary.
b. The institution should decide who will be responsible for making public statements.
c. The institution should inform its personnel who is authorized to grant interviews or answer questions from the press.
d. Discuss beforehand in problem situation which media will be contacted and who will contact them.

Conclusion

The risk of business disruption as a result of the Year 2000 remains notwithstanding the renovation and replacement efforts of most institutions. Institutions should prepare a business continuity plan to ensure the institution's ability to function normally after December 31, 1999.

Contingency planning is a process and it does not stop with the preparation of the Business Continuity Plan. Institutions should make it a continuous process to update and modify the plan.

By the end of the second quarter of 1999 each institution should be informed on the Year 2000 status of their major third parties such as: government agencies from which it receives information, its major clients, utility and telecommunication companies. In this context, an institution should be prepared to take the necessary steps if the companies on which it depends on are not compliant on time.

As part of the examination process, the Bank van de Nederlandse Antillen will address the contingency planning process to review all supervised institution's readiness and ensure that the institution will continue to function after the Year 2000.

Finally, it is the hope of the Bank that the majority of financial institutions and public infrastructure entities in the Dutch Caribbeanachieve Year 2000 compliance so that activation of contingencies will prove to be unnecessary.

It is nevertheless necessary, to prepare contingency plans now, rather than discovering on January 1, 2000 that they should have been prepared.

BANK VAN DE NEDERLANDSE ANTILLEN

Example Possibilities of Failure in Different Industries

	Possible Failure	**Examples of Possible Contingencies**
Tele-communications	Disruption in international calls switching	Cellular
	Disruption in domestic calls switching	CB radio

	Possible telephone service loss	Satellite phone
	Billing records error	Keep paper records
Utilities	Failure to distribute or loss of electric power	Generator /fuel supply
	Electric power cut off	Maintain records of 1999
	Loss of water pressure	Bottled drinking water
	Electric and water meter malfunction	Maintain records of 1999
Health/ Medicine	Malfunction of medical instruments (MRI,Cat)	If possible have insureds avoid surgery until mid '00
	Malfunction of patient monitoring devices	
	Problems with prescription refills	Refill in December 1999
	Possible shut down of pharmaceutical labs	Refill in December 1999
	Drug lot expiration errors	Check expiration date to prevent sickness
Central	Miscalculation of pensions	Save paper records in 1999
	Possible errors in social security	Save paper records in 1999
	Miscalculation of taxes	Save paper records in 1999
Island	Miscalculation in financial transactions	Save paper records in 1999
Insurance	No payment of Y2K claims	Seek special Y2K coverage
	Payments miscalculation	Save paper records in 1999
Banking Industry	Interest calculations errors	Review statements
	Miscalculation of credit card charges	Save paper records of 1999
	Account balances thrown off	Check balance regularly

	Bank/ATM Failures	Keep more cash at hand More personnel to perform transactions Decrease active ATM 's

Example Year 2000 Contingency Calendar

February– June '99	July-October '99	As of January 1, 2000
Approval of Contingency Plan by Management	Public Participation of :	All applications monitored for problems
Emergency Response Team Instituted	- Y2K readiness	All external (vendor) applications monitored
Preparation of Contingency Budget	- Contingency plan	Start emergency Y2K reparations if necessary
Revision of Contingency Plan	All back-up equipment deployed:	Provide weekly report on progress of emergency reparations
Prepare status reports on:	- generators	Updating of Post Y2K budget
-Institution's Year 2000 project	- fuel supplies	Prepare financial analysis Y2K impact
-Public Infrastructure and Government	- satellite telephones	All billing and account errors corrected
-Clients and Vendors		All insurance claims on the organization analyzed
-Legal and liability position		
Updating of Contact Lists		

Appendix C:

Example Planning Steps for a Business Continuity Plan

1 Obtain Senior Management's Commitment and Support to Develop the Plan

- Commitment to the process
- Assigning of resources to develop and implement the process
- Monitoring of progress

2 Establishment of a Business Contingency Committee

- Select qualified personnel
- Define the role and responsibilities for each member

- Develop the committee's project plan to manage the process
- Establish regular committee meetings
- Set up a schedule to report the progress of the project regularly to management

3 **Perform a Business Risk Analysis**
- Establish a planning strategy
- Define Year 2000 risk scenarios
- Perform a risk analysis of each core business process
- Assess public infrastructure risks
- Prioritize core business processes
- Determine minimum level of service and output for each core business process

4 **Contingency Planning**
- Select a contingency strategy for each core business process
- Identify and document contingency plans and implementation modes
- Establish trigger dates to activate contingency plans
- Establish a documentation strategy for the "rollover"
- Establish an emergency response team

5 **Testing**
- Validate the business contingency plan
- Develop test plan
- Document the testing process
- Determine the test scenario
- Evaluation

6 **Maintenance and updating of the plan**
- Review plan for changes
- Modify plan based on test results
- Incorporate new safety requirements

7 **Crisis Coordination and Public Relation**
- Develop and coordinate plans to handle the public, clients and the media during crisis
- Develop and coordinate plans to handle employees during crisis.
- Determine who will be responsible for making public statements and who will replace this person if necessary.
- Inform the institution's personnel who is authorized to grant interviews or answer questions from the press.
- Discuss beforehand in situation of crisis which media will be contacted and who will contact them.

GENERAL ADMINISTRATIVE RULES
GAR 2000/1
PART 1

GENERAL ADMINISTRATIVE RULES FOR PROVIDING INFORMATION AND DATA TO THE BANK OF THE DUTCH CARIBBEAN (GAR 2000/1)

For the execution of its tasks, the Bank of the Dutch Caribbean(hereafter to be called: the Bank), determines the following, pursuant to article 8 of the Foreign Exchange Transactions Act (P.B. 1981, no. 67):

A. Providing information to foreign exchange banks and other institutions authorized by the Bank of the Netherlands Antilles, among which the cash couriers for the settlement of international payment transactions.

1. Residents who make payments to or collect receipts from non-residents through the intermediary of foreign exchange banks are obliged, for statistical reasons, to supply the requested corresponding data. In the case of payments to and receipts from foreign countries, it will suffice in general to submit proofs and/or provide data to the mediating institution. Any possible required separate licenses granted to the resident for these transactions must also be submitted to the mediating institution. Also if foreign means of payment or customary monetary papers in tourist traffic are bought or sold by a resident at a foreign exchange bank, he is obliged to provide the foreign exchange bank in question with the data which are required by the Bank.
2. When receivables from and debts to non-residents are cleared, the resident in question, on paying his debt, has to provide the relevant information on the gross transactions to the Bank or to a foreign exchange bank (or other authorized financial institution) upon request and without delay.
3. If the foreign exchange bank to which the documents and other records are submitted establishes that the information and data supplied are incomplete, the resident is obliged upon request to provide further information and data timely upon request, or take care of the completeness of the information as the case may be.
4. Those who object to providing certain data and information through the intermediary of foreign exchange banks, can provide the Bank directly with these data and information after submitting a written request to that effect.

B. Reporting (current) accounts with non-residents to the Bank
Residents are obliged to report to the Bank without delay:

1. opening and holding accounts in their own name in any currency with non-residents;
2. opening and holding current-accounts with non-residents (including non-banks) for the clearing of mutual receivables and debts, stating the nature of their

business or the nature of the transactions that are paid, or cleared as the case may be. In doing so, the reporting guidelines of the Bank have to be observed.

C. Providing data concerning the settlement or execution of transactions with non-residents in a different manner than mentioned under A and B

Residents are obliged to report this different manner of settlement or execution directly and in writing to the Bank without delay, while stating all relevant data, and to observe the administrative rules given by the Bank. In doing so, the following should be considered:

1. Equity participations (direct investments)

   Pursuant to the Foreign Exchange Transactions Act, residents are obliged to report changes in equity participations abroad or in the Dutch Caribbeanto the Bank without delay, if these transactions result from dealings of or with non-residents.

   Such changes can result from (co)-founding, acquiring, extending or (co)-participating in enterprises and branches, and also decreasing or alienating the interests acquired earlier.

   Insofar as participations are effected in different manners than by payment via a foreign exchange bank or another authorized financial institution, or by payment or clearing via a (current)-account held abroad, residents have to report this per case directly and in writing to the Bank. In doing so, the following can be considered:

- contribution of corporeal matters (for example, goods or industrial buildings), incorporeal matters (for example, licenses, know-how) and services;
- converting foreign (commercial) receivables, debts and profits, dividends, loans, credits, current-account receivables and debts;
- exchanging stocks or other securities;
- reinvestment of funds becoming available elsewhere on account of disinvestment;
- retention of profit and writing off losses.

Whatever the manner in which these transactions are effected, residents have to observe the reporting guidelines of the Bank.

2. Loans

a. contracting loans abroad and relending the funds loaned to third parties abroad;
b. contracting loans abroad for the payment of debts abroad;
c. the contracting of loans in the Dutch Caribbeanby non-residents at non-banks for the payment of their debts to residents in the Netherlands Antilles.

3. Other manners of settlement

a. settlement, resulting from novation agreements, for example by converting short-term loans into long-term loans, or by debtor or creditor substitution;

b. compensation and settlement of outstanding receivables against debts;
c. non-monetary payment.

If for the transactions and settlements mentioned under 1, 2 and 3 a license must have been granted, the reporting has to take place as soon as possible after effectuation.
D. Supplier and buyer credit
Residents are obliged to report without delay and in writing to the Bank: contracting an agreement for the purchase and sale of goods from, respectively to, non-residents, if in doing so a supplier or buyer credit has been stipulated. In that case, the following data must be provided:

a. name and address of the non-resident with whom the agreement has been concluded;
b. nature, quantity and value (price) of the goods;
c. the terms of payment agreed on (including the currency in which the payment will be made);
d. the presumable month(s) of import, respectively export, of the goods.
e. Country of origin of the goods.

This reporting does not release residents from the possible obligation to request an exchange permit.
E. Data on the financial relation with non-residents
Upon request, residents are obliged to report to the Bank the balances of and changes in:

a. their participations in the capital of enterprises abroad;
b. the participations by non-residents in the capital of enterprises established in the Netherlands Antilles;
c. their loans/credits extended, within an intra-group, to foreign countries;
d. loans/credits raised by them abroad within an intra-group;
e. other international credit and debit equity ratios.

F. Registration of residents who effect certain foreign exchange transactions
Unless already registered at or designated by the Bank, the following residents/ enterprises/ institutions will have to report to the Bank for registration:

1. residents who are going to participate in transit and tripartite trade (among others, Free Zone companies);
2. residents who, in conducting their business, intend to trade goods with residents and non-residents, in which case the goods are not in free trade, nor will be taken out of bond (among others, ship-chandlers);
3. enterprises and institutions, irrespective of the legal form, that are residents and in which non-residents participate directly or indirectly via capital stock or otherwise and whose objective is to be occupied to a considerable extent with receiving means from non-residents and paying them on to non-residents;
4. other residents to be designated by the Bank.

The residents mentioned under 1 through 4 are obliged to observe the reporting guidelines of the Bank.
These instructions will become effective on July 1, 2000.

Extension of credit to Executive Officers, Supervisory Directors, Principal Shareholders and their related interests and to employees of a credit institution

I.1 Nature of Regulation I

1. With Supervisory Regulation I the Bank seeks to formally limit the amount of lending to executive officers, supervisory directors, principal shareholders being natural persons (including the related interests of those persons) and employees of the institution.
2. The intended limitation will be applied to mentioned persons individually in relation to the equity of the credit institution. However, for employees the limitation is on an aggregate basis for all employees.

I.2 Legal basis, purpose and scope

1. This regulation is issued pursuant to article 21, paragraph 2, letter c of the National Ordinance on the Supervision of Banking and Credit Institutions 1994 and draws therefore on the authority of subject ordinance.
2. This regulation governs any extension of credit by a credit institution to the persons (mentioned above) employed in the institution itself, the holding company (if any) of which the credit institution is a subsidiary and other subsidiaries of the holding company.
3. The regulation also applies to any extensions of credit by the credit institution to a company controlled by such persons or a committee or party that benefits from or is controlled by such persons.

I.3 Definitions

For the purpose of Supervisory Regulation I, the following definitions apply:

1. **"Equity"** is defined as Tier I capital as defined in the Chart of Accounts. For purposes of this regulation equity is considered at the end of the quarter preceding the date of the transaction.
2. **"Covered parties"** are the parties being subject to the regulation. These are executive officers, supervisory directors, principal shareholders and their respective related interests.
3. **"Interest party"** is a covered party that has made a request for extension of credit by the credit institution.
4. **"Control"** of a company or credit institution means that a person directly or indirectly, or acting through or in concert with others:
    a. owns or has the power to vote 20% or more of any class of voting securities of the company or credit institution;
    b. controls in any manner the election of the majority of the directors of the company or credit institutions

c. has the power to exercise a controlling influence over the management or policies of the company or bank. Based hereon, an executive officer or director is presumed to have control.

A person may rebut a presumption of control established as per a, b, or c above by submitting to the Bank written material that, in the Bank's judgment, demonstrate effectively the absence of control.

5. **"Director"** of a credit institution includes any supervisory director whether or not receiving compensation, any supervisory director of a bank holding company of which the institution is a subsidiary, and any supervisory director of any other subsidiary of that holding company.
6. **"Executive officer"** of a company or credit institution includes all individuals who participate or have the authority to participate (other than in the capacity of a director) in major policy-making functions of the company or credit institution whether or not the officer has an official title (such as Managing Director), the title designates the officers as an assistant or the officer is serving without compensation.

An officer who is presumed to be an executive officer in the meaning of this regulation may be effectively excluded from participation in major policy-making functions of the company or institution by unanimous resolution of the Board of Directors or by the articles association of the company or credit institution and this person actually does not participate in policy making. Consequently, the excluded executive officer will not be regarded as an officer (exercising control) in the sense of this regulation.

7. **"Immediate family"** means the individual's spouse, minor children and any of the individual's children (including adults) residing in the individual's home, whether adopted or not.
8. **"Principal shareholder"** means an individual or a company that directly or indirectly, or acting through or in concert with one or more persons, owns, controls or has the power to vote 10% or more of any class of voting shares of a company or credit institution. Shares owned or controlled by a member of an individual's immediate family are considered to be held by the individual.
9. **"Persons"** means both natural persons and corporate persons.
10. **"Related interests"** means a company or any other organization that is controlled by a person. In case there is no control by a person, the criterium for a related interest is whether the person benefits from the organization acting as an interested party.
11. **"Subsidiary"** is a company or credit institution in which a person holds a majority of the shares.
12. **"Extension of credit"** is a making or renewal of any loan, a granting of a line of credit in any manner whatsoever. Extensions of credit also include:
    a. a purchase under an irrevocable repurchase agreement of securities, other assets or obligations;
    b. an advance by means of an overdraft, cash or otherwise;

   c. issuance of a standby letter of credit or other similar arrangements regardless of names or description;
   d. an acquisition of any note, draft, bill of exchange or other evidence of indebtness;
   e. an increase in the existing indebtness;
   f. an advance of unearned salary or other compensation for a period in excess of 30 days and
   g. any other transaction as a result of which a person becomes obligated to pay money or its equivalent to a credit institution.
13. **"Employees"** are all other persons employed by a credit institution not being an executive officer or director.

    If an employee is also a principal shareholder, the employee is not considered to be an employee but a principal shareholder.

14. **"Credit institution"** is defined in article 1, paragraph 1, sub c and d of the National Ordinance on Supervision of Banking and Credit Institutions of 1994.

I.4 Applicability and exemptions

1. Supervisory Regulation I will be applicable to all credit institutions falling under the supervision of the Bank, except for those classes of institutions having an exemption under the regulation as mentioned in paragraph I.4.2.
2. This regulation shall not apply to any branches of foreign banks which are consolidated in their home country and for which branch the Bank has received a guarantee for all liabilities.

I.5 Extension of credit to executive officers, directors, principal shareholders and their related interests.
The requirements under the regulation for above mentioned parties are as follows:

1. Extensions of credit by a credit institution to executive officers, directors, principal shareholders being a natural person and their related interests are subject to the following limits:
   a. Executive officer: 50% the officer's net annual salary;
   b. Directors: reasonable current account overdraft facility in line with established internal policy;
   c. Principal shareholders: 2.5% of equity
2. An additional 2.5% of equity may be extended to the parties mentioned under 1.5.1. only if it is fully secured by adequate collateral.
3. Additionally, a credit institution is authorized to extend credit to any **executive officer** of the institution:
   a. to a reasonable amount to finance the education of the officer's children where these children, due to the executive officer's position, would not ordinarily qualify for a government scholarship and
   b. to a reasonable amount to finance the purchase, construction or improvement of residence, of the extension of credit is secured by a first

lien on the residence and the residence has been adequately appraised and is owned by the executive officer.

Hence, for any other purpose not specified in a and b above, the aggregate amount of the credits to that officer must not exceed the lending limits specified above.

4. Extension of credit to executive officers are made by the credit institution subject to the following conditions:
    a. the officer will report all requests for credit from other credit institutions;
    b. prior approval is received from the Board of Directors;
    c. unsecured loans become immediately due and payable upon the officer leaving the credit institution.
5. An extension of credit does not include an advance against accrued salary or other accrued compensation (earned but not disbursed) or an advance for the payment of authorized travel or other expenses on behalf of the institution.

I.6 Extension of credit to employees of a credit institution

1. Extension of credit to employees of a credit institution should be performed by the institution according to a proper lending policy for employees, considering the limits of paragraph I.6.2.
2. The requirement for loans to employees is as follows:
   Total loans to employees of an institution may not exceed 10% of equity, of which up to 5% of equity may be left unsecured.

I.7 Terms and Creditworthiness

1. No credit institution may extend credit to any of its directors, principal shareholders or their related interests and the related interest of executive officers unless the extension of credit is made on substantially the same terms, including interest rates and collateral, as those prevailing at the time for comparable transactions by the credit institution with other persons that are not covered parties and who are not employed with the institution. The extension of credit should furthermore not involve more than the normal risk of repayment or present other unfavorable features for the institution.
2. With regard to the lending terms, credit institutions may adopt in the context of the specified lending limits, preferential interest rates only for their **employees** and **executive officers**. These preferential rates for employees and executive officers must be approved by the Board of Directors.

I.8 Prior approval of extension of credit to covered parties (excluding employees)

1. No credit institution may extend credit to any of its executive officers, directors, principal shareholders or their related interests in an amount that, when aggregated with the amount of all other extensions of credit to that person and all its related interest, exceeds 50% of the limits specified under I.5.1 unless a line

of credit in excess hereof has been approved in advance by a majority of the board of directors and the interested party has abstained from participating directly or indirectly in the voting.

2. However, in no event may a credit institution extend credit to any one of the covered parties, in an amount that, when aggregated with all other extensions of credit to the interested party and its related interests, exceeds NAf.100.000 except by complying with the requirements of I.8.1 above (prior Board of Directors' approval and no participation in voting by the interested party).
3. Participation in the discussion by an interested party or any attempt to influence the voting by the board of directors regarding an extension of credit constitutes indirect participation in the voting on an extension of credit. Consequently, the credit institution is in non-compliance and the credit extended will have to be repaid immediately.

I.9 Records of credit institutions with regard to extensions of credit to covered parties

1. Each credit institution shall maintain the necessary records for compliance with the requirements of this regulation. These records identify all executive officers, directors, principal shareholders and their related interests and specify the amount and terms of each extension of credit by the credit institution to these covered parties.
2. Each credit institution shall request at least annually that each executive officer, director or principal shareholder identify by means of a written statement their related interests with a loan from the credit institution. These records should be readily available for the Bank's inspection at any time.

I.10 Report by executive officers

1. Each executive officer who has a loan with a credit institution and who becomes a debtor of any other credit institution in an aggregate amount in excess of NAf.50.000 shall, within 10 days of the date the indebtness reaches such level, make a written report to the board of directors of the officer's credit institution. The report shall state the lender's name, the date and amount of each extension of credit, any security for it, and the purposes for which the proceeds have been or are to be used.
2. Subject reports should be filed as an integral part of the documentation requested under paragraph 1.9.

I.11 Grandfathering provision

1. A lending relationship of an executive officer, director, principal shareholder that becomes unpermitted as a result of the implementation of this regulation may continue for a period desired by the institution after consultation with the Bank, but may not continue for a period longer than 12 months after the implementation date of the regulation.

2. Existing loans maturing in a period longer than 12 months shall be respected, provided a written request is done by the institution and which loan is found to be reasonable and sound by the Bank, based on the underlying documentation.

Restrictions on transactions with affiliates and loans to affiliates

II.1 Nature of Regulation I

1. Because of the risk of contagion by affiliates it is necessary to place restrictions on the type and volume of transactions with affiliates and the resulting receivables from these affiliates.
2. Therefore, the requirements of this regulation are aimed at restrictions on transactions with (unconsolidated) affiliates and a limit on net balances due from (unconsolidated) affiliates.

II.2 Legal basis, purpose and scope

1. This regulation is issued pursuant to article 21, paragraph 2, sub c of the National Ordinance on the Supervision of Banking and Credit Institutions 1994 and governs certain transaction with an affiliate. The regulation draws on the authority of subject ordinance.
2. The aim of this regulation is to provide a sound basis for transactions with affiliates. All unconsolidated affiliated companies fall within the scope of the requirements.

II.3 Definitions
For the purpose of Supervisory Regulation II, the following definitions apply:

1. **"Equity"** is defined as Tier I capital as defined in the Chart of Accounts. For purposes of this regulation equity is considered at the quarter preceding the date of the transaction.
2. An **"Affiliate"** of a supervised credit institution is defined for the purpose of the regulation to be:
   a. Any company for which commonality of ownership exists with the credit institution: any company that controls the credit institution (parent company or other) and any other company that is controlled by the company that controls the credit institution (sister companies) and any company that controls the company that controls the credit institution (ultimate parent company or companies);
   b. Subsidiaries of the credit institution:
   c. Any company for which a commonality of directors exists with the credit institution: any company in which the majority of its (supervisory or managing) directors constitute a majority of the directors of the credit institution or any company that is controlled by the credit institution;
   d. Any company that de Bank determines to have a relationship with the credit institution or its subsidiaries and affiliates, such that transactions

with that company may be affected by the relationship of the company with the credit institution, its subsidiaries or affiliates.

The definition of affiliate does not include:

Companies engaged solely in the following activities: holding the premises of the credit institution, conducting a safe deposit business, holding obligations of governments or holding real estate for execution on the short term. However, no transaction should be concluded with these affiliates other than those which are strictly necessary for the facilitation of their respective businesses to the benefit of the credit institution.

3. **"Covered transactions"** mean with respect to an affiliate of a credit institution all transactions mentioned below which are subject to the enforcement of this regulation and the resulting restrictions. The following transactions are 'covered' and hence subject to restrictions:
    a. an extension of credit to or the placement of a deposit with an affiliate;
    b. the issuance of a guarantee, acceptance or letter of credit (including a standby letter of credit) on behalf of an affiliate;
    c. a purchase of securities issued by an affiliate;
    d. a purchase of assets, including assets subject to a repurchase agreement, from an affiliate;
    e. the acceptance of securities issued by an affiliate as collateral for an extension of credit to any person or company.
4. **"Company"** is defined as any form of business organization irrespective of its orientation to profit and trusts (business or otherwise). However, the term does not include supervised credit institutions, supervised insurance companies and corporations of which the majority of the shares are owned by the government.
5. **"Control"** of a company or credit institution means that a person directly or indirectly, or acting through or in concert with others:
    a. owns or has the power to vote 20% or more of any class of voting securities of the company or credit institution;
    b. controls in any manner the election of the majority of the directors of the company or bank;
    c. has the power to exercise a controlling influence over the management or policies of the company or bank.
6. **"Persons"** means both natural persons and corporate persons.
7. **"Subsidiary"** is a company or institution in which a person holds a majority of the shares.
8. **"Securities"** means stock, bonds, debentures, notes or other similar obligations.
9. **"Low quality assets"** means an asset that falls into one or more of the following categories:
    a. an asset qualified as "substandard", "doubtful" or "loss" in the most recent report of examination of an affiliate by its supervisor (in case of a supervised institution) or assessed to fall into one of these categories by the Bank;
    b. an asset in non-accrual status;

   c. an asset on which principal or interest payments are more than 60 days past due;
   d. an asset whose terms have been renegotiated or compromised due to the deteriorating financial condition of the obligator.
10. **"Credit institution"** as defined in art. 1 paragraph 1 sub c and d of the National Ordinance in the Supervision of Banking and Credit Institutions of 1994.

II.4 Applicability and Exemptions

1. Supervisory Regulation II will be applicable to all credit institutions falling under the supervision of the Bank, except for those classes of institutions having an exemption under the regulation as mentioned in paragraph II.4.2.
2. This regulation shall not apply to any branches of foreign banks which are consolidated in their home country and for which branch the Bank has received a guarantee for all liabilities of the branch.

II.5 Covered transactions with and balances due from (unconsolidated) affiliates.
The requirements under the regulation are as follows:

1. A credit institution and its consolidated subsidiaries may engage in a covered transaction with an affiliate only if the **balances due from unconsolidated affiliates are limited to 10% of equity for individual affiliates and 20% of equity in the aggregate for all affiliates.**
2. For the purpose of this regulation, any transaction by a credit institution with any person shall be deemed to be a transaction with an affiliate to the extent that the proceeds of the transaction are used for the benefit of, or effectively transferred to, that affiliate.
3. A credit institution and its consolidated subsidiaries may not purchase a low quality asset from an affiliate unless the credit institution or such subsidiary, pursuant to an independent credit evaluation, has committed itself to purchase such an asset **prior** to the time such asset was acquired by the affiliate.

II.6 Exempted transactions with affiliates
The requirement for restrictions on (covered) transactions with affiliates shall not be applicable to:

a. any transaction (not involving low quality assets) of the credit institution with:
   - a local bank which controls 75% or more of the voting shares of the credit institution;
   - any bank in which the credit institution controls 75% or more of the voting shares;
   - a local bank in which 75% or more of the voting shares are controlled by the (holding) company that controls 75% or more of the voting shares of a credit institution.
b. making deposits in an affiliated bank or affiliated foreign bank in the ordinary course of correspondent business, subject to a restriction of 20% of equity per affiliated correspondent bank and 40% of equity in the aggregate for all affiliated correspondent banks.

c. extension of credit or the issuing of a guarantee or letter of credit on behalf of an affiliate that is fully secured by acceptable obligations of a government c.q. fully guarantees by a government, or by a segregated earmarked deposit account with the credit institutions;
d. purchasing assets having a readily identifiable and publicly available market quotation and purchased at market value or purchasing loans of sound quality from affiliate banks on an non-recourse basis;
e. purchasing from an affiliate a loan or extension of credit that was originated by the credit institution and sold to the affiliate subject to a repurchase agreement or with recourse.

II.7 Terms of transactions

1. A credit institution may engage in a transaction (covered or exempted) with an affiliate only:
    a. on the terms and under the circumstances, including credit standards, that are substantially the same, or at least as favorable to the credit institution or its subsidiaries, as those prevailing at the same time for comparable transactions with or involving non-affiliated companies and
    b. in the absence of comparable transactions, on terms and under circumstances, including credit standards, that in good faith would be offered, or would apply to, non affiliated companies.
2. In addition, any transaction (covered or exempted) between a credit institution and an affiliate shall be on terms and conditions that are consistent with safe and sound banking practices.

II.8 Grandfathering provision

1. An affiliate relationship that becomes unpermitted as a result of the implementation of this regulation may continue for a period desired by the institution after consultation with the Bank, but may not continue for a period longer than 12 months after the implementation date of the regulation.
2. Transactions maturing in a period longer than 12 months shall be respected, provided a written request is done by the institution and which transactions are found to be reasonable and sound by the Bank based on the underlying documentation.

Limitations on extensions of credit to any one borrower or group of connected borrowers ("large exposure regulation")

III.1 Nature of Regulation III

1. At the very center of a credit institution lies the extension of credit to borrowers. This regulation deals with the restriction of the amounts owed by one debtor or a group of connected debtors to a credit institution in order to avoid overexposure to one single entity.

2. Monitoring and controlling the exposures of a credit institution is an integral part of prudential supervision because excessive concentration of exposures to a single client or group of connected clients might result in an unacceptable degree of concentration risk and such a situation may be deemed to be prejudicial to the solvency of a credit institution.

III.2 Legal basis, purpose and scope

1. This regulation is issued pursuant to article 21, paragraph 2, letter c of the National Ordinance on the Supervision of Banking and Credit Institutions 1994 and governs any transaction with a single borrower.
2. The aim of this regulation is to provide a sound basis for transactions with large borrowers.

III.3. Definitions

For the purposes of Supervisory Regulation III, the following definitions apply:

1. **"Equity"** is defined as Tier I capital as defined in the Chart of Accounts. For purposes of this regulation equity is considered at the end of the quarter preceding the date of the transaction.
2. **"Credit institution"** is defined in accordance with article 1, paragraph 1, sub c and d of the National Ordinance on the Supervision of Banking and Credit Institutions of 1994;
3. **"Exposure"** is defined as any facility granted, whether drawn or undrawn, by a credit institution to a client or group of connected clients, on or off balance sheet, and includes those commitments and contingent items deemed to be relevant deemed to be relevant by the Bank when assessing the identifiable risks of the credit institutions. Exposure elements include but are not limited to:
    a. loans and advances, including overdrafts;
    b. leases;
    c. bills and promissory notes received;
    d. guarantees and similar contingent liabilities as acceptances, 	documentary credits issued and confirmed, irrevocable standby letters 	of credit and
    e. commitments such as repurchase agreements, irrevocable revolving lines of credit, underwriting (including note issuance facilities and revolving underwriting facilities), irrevocable undrawn overdraft facilities, lending commitments.
4. **"Group of connected clients"** means two or more persons, whether natural or legal, holding exposures from the same credit institution and any of its subsidiaries, whether on a joint or separate basis, but who are mutually associated through the control of one of them by the other. Moreover, the interconnection between the persons also implies that their cumulated exposure actually represents a single risk to the credit institution, with the likelihood that if one of them experiences financial problems the other or all of them are likely to encounter repayment difficulties.
5. **"Control"** as defined in Supervisory Regulation I and II.

III.4 Applicability and exemptions

1. Supervisory Regulation III will be applicable to all credit institutions falling under the supervision of the Bank, except for those classes of institutions having an exemption under the regulation as mentioned in paragraph III.4.2.
2. This regulation shall not apply to any branches of foreign banks which are consolidated in their home country and for which branch the Bank has received a guarantee for all liabilities.

III.5 Reporting of large exposures to the Bank

1. In the Supporting Schedules of the Chart of Accounts a report of every large exposure shall be made by the credit institution to the Bank on a periodic basis as required by the Bank.
2. An exposure of a credit institution to a client or group of connected clients is considered to be a large exposure when its value has reached or exceeded 15% of equity.
3. Regardless of whether large exposures exist in a credit institution the Bank requires the credit institution to report on the appropriate Chart of Accounts schedules a minimum of 25 exposures with the highest percentage value of equity.

III.6 Transactions with and balances due from large (connected) borrowers

1. In the determination of the interconnection between borrowers a credit institution should take at least the following criteria into consideration:
    a. common ownership of clients;
    b. common directors of clients;
    c. cross guarantees provided by one client for the other;
    d. direct commercial interdependency which cannot be substituted in the short term.
    If on the basis of these criteria interconnections between clients is observed by a credit institution, the aggregate credits of these clients should be classified as a single risk.
2. With regard to large exposures to one borrower or group of connected borrowers the following limits apply:
    a. Exposures to any one borrower or group of connected borrowers should be limited to 25% of equity.
    b. Exposures to all large borrowers may in the aggregate not exceed 600%;of equity.

III.7 Exceptions on and prior approval for large exposures

1. The aggregate exposure limit of 600% referred to in paragraph III.6.2. sub b may be exceeded only in exceptional cases with the distinct prior approval of the Bank.

2. In such cases the Bank shall require the credit institution either to increase the volume of equity or to take other remedial measures such as a substantial coverage with solid additional collateral, the value of which is not likely to deteriorate during the term of the commitment.
3. Under no circumstances will an individual exposure to one client or group of connected clients be allowed to exceed 35% of equity.

III.8 Exemptions to the large exposure rule.

1. The Bank may fully or partially exempt from the application of the exposure limits in paragraph III.6. the following clients or group of connected clients:
    a. the government of the Dutch Caribbeanand the Islands of the Dutch Caribbeanand
    b. public authorities of certain countries to be designated by the Bank ona case by case basis.
2. Furthermore, the Bank will in principle fully or partially exempt from the application of the exposure limits in paragraph III.6:
    a. exposures secured by an explicit and irrevocable guarantee or pledge of the public authorities referred to under a) and b) above;
    b. exposures fully secured by cash deposits or securities listed on a Stock Exchange acknowledged by the Government of the Netherlands Antilles, provided that the exposure is less than the average market value in the last 12 months;
    c. interbank exposures having a maturity of six months or less.

III.9 Consolidation
The exposures of a credit institution which has one or more subsidiary credit institutions and foreign branches shall be monitored and controlled on a consolidated basis by subject credit institution.
III.10 Grandfathering provision

1. A large borrower relationship that becomes unpermitted as a result of the implementation of this regulation may continue for a period desired by the institution after consultation with the Bank, but may not continue for a period longer than 12 months after the implementation date of the regulation.
2. Existing loans maturing in a period longer than 12 months shall be respected, provided a written request is made by the institutions and which loans are found to be sound by the Bank based on the underlying documentation.

Regulation concerning General and Specific Provisions of credit institutions.

V.1 Nature of Regulation V

1. Supervisory Regulation V is aimed at the establishment of effective provisioning guidelines for credit institutions in respect of the lending activities conducted by these institutions. The regulation deals with provisioning policies at two levels, general as well as specific provisions.

2. The General Provision covers the bulk of risks in a given loan portfolio, whereas Specific Provisions are geared towards the setting op of appropriate cushions for potential, but already identified, losses in certain loans.

V.2 Legal basis, purpose and scope

This regulation governs the provisioning policy of institutions under the supervision of the Bank and is issued pursuant to article 21, paragraph 2, sub c of the National Ordinance on the Supervision of Banking and Credit Institutions 1994.

V.3 Definitions

For the purposes of Supervisory Regulation V, the following definitions apply:

1. **"Equity"** is defined as Tier I capital as defined in the Chart of Accounts.
2. **"Subsidiary"** is a company or credit institution in which a person holds a majority of the shares.
3. **"Credit institution"** is defined in article 1, paragraph 1, sub c and d of the National Ordinance on the Supervision of Banking and Credit Institutions of 1994.
4. **"Net loan portfolio"** is calculated as gross loans minus compensations (as per Appendix A of the General Guidelines of the Chart of Accounts) and specific provisions.

V.4 Applicability and exemptions.

1. Supervisory Regulation V will be applicable to all credit institutions falling under the supervision of the Bank, except for those classes of institutions having an exemption under the regulation as mentioned in paragraph V.4.2.
2. The regulation shall not apply to any branches of foreign banks which are consolidated in their home country and for which branch the Bank has received a guarantee for all liabilities.

V.5 Provisioning policy concerning the General Provision for Loan Losses.

1. The General Provision for Loan Losses (GPLL) should be set up by credit institutions to provide for potential, but as yet unidentified or unexpected, losses in the loan portfolio.
2. Every institution under the supervision of the Bank should maintain appropriate policies to set up the GPLL and to determine the adequacy thereof.
3. The GPLL should normally be reviewed by the institution periodically in relation with the level of risks and the equity position of the institution, because prudent bank policy requires the maintenance of a GPLL that sufficiently accommodates the inherent credit risks affecting a loan portfolio as a whole.
4. In light of the above, the Bank maintains the policy that under normal economic circumstances and market conditions, with no substantial concentrations of risks and an overall soundness of the loan portfolio, the GPLL should be approximately 1.5 @ 2% of the Net Loan Portfolio.

5. However, under certain circumstances for a particular institution, a higher GPLL percentage may be necessary. Such circumstances that may warrant a higher provision percentage are, but not limited to, the following:
   a. depressed conditions in one or more sectors of the economy in which the institution operates;
   b. the level of unsecured loans in relation to the total loan portfolio and equity;
   c. number and size of large loans;
   d. the overall condition of the loan portfolio which is measured by the extent of loans classified as substandard, doubtful or loss.
6. In case a higher GPLL percentage is required than the norm mentioned in V.5.4, the Bank will advise the institution after an examination. Viewing the existence of the circumstances mentioned under a to d, the institution should review its GPLL and consider a GPLL percentage in excess of the above mentioned norm.

V.6 Provisioning policy concerning Specific Provisions for loan losses.

1. **Credit reviews**
   As part of its on-site examinations, the Bank performs a credit review at the institution under supervision. Credit reviews conducted by the Bank usually results in classification of the loan portfolio according to the following classifications: Satisfactory, Special Mention, Substandard, Doubtful and Loss. In order for credit institutions to anticipate on the Bank's classifications and the specific provisions required by the Bank after one such examination, the Bank's provisioning policy is hereby disclosed.
   All credit institutions are advised to review their own provisioning policies and bring these in line with the policies mentioned below.
2. **Loan classifications**
   Following is a description of the five loan classifications and the extent of specific provisions required in each case.

a. **Satisfactory**
   Loans classified satisfactory are loans which do not possess any weaknesses. These loans are performing according to the loan agreement and are well protected by the current sound worth and paying capacity of the borrower or by the collateral pledged. No specific provision is required by the Bank.
b. **Special Mention**
   Included in this category are loans which do not presently expose the bank to a sufficient degree of risk to warrant adverse classification, but these loans do possess credit deficiencies deserving management's close attention. Failure to correct deficiencies could result in greater credit risk in the future.
   Ordinarily, such borderline credits have characteristics which timely corrective management action would remedy. Often in credit lines warranting Special Mention, it is the bank's weak origination and/or servicing policies which constitute the cause for criticism. No specific provision is required by the Bank.
c. **Substandard**
   Substandard loans are inadequately protected by the current sound worth and

paying capacity of the borrower or by the collateral pledged, if any. Loans so classified have a well-defined weakness or weaknesses that jeopardize the liquidation of the debt.
These loans are characterized by the distinct possibility that the bank will sustain some loss if the deficiencies are not corrected. The required specific provision is 10%-25% of the loan depending on the severity of the weaknesses.

d. **Doubtful**
Loans classified Doubtful have all the weaknesses inherent in those classified Substandard with the added characteristic that the weaknesses make collection or liquidation in full, on the basis of currently known facts, conditions and values, highly questionable and improbable. Therefore, a specific provision of at least 50% is required to be maintained by the institution.

e. **Loss**
Loans classified Loss are considered uncollectible and of such little value that their continuance as bankable assets is not warranted. This classification does not mean that the loan has absolutely no recovery or salvage value, but rather it is not practical or desirable to defer writing off these basically worthless assets even though partial recovery may be effected in the future. The required specific provision for loans classified as "loss" is 100%.

V.7 Grandfathering provision.
Institutions that have provisions lower than the levels required above are advised to contact the Bank for a phase-in program. However, items classified as loss should be immediately provided for.

V.8 Consolidation.
This Regulation also applies to subsidiaries and foreign branches of credit institutions under the supervision of the Bank.

FOREIGN EXCHANGE REGULATIONS

INSTRUCTIONS FOREIGN EXCHANGE BANKS
Publication concerning
Foreign Exchange Transactions AW/2000-1

The Bank of the Netherlands Antilles,

considering

the provision in article 6, paragraph 2 of the Foreign Exchange Transactions Act (P.B. 1981, no. 67), announces that the foreign exchange banks have been given the following instructions:

Instruction no. 1: General provisions

1.1 The definitions of article 1 of the Foreign Exchange Transactions Act (P.B. 1981, no. 67) are applicable to all instructions that were or are given to foreign exchange banks.

1.2 In all the instructions that were or are given to the foreign exchange banks, foreign exchange is understood to be: foreign monetary instruments, foreign means of payment, receivables from non-residents and foreign securities, all as described in article 1, sub 6 through 10 of the Foreign Exchange Transactions Act (P.B. 1981, no. 67).

1.3 The foreign exchange banks are obliged to observe the administrative rules in all their foreign exchange transactions. They are given pursuant to article 8 of the Foreign Exchange Transactions Act (P.B. 1981, no. 67).

Instruction no. 2: Authority foreign exchange banks

2.1 Without prejudice to the other instructions, rules and provisions given with or pursuant to the Foreign Exchange Transactions Act (P.B. 1981, no. 67), foreign exchange banks are authorized to perform the following activities:

a. acquiring, holding, encumbering and alienating foreign exchange, both for themselves and for residents and non-residents;
b. opening, holding and closing accounts in their own names with banking or giro institutions abroad;
c. crediting, respectively debiting, the accounts referred to sub b. for, among other things, commissions, interests, dividends, means of payment sent and mediation in payment transactions;
d. acting as an intermediary in international payment transactions and in other financial transactions between residents and non-residents;
e. concluding financial transactions with non-residents in the course of conducting their foreign banking business, such as granting or raising credits and opening deposits, provided these transactions are in a foreign currency;
f. paying, respectively receiving, interest on the financial transactions referred to sub e.

2.2 The foreign exchange banks must see to it that each of the accounts referred to sub 2.1, b. do not show an overdraft without a permit to that effect from the Bank; momentary debit balances awaiting cover remittances are, however, allowed.

2.3 Foreign exchange is acquired, held and alienated by the foreign exchange bank for own account and risk.

2.4 Without a license to that effect from the Bank, foreign exchange banks are not allowed to hold other foreign currencies than currencies which the Bank quotes and publishes and the Venezuelan Bolivar.

2.5 Foreign exchange banks are allowed to open, hold and close accounts in the name of non-residents in their books:

a. denominated in one of the foreign currencies permitted in 2.4;
b. denominated in guilders, in which;

- the credit balance may not be acquired by depositing domestic bank notes and coins;

- the total credit balance in guilders of one and the same non-resident does not exceed NAf. 200,000.00.

These accounts must be entered in the foreign countriescolumn of the Chart of Accounts. The Bank reserves the right tochange or withdraw this facility, if it considers this desirable on account of monetary developments.

2.6 Foreign exchange banks are allowed to open, hold and close guilder accounts in their books in the name of natural persons or legal entities who have been granted an exemption from the obligations in article 9 through 15 of the Foreign Exchange Transactions Act (P.B. 1981, no. I67). The account holders in question may only make payments to residents (insofar as the transactions are permitted), to the debit of these accounts, and also pay taxes to the Collector of Taxes of the Central/Island Government. These accounts have to be entered in the column "domestic" of the Chart of Accounts.

2.7 An account as referred to sub 2.6 may not show a debit balance. Whenever a debit balance threatens to arise, the account holder in question is obliged to supplement the account by selling foreign currency referred to in 2.4. Moreover, it is not allowed to supplement the guilder account with guilders, whether a debit balance is threatening to arise or not.

2.8 Insofar as Antillean bank notes are offered by non-residents for conversion, it is prohibited for the foreign exchange banks to change more than NAf. 10,000.00 per non-resident per calendar quarter into a foreign currency. This restriction does not apply, if these bank notes have been acquired from current transactions with residents.

Instruction no. 3: foreign currency rates

3.1 The buying and selling rates of the most important foreign currencies are officially quoted and published every day by the Bank.
3.2 The rates of foreign currencies fixed and published daily by the Bank must be adhered to by the foreign exchange banks, respectively calculated in payment transactions between residents mutually, between residents and non-residents and between foreign exchange banks mutually. The foreign exchange banks are, however, allowed to determine the rates themselves for transactions exceeding NAf. 5,000.00. The rates for transactions exceeding Naf.5,000.00 must be reported daily to the Bank at 15:00 hours at the latest. For the record, the Bank wishes to point out to you that, in spite of the above-mentioned, reporting transactions to the Bank must take place by making use of the official rates.

3.3 The rates of foreign currencies fixed and published daily by the Bank need not be calculated crosswise by the foreign exchange banks when conducting their foreign banking business as referred to in instruction 2, sub 2.1, sub b.

3.4 The Bank can verify at the foreign exchange banks whether they comply with the obligations described under 3.2.

Instruction no. 4: currency transactions with the Bank

4.1 Until further notice, the Bank is prepared to sell non-cash dollars to, respectively buy from the foreign exchange banks at the buying and selling rates applicable to foreign exchange banks, with due observance of the provision in instruction no.

5.2. The Bank will immediately inform the foreign exchange banks of a decision to postpone or change this possibility.
4.2 With respect to the other officially quoted foreign currencies, the Bank is free to sell, respectively buy, them, if a request to that effect is made by one or more foreign exchange banks.
4.3 In the event of supplying foreign currencies, both in the case of selling and buying, the risk of interrupted communications will not be to the account of the Bank.
4.4 In the event of a rush purchase of US dollars by the Bank, the value-dating will take place on the same day, if the Bank is informed of this before 10:00 a.m. and the supply by the Federal Reserve Bank in New York takes place before 11:00 a.m., New York time. In the event of a normal purchase of US dollars by the Bank, the value dating will take place on the work day following the day on which the foreign exchange bank gives the Bank the selling-order, provided the Bank receives the order before 15:00 hours. The value-dating in the event of selling U.S. dollars takes place on the work day following the day on which the foreign exchange bank gives the Bank the selling-order, provided the Bank has received the order before 15:00 hours. A selling-order, respectively buying-order, which has been received by the Bank after 15:00 hours is considered to have been received on the next work day.
4.5 The value-dating in the event of buying and selling the other officially quoted foreign currencies is determined by the Bank per transaction.
4.6 Means of payment and receivables payable on demand in a currency other than that of which the rates are quoted and published daily, are, in principle, not sold to, respectively bought from, foreign exchange banks by the Bank.

Instruction no. 5: working balance foreign exchange banks
5.1 Foreign exchange banks are obliged to report weekly, on Monday, their foreign net working balance of the past Friday at 11:00 hours to the Bank. In the event of late receipt of the report, that is to say after Monday, the Bank will charge an administration fee of NAf. 1,000.00 per day for late receipt of the report.

5.2 A foreign exchange bank is not permitted to have its total foreign obligations exceed its total foreign receivables. In the event of a foreign exchange bank having a negative balance, the Bank will charge this bank an administration fee which is calculated on a weekly basis as follows: the interest rate for special loans on the negative balance multiplied by 7 days and divided by 360 days. These fees will be charged monthly.

CAPITAL PAYMENT TRANSACTIONS
Publication concerning
Foreign Exchange Transactions 2000/K.1.A.

Concerning: purchase and sale of foreign securities.

The Bank of the Netherlands Antilles,

considering

the provision in article 10, paragraph 1 of the Foreign Exchange Transactions Act (P.B. 1981, no. 67),

announces that

a general license has been granted to residents to buy, acquire in ownership, keep in custody and sell foreign securities. These securities have to be quoted at a recognized stock exchange as referred to in the Control on Corporations Quoted on the Stock Exchange Act *(Landsverordening Zeggenschap in ter Beurze genoteerde Vennootschappen)* (P.B. 1991, no. 5) with due observance of the following provisions:

a. the purchase and sale of foreign securities must take place through the intermediary of a foreign exchange bank in the Netherlands Antilles;

b. a resident is allowed to have the sales proceeds of foreign securities, and also of foreign stock-dividends and of receivables deposited on an E-account at a foreign exchange bank in the Netherlands Antilles;

c. a resident is allowed to buy foreign securities to the debit of an E-account in his name, insofar as the E-account does not show a debit balance;

d. except for the possibility sub c., a resident is allowed to buy securities as referred to in respectively Publication 2000/K.1.A and/or 2000/K.1.B without a special license per calendar year not exceeding the equivalent of an amount of at most NAf. 100,000.00 (insofar as this amount has not been acquired from domestic granting of credit).

This Publication concerning Foreign Exchange Transactions will take effect on July 1, 2000 and is, subject withdrawal, valid for an indefinite period of time.

Willemstad, July 1, 2000
THE BANK OF THE NETHERLANDS ANTILLES

Dr. E.D. Tromp
Governor

Publication concerning
Foreign Exchange Transactions 2000/K.1.B

The Bank of the Netherlands Antilles,

considering

the provision in articles 10, paragraph 1, and 15, paragraph 2 of the Foreign Exchange Transactions Act (P.B. 1981, no. 67),

announces that

1) a general license has been granted to residents to open and hold shareholders' accounts in the event of so-called open-end investment companies, whose stocks are quoted on a recognized stock exchange as referred to in the Control on Corporations Quoted on the Stock Exchange Act (P.B. 1991, no. 5), with due observance of the following provisions:

a. the purchase and sale of these stocks must take place through the mediation of a foreign exchange bank in the Netherlands Antilles;

b. a resident is allowed to have the dividends and/or the sales proceeds from stocks, and also the sales proceeds from stock dividends and/or receivables from those stocks reinvested in his name at another or the same open-end investment company, whose stocks are quoted on a recognized stock exchange;

c. except for the possibility sub b., a resident is allowed to buy securities as referred to in respectively Publication 2000/K.1.A and/or 2000/ K.1.B without a special license per calendar year up to the equivalent of an amount not exceeding NAf. 100,000.00 (insofar as this amount has not been acquired from domestic granting of credits).

2. that residents, for the stocks pertaining to them, of which they hold shareholders' accounts in their name as referred to sub 1 above, have been granted exemption from the obligation to give these stocks into open custody abroad to a non-resident for addition to a custody account in the name of the Bank or in the name of a foreign exchange bank.

This publication will take effect on July 1, 2000 and is, subject to withdrawal, valid for an indefinite period of time.
Willemstad, July 1, 2000
THE BANK OF THE DUTCH CARIBBEAN
Dr. E.D. Tromp
Governor

****

Publication concerning
Foreign Exchange Transactions 2000/K.2.

Concerning: exemption from the prohibition to import and export precious metals.

The Bank of the Netherlands Antilles,
considering
the provision in article 15 of the Foreign Exchange Transactions Act (P.B. 1981, no. 67),
announces that

all residents are granted a license to import or export precious metals, gold and precious stones. This publication concerning foreign exchange transactions will take effect on July 1, 2000 and is, subject to withdrawal, valid for an indefinite period of time.

Willemstad, July 1, 2000
THE BANK OF THE NETHERLANDS ANTILLES
Dr. E.D. Tromp
Governor

****

Publication concerning
Foreign Exchange Transactions 2000/K.3.

The Bank of the Netherlands Antilles,
considering
the provision in article 10 of the Foreign Exchange Transactions Act (P.B. 1981, no. 67),
announces that
that corporations established in the Netherlands Antilles, being trust companies, are allowed to transfer stocks in corporations that have been granted an exemption, as referred to in article 19 of the Foreign Exchange Transactions Act (P.B. 1981, no. 67), to non-residents.
This publication concerning foreign exchange transactions will take effect on July 1, 2000 and is, subject to withdrawal, valid for an indefinite period of time.

Willemstad, July 1, 2000
THE BANK OF THE NETHERLANDS ANTILLES
Dr. E.D. Tromp
Governor

****

Publication concerning
Foreign Exchange Transactions 2000/K.4.

The Bank of the Netherlands Antilles,
considering
the provision in article 10 of the Foreign Exchange Transactions Act (P.B. 1981, no. 67),
announces that
a general license has been granted to residents to alienate to non-residents immovable property situated in the Dutch Caribbeanor abroad or acquire such from non-residents, and to receive payments from, respectively make payments to, non-residents for alienating, respectively acquiring, immovable property situated in the Dutch Caribbeanor abroad.
This publication concerning foreign exchange transactions will take effect on July 1, 2000 and is, subject to withdrawal, valid for an indefinite period of time.

Willemstad, July 1, 2000
THE BANK OF THE NETHERLANDS ANTILLES
Dr. E.D. Tromp
Governor

Publication concerning
Foreign Exchange Transactions 2000/K.5.

The Bank of the Netherlands Antilles,
considering
the provision in article 12, paragraph 4 of the Foreign Exchange Transactions Act (P.B. 1981, no. 67),

announces that
residents are granted exemption from the obligation to collect and deposit as described in article 12, paragraphs 2 and 3 of the Foreign Exchange Transactions Act (P.B. 1981, no. 67). Insofar as it will be decided to collect the foreign monetary instruments or foreign receivables that have become payable, credit balances can be deposited on an account in their name with a non-resident bank or giro institution, provided the balances of, and the transactions on, the account as referred to above are reported upon request to the Bank per quarter.
This publication concerning foreign exchange transactions will take effect on July 1, 2000 and is, subject to withdrawal, valid for an indefinite period of time.

Willemstad, July 1, 2000
THE BANK OF THE NETHERLANDS ANTILLES
Dr. E.D. Tromp
Governor

****

Publication concerning
Foreign Exchange Transactions 2000/K.6.

The Bank of the Netherlands Antilles,
considering
the provisions in articles 10, 11 and 12 of the Foreign Exchange Transactions Act (P.B. 1981, no. 67),
announces that
resident natural persons are granted a license to open and hold an account in their name with a non-resident banking or giro institution, with due observance of the following conditions:

1. that the resident natural persons holding an account with a non-resident banking or giro institution may not deposit more than the equivalent of NAf. 50,000.00 per quarter, up to a maximum of the equivalent of NAf. 200,000.00 per year, per resident through the intermediary of a foreign exchange bank from the Dutch Caribbeanon this account;

2. that the account, as referred to above, must be reported to the Bank;

3. that the residents in question are obliged to report the balances of and the transactions on the account as referred to above to the Bank upon request.

This publication concerning foreign exchange transactions will take effect on July 1, 2000 and is, subject to withdrawal, valid for an indefinite period of time.

Willemstad, July 1, 2000
THE BANK OF THE NETHERLANDS ANTILLES
Dr. E.D. Tromp
Governor

****

Publication concerning
Foreign Exchange Transactions 2000/K.7

The Bank of the Netherlands Antilles,
considering
the provision in articles 10 of the Foreign Exchange Transactions Act (P.B. 1981/No. 67),

announces that
residents who conduct life operations or non-life operations and also residents acting as a company pension fund are granted a license to lend annually the capital to be invested by them with non-residents, provided the following investments with residents are minimally made:

- 40% of the sum of the first NAf. 10 million of the total reserves and debts;
- 50% of the sum of the following NAf. 10 million of the total reserves and debts; and
- 60% of the rest of the sum of the total reserves and debts.

This publication concerning foreign exchange transactions will take effect on July 1, 2000 and is, subject to withdrawal, valid for an indefinite period of time.

GENERAL ADMINISTRATIVE RULES
GAR 2000/1
PART 1

GENERAL ADMINISTRATIVE RULES FOR PROVIDING INFORMATION AND DATA TO THE BANK OF THE NETHERLANDS ANTILLES (GAR 2000/1)

For the execution of its tasks, the Bank of the Dutch Caribbean(hereafter to be called: the Bank), determines the following, pursuant to article 8 of the Foreign Exchange Transactions Act (P.B. 1981, no. 67):

A. Providing information to foreign exchange banks and other institutions authorized by the Bank of the Netherlands Antilles, among which the cash couriers for the settlement of international payment transactions.

1. Residents who make payments to or collect receipts from non-residents through the intermediary of foreign exchange banks are obliged, for statistical reasons, to supply the requested corresponding data. In the case of payments to and receipts from foreign countries, it will suffice in general to submit proofs and/or provide data to the mediating institution. Any possible required separate licenses granted to the resident for these transactions must also be submitted to the mediating institution. Also if foreign means of payment or customary monetary papers in tourist traffic are bought or sold by a resident at a foreign exchange bank, he is obliged to provide the foreign exchange bank in question with the data which are required by the Bank.
2. When receivables from and debts to non-residents are cleared, the resident in question, on paying his debt, has to provide the relevant information on the gross transactions to the Bank or to a foreign exchange bank (or other authorized financial institution) upon request and without delay.
3. If the foreign exchange bank to which the documents and other records are submitted establishes that the information and data supplied are incomplete, the resident is obliged upon request to provide further information and data timely

upon request, or take care of the completeness of the information as the case may be.

4. Those who object to providing certain data and information through the intermediary of foreign exchange banks, can provide the Bank directly with these data and information after submitting a written request to that effect.

B. Reporting (current) accounts with non-residents to the Bank

Residents are obliged to report to the Bank without delay:

1. opening and holding accounts in their own name in any currency with non-residents;
2. opening and holding current-accounts with non-residents (including non-banks) for the clearing of mutual receivables and debts, stating the nature of their business or the nature of the transactions that are paid, or cleared as the case may be. In doing so, the reporting guidelines of the Bank have to be observed.

C. Providing data concerning the settlement or execution of transactions with non-residents in a different manner than mentioned under A and B

Residents are obliged to report this different manner of settlement or execution directly and in writing to the Bank without delay, while stating all relevant data, and to observe the administrative rules given by the Bank. In doing so, the following should be considered:

1. Equity participations (direct investments)

   Pursuant to the Foreign Exchange Transactions Act, residents are obliged to report changes in equity participations abroad or in the Dutch Caribbeanto the Bank without delay, if these transactions result from dealings of or with non-residents.

   Such changes can result from (co)-founding, acquiring, extending or (co)-participating in enterprises and branches, and also decreasing or alienating the interests acquired earlier.

   Insofar as participations are effected in different manners than by payment via a foreign exchange bank or another authorized financial institution, or by payment or clearing via a (current)-account held abroad, residents have to report this per case directly and in writing to the Bank. In doing so, the following can be considered:

- contribution of corporeal matters (for example, goods or industrial buildings), incorporeal matters (for example, licenses, know-how) and services;
- converting foreign (commercial) receivables, debts and profits, dividends, loans, credits, current-account receivables and debts;
- exchanging stocks or other securities;
- reinvestment of funds becoming available elsewhere on account of disinvestment;
- retention of profit and writing off losses.

Whatever the manner in which these transactions are effected, residents have to observe the reporting guidelines of the Bank.

2. Loans

a. contracting loans abroad and relending the funds loaned to third parties abroad;
b. contracting loans abroad for the payment of debts abroad;
c. the contracting of loans in the Dutch Caribbeanby non-residents at non-banks for the payment of their debts to residents in the Netherlands Antilles.

3. Other manners of settlement

a. settlement, resulting from novation agreements, for example by converting short-term loans into long-term loans, or by debtor or creditor substitution;
b. compensation and settlement of outstanding receivables against debts;
c. non-monetary payment.

If for the transactions and settlements mentioned under 1, 2 and 3 a license must have been granted, the reporting has to take place as soon as possible after effectuation.

D. Supplier and buyer credit

Residents are obliged to report without delay and in writing to the Bank: contracting an agreement for the purchase and sale of goods from, respectively to, non-residents, if in doing so a supplier or buyer credit has been stipulated. In that case, the following data must be provided:

a. name and address of the non-resident with whom the agreement has been concluded;
b. nature, quantity and value (price) of the goods;
c. the terms of payment agreed on (including the currency in which the payment will be made);
d. the presumable month(s) of import, respectively export, of the goods.
e. Country of origin of the goods.

This reporting does not release residents from the possible obligation to request an exchange permit.

E. Data on the financial relation with non-residents

Upon request, residents are obliged to report to the Bank the balances of and changes in:

a. their participations in the capital of enterprises abroad;
b. the participations by non-residents in the capital of enterprises established in the Netherlands Antilles;
c. their loans/credits extended, within an intra-group, to foreign countries;
d. loans/credits raised by them abroad within an intra-group;
e. other international credit and debit equity ratios.

F. Registration of residents who effect certain foreign exchange transactions

Unless already registered at or designated by the Bank, the following residents/ enterprises/ institutions will have to report to the Bank for registration:

1. residents who are going to participate in transit and tripartite trade (among others, Free Zone companies);
2. residents who, in conducting their business, intend to trade goods with residents and non-residents, in which case the goods are not in free trade, nor will be taken out of bond (among others, ship-chandlers);
3. enterprises and institutions, irrespective of the legal form, that are residents and in which non-residents participate directly or indirectly via capital stock or otherwise and whose objective is to be occupied to a considerable extent with receiving means from non-residents and paying them on to non-residents;
4. other residents to be designated by the Bank.

The residents mentioned under 1 through 4 are obliged to observe the reporting guidelines of the Bank.
These instructions will become effective on July 1, 2000.

PART 2

GENERAL ADMINISTRATIVE INSTRUCTIONS FOR REPORTING

For the execution of its tasks, the following is stipulated by the Bank of the Dutch Caribbean(hereafter to be called: the Bank) for reporting, pursuant to article 8 of the Foreign Exchange Transactions Act (P.B. 1981, no. 67):

A. MANNER OF REPORTING

For the layout of the balance of payments and obtaining insight into the nature of the payment transactions between residents and non-residents, a reporting system has been developed, in which residents, pursuant to article 8 of the 1981 Foreign Exchange Transactions Act are obliged to supply the Bank with data on these transactions (Current transactions and Capital transactions). The data to be reported must be submitted by the foreign exchange banks and other institutions authorized by the Bank for the settlement of international payment transactions to the Bank on diskette or via another medium to be designated by the Bank.

All diskettes must be accompanied by:

a. an accompanying letter on official letter paper of the foreign exchange bank and signed by an authorized employee, or
b. an accompanying letter which is provided with the official identification stamp of the foreign exchange bank and signed by an authorized employee. The foreign exchange bank has to supply the Bank with proofs that the employee who signs the accompanying letter is authorized to do so.
c. A certified print-out of the processed data.

The data must be reported accurately, completely and truthfully. On account of this, it will be possible for the Bank to group the components of the balance of payments and verify the report. It is also of the utmost importance that the report is submitted on time. Point of departure when reporting is that all payments between residents and non-residents are reported to the Bank by the foreign exchange bank performing the international payment transactions (and consequently sees its foreign position change). The payments can take place in foreign currency as well as Antillean currency. The Bank decides whether the payments may be reported in an authorized form or not. In principle, payments between residents mutually, even though they take place in a foreign currency, and also the payments between non-residents, remain out of consideration. **For administrative reasons, an exception has been made for cash transactions in foreign currency, that is to say, cash transactions in foreign bank notes and coins.**

1. On behalf of residents, the following transactions and statements are reported by the foreign exchange banks to the Bank of the Netherlands Antilles:

a. A-transaction: making payments, both cash (AC-transactions) and cashless (AG-transactions), to non-residents.
b. B-transaction: receiving payments, both cash (BC-transactions) and cashless (BG-transactions) from non-residents.
c. Negative A and B-transactions: executing corrections of A- and B-transactions reported earlier and the cash transactions of non-residents.
d. C-statement: a statement of the negotiated foreign bank notes and coins and the total amounts of cash transactions in the various currencies. That is to say: cash transactions in foreign bank notes and coins without making a distinction between currency amounts that are related to residents or non-residents.
e. D-statement: the verification of all transactions performed in the month in question. Here, the receipts and expenses mentioned under a. through d. and the amounts of the foreign exchange transactions between the foreign exchange banks mutually and between the Bank and the foreign exchange banks are mentioned.
f. G-statement: the summary of all foreign exchange cash transactions in foreign bank notes and coins.

It is expressly brought to your attention that making a correct distinction between residents and non-residents is of the utmost importance for correct reporting. You will find a definition in article 1, sub 1, a. through e. of the Foreign Exchange Transactions Act, P.B. 1981, no. 67. In short, a resident is a natural person who has lived for more than a year in the Dutch Caribbeanor a legal entity established in the Dutch Caribbeanand also conducting its principal activities within this territory. Thus, for example, investment and financial companies that have only their seat in the Netherlands Antilles, but conduct their activities mainly elsewhere (the offshore companies) can be considered non-residents of the Dutch Caribbeanfor the balance of payments registration.

Reporting can be rendered more difficult if an international payment transaction is performed by order of a resident who is a client at another local bank than the one via which the settlement with the foreign country takes place. Two possibilities can be distinguished here:

1. Payment to foreign countries by debiting a nostro-account or

crediting a loro-account. This possibility will occur, among other things, if a collection from abroad has been received on a resident who has an account as another local bank and makes the collection payable there.

2. Payment from abroad by crediting a nostro-account or debiting a loro-account. This latter account will mostly be in Antillean curency.
In both cases, the bank at which the change in the foreign position occurs, in this case the nostro or loro-account, will have to report this payment as an A-, respectively B-transaction. It is, therefore, not permitted for this bank to process only the payment in the D-statement ("Foreign exchange banks" entry) and assume that the bank, with which the payment is settled, will report the required A- or B-transaction.
In the first case, no difficulty will occur, according to us, when determining the nature of the payment, because it will become sufficiently clear from the description on the collection or the attached documents.

In the second case, it will not always be possible to determine the nature of the transaction. The bank has to see to it, however, that the reported description is carefully chosen. If the nature of the transaction is not known at the reporting bank, it must request the bank relation of the beneficiary/resident to make this known to it.

EXPLANATION OF THE INFORMATION TO BE SUBMITTED
A-transaction:
An A-transaction is the registration of each separate cashless (money orders, banker's checks, traveler's checks, etc.) and cash payments of residents to non-residents. The transfer to a resident who is temporarily abroad is also an A-transaction, because it may be assumed that he will use the amount for payments abroad.

In other words: no reporting is necessary of payments of residents to residents and payments of non-residents (whether or not residing temporarily in the Netherlands Antilles) to non-residents, no matter whether these payments are in foreign currencies or in Antillean guilders (see also the explanation of the D-statement under Foreign Exchange Banks);

Reporting the A-transaction takes place as follows:
Bank
The name of the reporting foreign exchange bank. If a branch office reports, the name of this office must be mentioned.

Name and address ordering client (resident) Both the name and the complete address of the client must be mentioned.

Name and address creditor (non-resident)
Both the name and the complete address (particularly the country) of the beneficiary must be mentioned.

Currency and amount
If the client wishes to transfer foreign currency, it must be mentioned here.

Equivalent in NAf.

The equivalent in Antillean guilders is obtained from the conversion against the exchange rate on the day of transfer. This rate has to correspond with the official quotation of the Bank, excluding the increment for license fees.

The A-transaction is also dated on this day.
Amount license fees
The license fees to be paid by the foreign exchange banks is 1 percent of the amount filled in at "equivalent in NAf.". If no license fees are due, "free of charge" must be mentioned. In that case, there must be an explanation under "explanation" why the payment must be considered free of charge.

Nature of payment
For the correct classification of the various entries of the balance of payments, the foreign exchange bank has to mention the code number of the transaction. For an extensive description of the entries, you are referred to the code list attached. In dubious cases, the code number that comes closest to the nature of the transaction has to be marked.

Although the international current payment transactions are free in principle, residents are obliged to report their payments to and receipts from non-residents (Current and Capital payment transactions) via the system established by the Bank and provide relevant data with respect to such. This has to take place by means of submission of documents by the client. If a resident client pays a sum of money to or receives a sum of money from a non-resident, the personnel of the foreign exchange bank has to see to it that the client submits the relevant data in order to be able to report the nature of the transaction correctly, regardless of it being a transaction subject to compulsory licensing. The foreign exchange bank has to take measures to prevent multiple use of the same documents.

IMPORTANT LAWS AND REGULATIONS

ON-LINE GAMING UNDER THE LAWS OF THE NETHERLANDS ANTILLES

On-line gaming is a legitimate business activity in the Netherlands Antilles, especially Curasao, provided the e-gaming company has obtained the proper license. The Dutch Caribbean(master) gaming licenses are based on the National Ordinance on Offshore Hazard Games.

There are two formats to be licensed:
a) having a master license or
b) having a sub-license.

A master license licenses the (e-)gaming company itself, and in addition opens the possibility to sub-license third parties subject to the responsibility and covenants under the master license. A sub-license – under a master license – offers equal possibilities to performing e-gaming business legitimately, however without the possibility to further sub-license.

Basic requirements for applying for a (sub-)license are compliance with due diligence and KYC policies, full identification of Ultimate Beneficial Owners (UBOs), satisfactory reference on UBOs as well as detailed and transparent description of the games to be offered. In the case of a master license application the decision is taken at the sole discretion of the Minister of Justice, based on the documentation submitted by the Dutch Caribbeancounsel.

The Dutch Caribbean(NA) combines a group of five islands (Curaçao, Bonaire, St. Eustatius, St. Maarten and Saba) in the Caribbean Sea. This former Dutch colony now forms part of the Kingdom of the Netherlands, a federation which also comprises the Netherlands and Aruba. The NA has an autonomous government, though responsibility for defence and external affairs is entrusted to the Dutch government. The NA is not a full member of the European Union. However, it has the status of an associate membership providing it with the following benefits: (i) duty-free imports of their products into the European Union and; and (ii) the grant of financial and technical aid by the European Union to promote the economic development of the NA.

It must be taken in account that the NA is going to be disbanded on October 2010. Curaçao and St.-Maarten are to become two separate and independent entities within the Kingdom of the Netherlands, with a status similar to that currently enjoyed by Aruba. Bonaire, Saba and St. Eustatius will become part of the Netherlands as special municipalities.

The NA has two important gaming sectors; terrestrial casinos and online gambling. There are approximately 24 land based casinos in NA, most of them located in the islands of Saint Maarten and Curacao. This industry benefits from the popularity of these islands as a holiday destination for US residents, Europeans and Latin Americans.

The NA was one of the first jurisdictions to regulate online gambling. While initially it was a very popular jurisdiction for online operators, the closure of the US market and its failure to obtain a "white list" status in the UK has seen the NA's popularity wane.

THE GAMING MARKET TODAY

In the NA gambling issues are regulated independently by each of the islands and there is no common policy approach.

NA's most important gambling sectors are land-based casinos and online gambling.

Land-based casinos were introduced to attract more tourists into the islands. Currently, NA has three islands that allow casino gaming, St. Maarten, Curacao and Bonaire. The requirements for obtaining a casino license vary on each island.

According to the Casino City's Gaming Business Directory there are 24 casinos in NA, most of them located in St. Maarten. Most of these casinos form part of hotel resorts and are predominately marketed to foreign clients, even though locals are allowed to gamble in them.

NA was one of the first jurisdictions to regulate online gambling, as it implemented specific legislation in the middle of the 1990s. Curacao was the island that most benefited from the dawn of the online gambling era, as hundreds of new operators applied for an online license looking to benefit from Curacao's competitive tax regime.

However, the closure of the US market, the prosecution of many NA operators and finally the non inclusion of NA in the UK's white list has made many gambling companies migrated to other jurisdictions. Currently, while there are still a number of companies licensed in the island, prominent operators have moved out to other online jurisdictions such as Malta or the Isle of Man.

ONLINE GAMBLING

STATISTICS

Internet gambling has become a central industry for the NA, especially for Curacao that now controls this activity in this jurisdiction. The introduction of the National Ordinance Offshore Games of Hazard in 1993 opened the door to the industry. In 1996 the first master license was granted to Cyberluck, which continues to provide e-gaming licensing and co-hosting services in Curacao.

For many years, Curacao was a prominent online hub, favored over other jurisdictions for its competitive tax regime and its proximity to the US.

However, in the late 1990s the US started indicting many operators of offshore online gambling sites licensed in Curacao for violations of US Wire Wagering Act. Some of the most prominent cases involving Curacao licensed sites were the following:

In 1999 Allen Ross was convicted for operating a sport book business (Island Casino) and accepting wagers from a site licensed in Curacao.
In January 2000, federal prosecutors in St. Louis, Missouri charged Marc Meghrouni and Scott Shaver, owners of Paradise Casino who operated an offshore sports book in Curacao, with violating the Wire Wagering Act, as well as tax fraud. Additionally, Paradise Casino was charged with money laundering relating to the spending of betting funds in the US. Meghrouni, Shaver and Paradise Casino pleaded guilty to all of the charges and agreed to forfeit a one million dollar condominium, and a 1995 Lamborghini.
In 2001 Duane Pede and Jeff D'Ambrosia pleaded guilty to gambling and tax charges in United States District Court in Madison. According to the prosecution, Pede and D'Ambrosia were engaged in the business of wagering and sports betting through an entity called Gold Medal Sports Book, located in Curacao, with US residents. Gold Medal Sports also entered a guilty plea to racketeering and a criminal forfeiture count. Gold Medal Sports agreed to forfeit more than US$ 3.3m in criminal earnings, and Pede and D'Ambrosia paid over US$ 1.4m in back taxes.
In 2006 Gerald Uvari and David Appelbaum pleaded guilty of operating an illegal gambling business in the United District Court for the Southern District of New York. Both acted as representatives of the Uvari Group, an intermediary between bettors and various offshore internet gambling sites, including sport books located in Curacao.

These cases affected the jurisdiction's reputation and many prominent operators decided to leave the island. Further damage was generated by the passing of the Unlawful Internet Gaming Enforcement Act in 2006 in the US effectively closing one of the most important target markets for operators located in NA.

Another issue that diminished NA's attractiveness was the jurisdiction's failure to obtain "white list" status in the UK. The NA was amongst the first to apply to become a member of the UK's white list. The UK's Department for Culture Music and Sport (DCMS) excluded NA for what they said to be an insufficient scale of regulatory presence regarding their gambling industry. In response, NA drafted legislation that was intended to resolve this issue, stating that they were "confident it will be rapidly and rightfully placed on UK white list." In spite of this confidence, NA has never been placed on the white list and its applications have been repeatedly denied.

Any aspirations the NA may have held of becoming a member of the white list in the near future have been dashed by the DCMS announcing in April 2009 that it would be putting a freeze on the number of white listed countries until the end of the year. Furthermore the DCMS in conjunction with the UK gambling commission has undertaken a review of the whole of the UK's gambling regulatory current system which includes the white listing process. It is likely that they would advise robust changes to the system which locally based operators feel places them at a considerable disadvantage. These changes may include capping the number of countries on the white list of the present number.

While major operators have left Curacao, there are still some companies licensed in the island. These companies offer mainly to Latin America and in some cases the US. Germany's Gaming VC has an online license in NA. After acquiring Betboo in July 2009, Betboo's operations have been moved into Curacao. Betboo provides bingo, sports-book, casino and poker to over 3,000 monthly customers located mainly in Brazil.

Other sites licensed in Curacao are Pinnaclesports and Microgaming's Progressive Jackpot Network.

The Cake Poker Network is also based in Curacao and hosted by Cyberluck. Some of the partners of this network are Sportbook.com, BetUS, Pokerworld and Doyles Room.

LEGISLATIVE FRAMEWORK

The primary legislation for internet gaming is the National Ordinance Offshore Games of Hazard enacted in 1993.

LICENSING

To operate online gaming activities in Curaçao at present, the government of the NA requires an operator to have either:

1. A license for offshore hazard games also known as a 'Master License', or
2. A sublicense under a master gaming license.

In the case of a master license application the decision is taken at the sole discretion of the Minister of Justice, based on the documentation submitted by the Dutch Caribbeancounsel, including full disclosure and representation of the UBO's ('Ultimate Beneficial Owners') and a detailed description of the games.

In order to receive a license from the Department of Justice a written application must be addressed to the Governor of NA and submitted to the Department of Justice stating the island territories from which the applicant wishes to operate.

The application must be accompanied by a certificate of registration with the Chamber of Commerce as a locally formed legal entity as well as all relevant details required for the screening of all the parties involved. This shall include shareholders, the managing directors, the executives, and all advisors, financiers or any person who can influence the operation of the legal entity. The application must also include a business plan and a financial feasibility study for the first three years.

In addition two legal opinions, one from an NA qualified lawyer and one from a US-qualified lawyer, stating respectively that the proposed activities do not contravene the National Ordinance Penalizing Money-laundering (O.G. 1993, no. 52) or the federal laws of the US concerning gambling must be attached.

Within five days from an application having been received, the Department of Justice will check whether the accompanying documents are complete. From the moment the application is complete, the department will take six weeks to conduct an investigation. If at the end of the six weeks the investigation has been completed and has yielded no objections, the applicant shall be granted a five-year license. A number of conditions shall attach to this license, among others a 60,000 ANG guarantee deposit (approx. US$ 33,333).

The license shall be limited to the island territory (territories) designated in the application. Consequently, in order to be allowed to offer games of hazard from another island territory, the license must be adapted.

Any foreign entrepreneur who is seeking to establish perform online gaming activities from the NA shall require a temporary residence permit with permission to work. Details relating to such an application can be found on CIGA's website.

The holder of a license pursuant to the National Ordinance Offshore Games of Hazard should also apply for an establishment permit and a related management permit, to be granted by the executive council of the island territory where he is established. Once again, further details relating to such an application can be found on CIGA's website.

Regarding the sub-licenses being granted by holders of a master license there is no uniform process. In case of a sub-license the decision will be taken at the discretion of the master licensor (such as Cyberluck), who will be responsible towards the Dutch Caribbeanauthorities for any performance of the sub-licensee. In both situations emphasis will be on the standing of the UBOs. The cost of a sub-license ranges from US$2,000 to US$4,000

A gaming license can only be issued to companies established in the Netherlands Antilles. Dutch Caribbeanlaw requires that the company is registered in the Dutch Caribbeanwith a local managing director. However, it is possible to hire a management services company as the managing director.

CASINO

STATISTICS

There are three islands that allow casino gaming, St. Maarten, Curacao and Bonaire. According to Casino's City Gaming Business Directory 2009 there are 24 casinos in the NA. The island with the highest number of casinos in the NA is St. Maarten with 13 casinos.

With 33,000 casino square footage, 26 poker tables and 400 slot machines, the Sonesta Maho Beach Resort and Casino Royal, (located in St. Maarten) is the biggest casino in NA. Other important casinos are the Princess Port de Plaisance Hotel and Casino, (with 600 slot machines and 15 table games), the Holiday Beach Hotel & Casino Royale (with 365 machines and 14 gaming tables) and the Atlantis Casino (400 slot machines and 30 gaming tables) all in St. Maarten.

The NA land-based casino market is dominated by domestic groups and small foreign investors. Atlantis World Group controls three casinos in NA, Atlantis World Casino, Paradise Plaza Casino, and the Beach Plaza casino, all in St. Maarten. They are also developing a new casino in St. Maarten (Dunes Casino) that will have 285 slot machines. The group also has casino operations in the Dominican Republic and Panama. Atlantis World Group is also present in the gaming industry in Italy thanks to a non-exclusive concession from the Italian Government that has enabled the company to network and monitor over 73,000 gaming machines and collect related gaming taxes on behalf of the Italian Government.

Another important group operating in the NA is Maho Group, a company based in the NA that was founded by the controversial Rosario "Saro" Spadaro. The company controls five casinos (i) Sonesta Maho Beach Resort & Casino, (ii) Sonesta Great Bay Beach Beach Resort & Casino, (iii) Casino Royale, (iv) Golden Casino and (v) Diamond Casino.

The NA casino industry has not lacked controversy over the years. In 2005, Rosario "Saro" Spadaro, the owner of the Maho Group was arrested in Italy on charges of money laundering and being part of a criminal organization. A 12 year investigation that led to the arrest of 16 people in Italy concluded that Spadaro, (who is from Messina) was the Caribbean partner in a ring to illicitly finance real-estate speculations with "Cosa Nostra" Mafia money, reinvesting the profits abroad to buy casinos and finance other criminal transactions in casinos.

LICENSING

Each island regulates casino gambling in an independent way. In the case of St. Maarten, casino licenses are given away by the Island Council and casino activities are controlled by the Department of Control, Inspection & Security. In Bonaire, casino licenses are granted by the Executive Council. In the case of Curacao, casino licenses are granted by the Curacao Gaming Board.

Requirements vary in every island. However, in most the cases companies that want to operate a casino in any of the island will need to obtain a (i) business license to operate in the island, (ii) a director's license for a non Antillean director (if its applicable) and (iii) a work and residence permit for the managing director. Also, the company must be registered in the Chamber of Commerce of the specific island.

The island of St. Maarten has established clear licensing requirements for casinos. St Maarten regulation differentiates between "stand alone" casinos from "full fledged" casinos. "Stand alone" casinos only operate a single game, for example slot machines. A "full fledged" casino operates more games.

St. Maarten has established a 10 "stand alone" casino limit that has already been reached. Therefore, no more "stand alone" licenses are granted."Full fledged" casinos can only be installed in hotels with at least 200 rooms.

Casinos cannot be located within a radius of 50 meters of churches and schools.

In order to give away a license, authorities will run a criminal and financial background check for directors and shareholders and also will investigate the sources of the initial investment capital.

An investor or directive can only be involved in a maximum of two casino projects.

In the case of St. Maarten, the island charges an upfront fee of 10,000 ANG (approx. US$ 5,830) for a stand alone casino license and 120,000 ANG (approx. US$ 69,000) for full casino license. Also, every year they will need to pay a 120,000 ANG annual license fee for a stand alone casino and a 600,000 ANG (approx. US$ 350,856) annual fee for a full casino.

NEW REGULATION IN CURACAO

In October 2009 Curacao regulators tried to introduce a 10 ANG guilder entrance fee applicable only to locals. This measure looked to collect an additional 20m ANG to straight up the government finances.

Tourists will be requested to show a pre-impressed valid ID-receipt provided by their hotel. The hotel guests should be clearly informed of the prevailing procedures upon entering the casino. The hotels will hand out the ID-receipts in compliance with the regulations provided by the Gaming Casino Board. The casinos will be given a detailed explanation with regard to the ordering, paying and issuance of casino entrance receipts.

Casinos have previously been exempt from the 5 percent sales tax for practical reasons. This entrance fee, which is also imposed on the consumer, is now being implemented in order to somewhat adjust aforementioned exemption.

However, at the end of October, the government announced that the application of the entrance fee will be postponed until November 2009.

TAX

TAXATION REGIME APPLICABLE TO ONLINE GAMING

Online gaming operations can establish themselves in denominated "e-zones". These special zones are regulated by the 2001 Economic Zone Ordinance. The Ordinance defines an e-zone as "a site or sites designated as such, where goods can be stored, processed, worked up, assembled, packed, displayed and cleared from bond, or can undergo other treatments, and where or from where services may be provided".

The Ordinance includes services offered internationally by means of electronic communication amongst those services that can be provided within an e-zone. As a result of this disposition e-gambling activities can be provided from the e-zone and benefit from its tax regime.

There are ten e-zones within the NA of which eight are designated for services. Only a legal entity with its capital divided into shares may perform activities within an e-zone. The activities of these companies must be focused principally in providing services outside the NA and have to contribute to the economic growth of the islands by generating either foreign currency or employment. These companies may conduct some business with companies located within the NA if they obtain the approval from the Department of Economic Affairs. The turnover generated through local business must not exceed 25 percent of the total turnover and this profit will be taxed under the regular income tax.

Online gaming operations performed in an e-zone will be subject to the following tax regime:

a) Profit tax

Profits derived from online gaming activities are subject to a reduced profit tax at a rate of 2 percent (including the island surcharge). This reduced profit tax rate is guaranteed until 2026.

b) Import duties and turnover tax

No import duties will be applicable to goods entering the e-zone. This means that online gambling companies may import all the necessary equipment to start operations inside the e-zone without any import duty cost.

On the other hand, services performed in an e-zone or received by a company located in an e-zone are not subject to the turnover tax.

c) Dividend tax

Even when the NA fiscal framework includes a dividends tax clause, this has not been brought into effect. As a result of this, there is no income tax relating to dividend payments.

d) Employees tax

Employees who have lived in excess of five years outside the NA before starting to work in an e-zone can qualify for expatriate status, which grants them access to certain tax-free benefits providing that certain conditions are met. An e-zone company can calculate the wage tax of an expatriate on the net salary of the employee without being required to 'gross up' the salary.

e) License payments

License holders will have to pay 10,000 ANG per month in license fees during the first two years. A new license fee can be determined after the first two years.

TAXATION REGIME APPLICABLE TO LAND-BASED CASINOS

a. Income Tax

The income tax rate for corporations is 30 percent, excluding the island surcharge. Corporations are additionally subject to the island surcharge, which is levied at the rate of 15 percent of the tax payable in all the islands. Therefore, the effective overall tax rate is 34.5 percent.

b) Turnover tax

The turnover tax is levied on the provision of services and deliveries by entrepreneurs and companies. A limited number of services and deliveries are exempted. The tax rate in Curacao and Bonaire amounts to 5 percent and the taxable base is equivalent to the revenue generated by the operation without considering the turnover tax.

c) Real property tax

Land-based casinos may be affected by the real property tax. This tax levies real property situated in the NA on the basis of its value. Valuation of property subject to the tax is carried out every 5 years. The tax is levied at a 0.3 percent flat rate. The local authority of the island where the property is located may add an island surcharge (15 percent) to the amount of the tax payable.

d) Casino tax

Land-based casinos are subject to gambling tax that is charged by the local governments of the islands that integrate the NA. The tax is calculated at a flat fee and in some islands as a percentage of the gaming turnover.

e) Tax incentives

Land-based casinos may benefit from a series of tax incentives if they operate in a hotel. These benefits are regulated by the Business and Hotel Promotion Ordinance (BHP Ordinance of 1953). This Ordinance provides tax benefits to the following companies:

• Companies engaged in the exploitation of hotels, villas, provision of tourist amenities and tourism promotion.

• Companies that renovate, extend or improve hotels and other facilities already in existence under the Hotel Renovation Ordinance.

To qualify, a company must, in addition to being engaged in the hotel and tourism sector, demonstrate that its investment can be expected to broaden the economic base of the Netherlands Antilles. The investment in hotels, like accommodation or tourist amenities, must be of at least approximately US$568,000 in Curaçao and St. Maarten and approximately US$284,000 in the other islands.Qualifying enterprises may obtain the following benefits:

• Exemption from import duties on materials and goods to be used in constructing or furnishing a business property;

• Exemption from real property tax (land tax) and usage tax on business property;

• Reduced profit taxation under the Profit Tax Ordinance at a minimum rate of 2 percent (inclusive of island surcharges);

• Exemption from income tax on profit distributions.

The exemptions may be granted for a maximum period of 11 years.

MONEY LAUNDERING

The National Ordinance Penalization of Money Laundering 1993 (Landsverordening strafbaarstelling witwassen van gelden) criminalizes money laundering. Master licenses will only be granted if the applicant submits, amongst other things, an opinion from a Dutch Caribbeanbased attorney. The opinion should include a declaration stating the following:

"We are of the opinion that the operations of the applicant, so far as they are known to us, do not appear to be specifically designed or appropriate for money laundering activities. They are not in violation of any Dutch Caribbeancode, regulation or law concerning on-line gaming and/or gambling and are not illegal from the point of view of the Penalization of Money Laundering Act 1993."

The opinion is rendered based on the applicant's description of his future activities, an example of which must always form part of the legal opinion.

Opening a customer account and making deposits thereon:

- Bets and wagers, whether for the online lottery and/or casino and/or online sportsbook or otherwise, can only be made by a customer from his customer account.
- A customer account will not be opened unless the customer gives his full name, address and phone number.
- Identification documents must be verified.
- Deposits on a customer account can only be made by the customer himself using one of the following methods of payment: credit card, bank wire, Western Union money transfer, or bank check issued by a bank located in Europe.
- Deposits are only permitted if the balance in the customer account is below US$40,000, in which case deposits are allowed up to the difference between the balance and US$ 40,000, and only deposits not in excess of US$ 1,000 at a time are permitted:
- Once a customer has used a certain method of payment or credit card (number), as the case may be, to make deposits, no other method of payment or credit card (number) can be used until the balance in the customer account (if any) has been refunded to the customer in full, using the same method of payment or credit card (number).
- Credit card transactions will be subject to on-line verification.

Bets, wagers and (re)payments:

- Bets and wagers, which can only be made by a customer from his customer account, can be made from a minimum of US$5.00 up to a maximum of US$50.00.
- All gains and profits made by a customer will be credited to his customer account.
- The applicant will not make repayments in excess of US$1,000 at a time.
- Any repayments to a customer will be made from the customer account in the same manner as the customer made his deposit(s), i.e. all information related to the addressee account must match with the information relating to the account from which the deposit(s) originated before such payment will be made.
- Repayments with bank checks will be cleared through banks located in Europe or any correspondent bank which is subject to supervision by the Central Bank in its jurisdiction.

Records:

- All transactions to which the applicant is a party, including without limitation payments made to and from a customer account, must have an electronic trail.
- The applicant keeps and maintains records of all its customer accounts and the transactions related thereto.
- Each and every action of the applicant and each and every bet or wager by a customer is recorded by computers, records of which must be kept and maintained for a period of five years.

REGULATING THE ONLINE CASINOS

Fraught with inconsistent regulatory laws from country to country, online gambling still has a long way to go in becoming internationally regulated, so to speak. Some jurisdictions fully license and regulate, like those of Gibraltar and the UK, while other jurisdictions, like Costa Rica, only provide offshore licenses and do not regulate at all.

Nonetheless, online gambling is a multi-billion dollar global industry that is effectively regulated in several jurisdictions, including premiere land-based gambling jurisdictions such as the UK. Whether or not online gambling is regulated in your specific country, the privelage of placing wagers at fully regulated offshore online gambling destinations is available to players from around the world. It is up to each individual online gambling operator whether or not bets from players in specific countries may or may not be permitted. And, it is up to your location whether or not online gambling is permitted in your jurisdiction of residence.

That said, if you are seriously considering placing real money wagers at an online casino, please take the time to first ensure the casino operator is being bound by online gambling regulations imposed by a reputable gaming jurisdiction. The following list of jurisdictions represent the online gambling industry's leading regulators of offshore online casinos accepting bets from players around the globe.

United Kingdom - Under the 2005 UK Gambling Act, Great Britain's Gambling Commission now regulates over 100 online gambling sites, in addition to over 150 land-based casinos. The top three concerns of the commission are to keep crime out of gambling, ensuring fair and open gambling operations, and prevent underage and problem gambling. New license conditions and codes of practice were published in October, 2008.

Gibraltar - Under the 2005 Gambling Act, the Gibraltar Regulatory Authority regulates 20 internet gaming operators as of February, 2009. Imposing practically identical regulations as that of the UK, Gibraltar is considered one of the premier online gambling regulatory jurisdictions today. Some of the top names in gaming are regulated here, including top UK online casino, 32 Red.

Malta - The Lotteries and Gaming Authority of Malta is one of the busiest online gambling regulatory jurisdictions today, licensing more online betting operations than any other jurisdiction. In fact, Malta was the first EU member State to regulate online gambling (under the Public Lotto Ordinace in 2000). Under Malta's Remote Gaming Regulations published in 2004, there are four licenses (Class 1 though 4) by which operators can offer remote gaming services. Inspired by the lead of the UK Gambling Commission, the Malta Remote Gaming Council was launched in 2005, helping to foster the closest thing to an international standard of online gambling currently available.

Dutch Caribbean(Curacao; CIGA**)** - The Curacao Gaming Control Board regulates over 250 online betting operations, many of which offer services to U.S. players, under the jurisdictional domain of The Netherlands Antilles. The Curacao Internet Gaming Association (CIGA) is a trade body of Curacao licensed operators focused on upholding responsible gaming standards and regulatory compliance as dictated by the 2002 National Ordinance Offshore Games of Hazard.

Alderney -Established in May of 2000, the Alderney Gambling Control Commission is an independent, non-political regulatory body operating on behalf of the States of Alderney. Part of the British Channel islands, (60 miles from mainland Britain), Alderney is a self-governing dependency of the British Crown, but is not a part of the UK or European Union. Under the eGambling Ordinance of 2006, the Alderney Gambling Control Commission upholds the highest international gaming standards as those fostered in the UK.

Isle of Man - Under the Online Gambling Regulation Act of 2001 and Gambling Amendment Act of 2006, the Gambling Supervision Commission of the Isel of Man regulates nearly twenty online betting operators as of July, 2009. Several Regulation Ordinances from 2007 have been published to keep legislation timely.

Kahnawake - One of the first independent online gambling regulatory bodies, the Kahnawake Gaming Commission was formed in 1996 at the dawn of the internet betting industry. Under the provisions of the Kahnawake Gaming Law (updated 1999), some 270+ online betting sites are regulated here. The Kahnawake Gaming Commission is empowered to regulate within the Mohawk Indian territory of Kahnawake (outside of Montreal, Canada). While scandal has surfaced at two online poker sites (Absolute Poker and Ultimate Bet) regulated in Kahnawake, the commission has taken steps to improve regulatory procedures closely aligned with international standards. Renowned testing facility, Gaming Associates, provides software risk analysis, and former New Jersey Division of Gaming Enforcement Director, Frank Catania, was instrumental in helping draft regulations.

Saskatchewan - The Saskatchewan Liquor and Gaming Authority (SLGA) i oversees the distribution, control and regulation of alcoholic beverages and most gambling in the

Saskatchewan province of Canada. It owns and manages every video lottery terminal (VLT), slot machine and five casinos operated by the Saskatchewan Indian Gaming Authority (SIGA). The SLGA also licenses and regulates other forms of gambling such as bingo, raffles, lotto tickets and horse racing. Gambling remains a big contributor to the Saskatchewan economy, accounting for more than $500 million in revenue every year.

Antigua & Barbuda (West Indies) - A longtime online gambling regulatory jurisdiction, the Directorate of Offshore Gaming, under the domain of the Financaial Services Regulatory Commission of Antigua, is charged with licensing and regulating online gambling operations. Over 100 operators are currently regulated under the Interactive Gaming and Wagering Regulations last amended in 2007. Following a banking scandal that involved the Director of Antigua's Financial Services Regulatory Division (non-gaming related) in early 2009, Antigua has improved its checks and balances and has managed to stay up to par with the strict regulatory standards imposed in the UK.

THE CONDITION OF OFFSHORE GAMING IN THE NETHERLANDS ANTILLES

By going offshore, the gaming industry has been able to surpass some of the greatest impediments in its road to success. In recent years, it has been battling with increasing costs as well as complications with the law particularly in its major hub in the U.S. With the help ofoffshore gaming, online gaming companies have been able to run their operations legally and more smoothly.

Through offshore gaming, the industry has been able to significantly reduce its costs and expenses. This means more profits for them. Aside from this, they could be able to provide better service by acquiring the services of skilled people for a much lesser price. This win-win situation has kept the world of gaming thriving together with the different locations that have decided to host these businesses.

Among the various offshore gaming sites of today, the Dutch Caribbeanis another important location where gaming companies have decided to transfer their business operations. While its economy relies so much on tourism and petroleum, the addition of these offshore gaming operations would definitely increase the island's economic value.

Under the legislated National Ordinance Offshore Games of Hazard, the Dutch Caribbeangovernor has been given the authority to issue licenses to worthy parties. These licenses would cover the different kinds of interactive gaming. Sub-licenses can also be procured for running Internet gambling. This move opened the gates for online gaming businesses to conduct their operations legally on the island.

With the fees and taxes that these gaming companies would pay to the island's government, the gaming industry would somehow repay the Dutch Caribbeanfor its warm acceptance. Aside from these financial opportunities, gaming companies could also provide sufficient jobs and employment to the numerous local residents. Based on these benefits and advantages, it can be concluded that offshore gaming can really contribute good things to society.

The offshore gaming in the Dutch Caribbeanis certainly a big help to the gaming industry as a whole. Without the acquisition of this practice, the various gaming companies would still have a very hard time in dealing with the issues and problems that are facing them. This seemingly temporary solution could somehow help the world accept more easily the good things that gaming can really offer.

Through offshore gaming, the various interactive and online casino games have been distributed more widely than ever. More people have been able to experience the real fun and excitement that gaming could bring. Expect more gaming companies to imbibe this practice to offer better service and save more money for their future operations.

GAMING INDUSTRY OPPORTUNITES

The Dutch Caribbeanwere previously called the Netherlands West Indies, the islands are a part of the Lesser Antilles just off the coast of Venezuela to the South-East of the Virgin Islands. The Dutch Caribbeanconstitute an autonomous part of the Kingdom of the Netherlands, and cover an area of 800 sq km. Willemstad is the capital of the Netherlands Antilles. Dutch, English and Papiamento are its official languages. Spanish is not an official language, but it widely used within the territory of the Netherlands Antilles.

The head of the Dutch Caribbeans the ruling monarch of the Netherlands, who appoints a governor to represent him within the jurisdiction. Executive power belongs to a Prime Minister who forms the government; the governor assigned by the monarch has a representative power, the Netherlands is responsible for defense and international relations of the Netherlands Antilles. Legislative power belongs to delegates of the islands who actively cooperate within the government, and local governors of every island who deal with everyday affairs at a local level. The Dutch Caribbeansare not a part of the EU.

Economy of the islands mostly depends on tourism, financial industry, international trade and shipping. The US, Venezuela and Mexico are main countries from which food products and other goods are imported to the Netherlands Antilles. Dutch government provides a significant aid to the development of the jurisdiction. Main problem to ensure a constant agricultural development of the Dutch Caribbeanis the lack of rain and poor soils.

Internet gaming became a central industry for the island of Curacao in 2002 when the regulation of online gambling was decentralized from the Curacao Gaming Control Board. Cyberluck Casino holds the longest standing Internet gaming license, which was granted under the old regulatory scheme in 1999.

The Governor of the Dutch Caribbeanmay award interactive gaming licenses pursuant to the National Ordinance Offshore Games of Hazard.

Applicants must first register with the Dutch CaribbeanChamber of Commerce as a locally formed legal entity, either onshore or offshore, and must state the island territories from which they wish to operate. Once an application is completed, the Department of Justice will conduct an investigation. If at the end of six weeks the investigation has been completed and yielded no objections then the applicant can receive a provisional license, which will be subject to a number of conditions, including a 60,000 (ANG) guarantee deposit.

Online gaming operators may also obtain sub-licenses to run Internet gambling operations from the Netherlands Antilles. Host businesses may sub-divide their existing gambling licenses for use by partner companies, provided the arrangement complies with applicable fees ranging from USD $2,000 to USD $4,000.

License holders pay 10,000 (ANG) per month in license fees during the first two years. A new license fee can be determined after the first two years.

The island territory on which a license holder is located is entitled to demand a contribution of up to 2% of the license holder's net gains from interactive gaming.

DUTCH CARIBBEANSONLINE GAMBLING LICENSING

Internet gaming became a central industry for the island of Curacao in 2002 when the regulation of online gambling was decentralized from the Curacao Gaming Control Board.
The Governor of the Dutch Caribbeanmay award interactive gaming licenses pursuant to the National Ordinance Offshore Games of Hazard.

On-line gaming is a legitimate business activity in the Netherlands Antilles, especially Curacao, provided the e-gaming company has obtained the proper license. The Dutch Caribbean(master) gaming licenses are based on the National Ordinance on Offshore Hazard Games.
There are two formats to be licensed:

a) master license
b) sub-license.
A master license licenses the (e-)gaming company itself, and in addition opens the possibility to sub-license third parties subject to the responsibility and covenants under the master license. A sub-license - under a master license - offers equal possibilities to performing e-gaming business legitimately, however without the possibility to further sub-license.

Basic requirements for applying for a (sub-)license are compliance with due diligence and KYC policies, full identification of Ultimate Beneficial Owners (UBOs), satisfactory reference on UBOs as well as detailed and transparent description of the games to be offered. In the case of a master license application the decision is taken at the sole discretion of the Minister of Justice, based on the documentation submitted by the Dutch Caribbeancounsel.

Applicants must first register with the Dutch CaribbeanChamber of Commerce as a locally formed legal entity, either onshore or offshore, and must state the island territories from which they wish to operate. Once an application is completed, the Department of Justice will conduct an investigation. If at the end of six weeks the investigation has been completed and yielded no objections then the applicant can receive a provisional license, which will be subject to a number of conditions, including a 60,000 (ANG) guarantee deposit.

Online gaming operators may also obtain sub-licenses to run Internet gambling operations from the Netherlands Antilles. Host businesses may sub-divide their existing gambling licenses for use by partner companies, provided the arrangement complies with applicable fees ranging from USD $2,000 to USD $4,000.

License holders pay 10,000 (ANG) per month in license fees during the first two years. A new license fee can be determined after the first two years.
The island territory on which a license holder is located is entitled to demand a contribution of up to 2% of the license holder's net gains from interactive gaming.

CURACAO GAMING JURISDICTION

Curacao Gaming Control Board
Address: Piscadera Bay z/n, WTC
Phone: (599-9) 463-6399 / (599-9) 463-6313

Curacao, an island in the southern part of the Caribbean, off the coast of Venezuela, is part of the group of islands known as the Dutch Caribbean– a self-governing part of the Dutch Kingdom. Curacao has a stable economy and is considered a highly attractive option for online gambling operators. In fact, it was one of the first jurisdictions in the world to regulate online gambling, which has been a central industry in the country since the decentralization of online gaming from the Curacao Gaming Control Board in 2002.

The longest standing internet gaming license was granted to Cyberluck Casino under old laws in 1999, and this casino has been the Master License Authority designated by the Department of Justice since then.

The are many reasons why operators are drawn to Curacao, among them a favorable tax regime, excellent technology across the board, part of the Dutch Kingdom, very little red tape and the fact that the island is situated outside the notorious hurricane belt. Curacao also has multiple fiber optic cables to facilitate the easy transfer of information, and has enough bandwidth offered at good rates. Combine all this with an outsourced network operation center that works around the clock, call center facilities and professional infrastructure in place such as banks, legal and audit firms, and it is easy to understand the attraction of Curacao.

Operators who wish to obtain a license from Curacao need to meet the strict requirements of the island state. Firstly, they need to register with the Dutch CaribbeanChamber of Commerce as a local, legal entity, stating the island territories from where they wish to operate. The Curacao Department of Justice then conducts an investigation into the company – a procedure that takes approximately 6 weeks.

A provisional license is granted to companies who manage to pass the Justice Department's investigation, subject to certain conditions, including a guaranteed deposit of around $35,000. Sublicenses are also available in order to run internet gaming operations from the Netherlands Antilles. Partner companies can share existing gambling licenses, again, subject to conditions. Licensees pay a monthly fee for two years, and a new license fee will be determined after this time period. A certain percentage of the company's net gains is usually taken as a subsequent monthly fee.

In May 2007, Curacao announced that it would be updating its e-gaming legislation and regulations in order to compete among the world's leading jurisdictions. Part of this move was to ensure that the island state would eventually be accepted onto the United Kingdom's prestigious 'white list' – a list of offshore jurisdictions that may operate within the UK market under the country's new gambling laws. To date, despite an application to be accepted onto the list, the UK has not granted Curacao white list status, but the country is working hard to move towards this goal.

GENERAL INFORMATION CONCERNING ON-LINE GAMING / GAMBLING

In 2002, internet gambling started playing a central role in Curacao's industry. The island decentralized online gambling from the Curacao Gaming Control Board, and they readily offer official licensing to all that pass the application process.

Cyberluck Casinos, the company dealing with licensing, has the longest standing internet gaming license in the industry, receiving it in 1999 under the old regulatory scheme. Although many revisions have been made to gambling law, Cyberluck's license is still valid. Dutch Caribbeanalso awards interactive gaming licenses at the governor's say so.

The island of Curacao has a very large number of gaming entities hosting their respective websites within the country's jurisdiction. Part of this has to do with very low licensing fees. Part of the popularity also has to do with Cyberluck Curacao's policies and insistence on fair game play.

Although Cyberluck does not offer any direct support between virtual casinos and players to resolve disputes, their regulatory authority and strict application process ensures that only the most trustworthy entities receive licensing through Curacao.

CIGA, a popular symbol on hundreds of online casinos, stands for the Curacao Internet Gaming Association. Under this banner, all operators must provide a forum for interested parties to address issues, advance common interests of members, and respect the global interactive gaming community and industry. All parties must also establish responsible and fair practices and guidelines that will enhance consumer confidence in all gaming products and services based in Curacao.

All CIGA Operator Members must agree to basic principles and act accordingly: entities must operate with an official license granted by the Netherlands Antilles. They must maintain a complete audit trail of individual transactions and wagers for every customer.

No resident of the Dutch Caribbeanwill be granted access to gambling sites, and all participants must be 18 years of age at a minimum. All sites must maintain sufficient financial resources in order to pay every winning wager on demand.

Within the jurisdiction of the Netherlands Antilles, Curacao, in association with Cyberluck, grants gambling licenses for three types of online gaming venues: virtual casinos, sports books, and poker rooms. These licenses are acquired by going through the country's Department of Justice.

Needless to say, Curacao's DOJ is intent on having only the most reputable would-be gambling hosts participate under the country's banner. All gambling licenses from the Department of Justice in Curacao last for a period of two years. The DOJ will conduct an investigation of up to six weeks. A deposit of 60,000 ANG is required.

Gambling licenses are also available in the form of sub-licensing. This is the process of procuring a license from a pre-existing license holder. These types of licenses range from $2,000 to $4,000 USD. All license holders pay a fee of 10,000 ANG per month, and at the end of the two year period, a new license fee will be negotiated.

Corporation Tax Rate
2% of Net profits; no import duties, no sales (turnover) tax. Expatriate employees working from E-Zone are entitled to a special income tax regime. E-Zone permit required. Apply through E-Zone area manager at www.curacao-egaming.com

Gaming Tax Rate
None

Minimum Share Capital for iGaming Company
No minimum share capital is required.

Security Requirements / Indemnity for Player Deposits
If an iGaming company operates under an existing licence, no deposit is required. Otherwise a NAf60,000 - guarantee deposit.

Licence Fee
The license holder shall owe the Central Government a license fee of US$5,600 per month unless approved gaming company secures licence via Master Licensing Authority under negotiated terms. Access to Master Licensing Authority at www.curacao-egaming.com

Licence Length
5 years

Software Testing Requirements
- Certification of RNG
- Games need approval of Minister of Justice
- Control system must be in Curacao at approved location

Reporting Requirements to Regulators
Requirements may vary according to circumstances. Copies of communications between company and client, including but not limited to result of game and pay-out to be available to Regulator or supervising authority for 5 years.

Anti-Money Laundering Policy
National Anti-money Laudering Regulations apply. International AML standards apply.

Country Restrictions
Netherlands Antilles

Contact Details
Dept of Justice of the Netherlands Antilles,
Wilhelminaplein z/n,
Curacao,
Netherlands Antilles
Attention: Mr Herbert Coffie
Herbert.coffie@gov.an

For the performance of gaming activities from the Dutch Caribbeanby means of util-ity-line services, a license pursuant to the National Ordinance Offshore Games of Hazard (Official Gazette 1993, no. 63) shall be required, to be granted by the Governor of the Netherlands Antilles. This information folder will furnish you with information on the terms and conditions to be met on applying for such a license, before the application can be dealt with. In addition, you will find other useful information.

1. THE FILING OF APPLICATIONS

In order to be considered for a license pursuant to the National Ordinance offshore games of hazard, the following conditions shall be fulfilled:
1° a written application, addressed to the Governor on stamped paper, stating the island territories from which the applicant wishes to operate, such application to be submit-ted to the Department of Justice, Wilhelminaplein z/n, Curaçao, Netherlands Antilles;

2° the application shall be accompanied by:
a. certificate of registration with the Chamber of Commerce as a locally formed le-gal entity, be this offshore or onshore, whether or not enjoying a tax holiday; all this accompanied by a description of the objects according to the articles of incor-poration;
b. full name and address of all the parties involved, their domiciles, nationality, passport number and if possible social security number, and other relevant data that shall be required for the purpose of screening these parties involved; by "par-ties involved" shall be understood:
(i) the shareholders of the legal entity and, insofar as corporate shareholders are involved, the ultimate individuals who hold shares via legal entities;
(ii) the managing directors of the legal entity, according to its articles of in-corporation;
(iii) the parties in charge of the daily management of the legal entity;
(iv) all others who are involved in the legal entity as advisor, financier or oth-erwise and who, as such, can influence the operation of the legal entity;
c. a business plan containing an explanatory memorandum concerning the place where and the manner in which and the games of hazard that shall be offered and operated; the number of employees expected to be engaged, recruited from both the local market and abroad, the number of information providers the legal entity contemplates using and the number of employees to be recruited by the informa-tion providers for these activities; a view as to the contribution the legal entity be-lieves it will be able to make towards the development of the Dutch Caribbeancommunity;
d. a financial feasibility study for the first three years;
e. some two legal opinions addressed to the Minister of Justice, to be submitted by:
1° a member of the Order of Lawyers or a local civil-law notary, giving a rea-soned statement to the effect that the proposed activities are not in contraven-tion of the National Ordinance Penalizing Money-laundering (O.G. 1993, no. 52); and
2° a lawyer registered with the Federal Bar of the United States, giving a rea-soned statement to

the effect that the proposed activities are not in contraven-tion of the federal laws of the United States concerning games of hazard.

(The costs attaching to the drawing up of these legal opinions shall be borne by the applicant.)

2. HANDLING OF APPLICATIONS

As regards the time for dealing with the applications for the granting of a license, the fol-lowing procedure applies. Within five days from an application having been received, the Department of Justice will check whether the accompanying documents are complete. If necessary, the applicant shall supplement these appendices. From the moment the appli-cation is complete, the department will take six weeks to conduct an investigation. If at the end of the six weeks the investigation has been completed and has yielded no objec-tions, the applicant shall be granted a five-year license. If after six weeks the investiga-tion has not been completed but there appear to be no objections, a provisional license may be granted for a period of six months (provided the applicant himself is not to blame for the delay in the investigation). A number of conditions shall attach to this license, among others a NA*f*.60,000.- guarantee deposit. If it should appear at the conclusion of the investigation that there are no objections, the provisional license shall be converted into a five-year license, and the guarantee deposit returned. At the expiration of the five-year term, the license may be extended.

In order to prevent the possibility of the Central Government and the island authorities working at cross purposes, the license applications shall be sent, for their information, to the executive council(s) of the island territory (territories) from where the potential li-cense holder wishes to offer his games of hazard.

3. AREA OF APPLICATION AND LICENSE FEES

The license shall be limited to the island territory (territories) designated in the applica-tion. Consequently, in order to be allowed to offer games of hazard from another island territory, the license must be adapted.

The license holder shall owe the Central Government a license fee of NA*f*.10,000.- per month during the first two years of the license. After that, the amount of the license fee shall be determined anew.

It has been agreed with the island territories that each island territory, from where games of hazard are being offered, shall be entitled to demand a contribution of up to 2% of the net gains from the activities to be performed by the license holder from that island terri-tory.

The license holder shall be bound to submit to the Minister of Justice each year (a) a copy of his annual accounts and (b) written information concerning the financial arrangement with his information providers for that year.

A license shall expire if not accepted within thirty days from the date of determination, against payment of the amount due in pursuance of the Stamp Ordinance 1908 (O.G. 1908, no. 52). (License to be obtained at the Central Bureau for Registration and Public Records (["Centraal Bureau voor Registratuur en Archiefzaken"] - "CBRA", Fort Amsterdam in Curaçao); stamps are to be purchased, affixed and stamped (cancelled) at the offices of the National Tax Collector).

4. RESIDENCE PERMIT FOR FOREIGN ENTREPRENEURS

For the performance of gaming activities from the Dutch Caribbeanby means of util-ity-line services, foreign entrepreneurs shall be required to dispose of a temporary resi-dence permit, with permission to work. The temporary residence permit is granted by the Lt.-Governor of the island territory.

In this connection entrepreneur shall mean the party in respect of whom the National Or-dinance on Admission and Expulsion (O.G. 1966, no. 17) shall apply, and who applies for a license for temporary residence in the Dutch Caribbeanin order to be admitted to the Netherlands Antilles, with the evident intention of establishing himself in connec-tion with the setting up or management of an enterprise, of which he is the owner or co-owner.

Immediately after an application has been submitted by an entrepreneur to obtain a li-cense for temporary residence in the Netherlands Antilles, a permit for temporary resi-dence shall be granted for the term of six months. The application shall be accompanied by a statement from a bank or credit institution, or by a notarial or similar deed, purport-ing to the set-up or management of an enterprise, from which it appears that the entrepre-neur must be deemed capable of setting up or managing the enterprise contemplated. At the same time a writing shall be submitted, proving that the entrepreneur is of impeccable character.

At the expiration of the six-month temporary residence permit, the same shall be con-verted into a permit for the same duration or for a longer period of time in accordance with the application of the entrepreneur, unless the National Ordinance on Admission and Expulsion should oppose this.

5. OTHER MATTERS

Establishment permit

The holder of a license pursuant to the National Ordinance Offshore Games of Hazard should also apply for an establishment permit and a related management permit, to be granted by the executive council of the island territory where he is established.

In order to come into consideration for an establishment permit casu quo management permit, the applicant shall fulfill the following conditions:
1° a written application on stamped paper addressed to the executive council of the is-land territory concerned, to be submitted to the Economic Affairs Bureau;
2° the application shall be accompanied by:
a. proof of the activities to be performed;
b. the address at which the legal entity is proposed to be established;
c. information on the financing of the legal entity, such to include the issued, or as the case may be, the authorized capital and the composition thereof;
d. personal data of the shareholder(s);
e. personal data of the managing director(s).

Telecommunication facilities

For the telecommunication facilities the license holder must depend on the supply by and contract with the long-distance concessionaire (Antelecom N.V.), and possibly the con-cessionaire for the local telecommunication (Telbo N.V. for Bonaire; Setel N.V. for Curaçao; Satel N.V. for Saba; Eutel N.V. for Sint Eustatius; and Telem N.V. for Sint Maarten).

Other information

The profit tax for offshore and tax holiday enterprises amounts to between 2 and 3% per annum pursuant to the National Ordinance on Profit Tax 1940 (O.G. 1965, no. 58) and the National Ordinance to Promote the Establishment of Businesses and the Construction of Hotels (O.G. 1953, no. 194).

For the aspects of banking, reference is made to the Bank van de Nederlandse Antillen [the Central Bank of the Netherlands Antilles].

POPULAR GAMBLING LICENSE JURISDICTIONS

To operate an online casino, poker room or sports betting gaming site legally you will need to obtain a gambling license first. The actual gambling license to operate online gaming site is issued by many governments worldwide, but the most popular jurisdictions issuing such offshore gambling licenses are from the Caribbean and Pacific Island Governments such as Antigua and Barbuda, Costa Rica, St Kitts, Dominica, Curacau and Vanuatu. When selecting a gambling license jurisdiction, you should select one with a sensible approach to taxation, and license cost in combination with a strong licensing law and technical standards.

GAMBLING LICENSE FOR YOUR ONLINE CASINO, POKER OR SPORTS BETTING SITE?

It is possible to make your online gaming business without a license, but most of major online casinos have license. Here are three main causes why it is worth to have a gambling license.

- In player's opinion gambling license guarantees reliability and straight dealing of the gaming company. Players have more confidence playing in casinos and poker rooms with license.
- In case of a settlement account opening banks insist on gambling license and especially while concluding agreements for receiving payments from bank cards.
- In many countries operating a gambling business without a gambling license is illegal and it may result in termination and criminal responsibilities.

You can apply for a gambling license in one of the countries listed below:

GAMBLING LICENSE ANTIGUA AND BARBUDA

Antigua and Barbuda is a twin-island nation located in the Eastern Caribbean. Antigua and Barbuda was one of the first jurisdictions to license interactive gaming and wagering companies in 1994. The internet gaming companies are classified as

"Financial Institutions" and are subject to all the Anti-Money Laundering (AML) and Caribbean Financial Action Task Force (CFATF) requirements of the jurisdiction.
The licensing and regulation of online gambling services on the islands of Antigua and Barbuda is handled by the Financial Services Regulatory Commission's Division of Gaming. The FRSC Gaming Division awards two types of licensees: interactive gaming and interactive wagering.
The gaming license is for casino and poker sites and the wagering license is for sports betting sites. It's one of the offshore jurisdictions which contain the biggest number of registered online casinos.
For more information on Antigua's interactive gaming and wagering laws and regulations see the following:
Interactive Gaming and Interactive Wagering Regulations, as Amended 2007
Control Systems Guidelines
Social Responsibility Commitment
-http://www.antiguagaming.gov.ag/files/Antigua_and_Barbuda_Gaming_Regulations-Final.pdf
The Antiguan gaming regulations are enforced by the Antiguan Directorate of Offshore Gaming (the "Directorate"). For more information on obtaining a gambling license in Antigua and Barbuda please visit www.antiguagaming.gov.ag

GAMBLING LICENSE COSTA-RICA

Costa Rica is the Mecca of online casinos and poker rooms because it has the best infrastructure available in the Caribbean basin - its reliable telecommunication system, its multilingual workers, and its lack of online gaming and Internet regulations. A lot of online casinos have chosen Costa Rica as registration country because of the fact that there are no direct prohibition on gambling business and no necessity to receive a special license.
There is no online gambling license in Costa Rica. A company incorporated under the laws of Costa Rica can operate an online gaming business. Companies operate under a "data processing" license.
Costa Rica is home to 200+ online gambling companies, without a legislation specifically dealing with gambling over the Internet. Legislation does exist to restrict land-based gambling, but these laws are not interpreted as extending to Internet gambling.
The requirements to obtain a license are:

- Office Lease Contract
- Health permit
- Workers insurance policy

For more information please visit http://www.meic.go.cr

KAHNAWAKE GAMBLING LICENSE

Kahnawake is an Indian (native American) territory in Quebec, Canada.
The Kahnawake Gaming Commission is an organization that licenses a large number of online casinos and online poker rooms. The Kahnawáke Gaming Commission was established in June 1996. The Commission is empowered to regulate and control

gaming and related activities within and from the Mohawk Territory of Kahnawáke. These gaming activities are regulated in accordance with the highest principles of honesty and integrity.
The fee for the initial application is C$15,000 plus an annual license fee of C$10,000 Visit http://www.kahnawake.com/gamingcommission for more information.

GAMBLING LICENSE PANAMA

Panama adopted regulations governing the licensing of electronic games of chance and wagering activities in late 2002. Internet gaming companies domiciled in Panama enjoy complete tax exemptions. Customs duty concessions are given for imports needed to carry on Internet gaming. As long as the income made from Internet operations are to jurisdictions outside of Panama, there is no income tax, withholding tax, sales tax or VAT taxes. Offshore companies, such as online gaming companies are not subject to foreign exchange control. There is also a new call center incentive and training program that boast numerous qualified bilingual workers.
The regulations allow master licenses to be granted that are valid for up to seven years upon payment of a license fee of US$40,000. There is also an annual license fee of US$20,000. Master license holders may grant sub-licenses, which are subject to the annual fee. Applicants must pay all investigation costs incurred in the processing of the application. Operators must comply with money-laundering regulations and notify the Financial Analysis Unit of any suspicious transactions above US$10,000. An account must be maintained to guarantee payment to winners. Until now a very few companies have applied for the license, mainly due to the huge paper work and the cost of the gambling license.

ANTILLES NETHERLANDS AND CURACAO

Within the Netherlands Antilles, Curacao offers gambling licenses for online casinos, poker rooms and sportsbooks. Gambling licenses are available through the Department of Justice or through sub-licensing from an existing gambling license holders. Licenses from the Department of Justice last for two years.

Gambling License Gibraltar

All gaming operations in Gibraltar require licensing under the Gambling Ordinance 2005. Remote Gambling licenses, including for telephone and internet betting, are issued by the Government of Gibraltar.
Only companies with a proven track record in gaming, of reputable standing and with a realistic business plan can be granted gambling licenses. Gibraltar gaming licenses are generally difficult to obtain.
For more information on obtaining a gambling license in Gibraltar visit http://www.gibraltar.gov.gi/gov_depts/internet_gaming/internet_gaming.htm

Isle of Man

The Isle of Man specifically encourages the location of online gambling businesses: "The Isle of Man Government actively encourages the development of gambling and e-gaming business on the Isle of Man. It remains committed to delivering a stable

government and strong regulatory environment, supported by a wide range of attractive Business Benefits."
The Commission requires independent testing of software to ensure games offered are not rigged and will make accurate payment of player winnings. Games may only be offered by licensed, corporate operators. All operators must also establish bond arrangements to guarantee players will be paid in the event the licensee ceased operations for any reason.

Fees

- GBP35,000 per annum
- GBP1000 one off administration fee which is non-refundable

Duty

- for gross gaming yield not exceeding £20 million per annum 1.5%
- for gross gaming yield of more than £20 million per annum, but not exceeding £40 million per annum 0.5%
- for gross gaming yield exceeding £40 million per annum 0.1%

For more information on how to obtain a gambling license in the Isle of Man please visit
http://www.gov.im/gambling/licensing/

Gambling License Malta
Class 1 – Remote Gaming Licence for online gaming
Class 2 – Remote Gaming Licence for online betting office
Class 3 – Promotion and abet gaming from Malta
Class 4 - Hosting and managing only gaming operations, excluding licences itself.
Licences are issued for a minimum period of five years and may be extended for further periods of five years each.

Licensing Requirements
Obtaining a gaming licence in Malta is a serious affair and in the interest of the consumers and the local reputation, the Authority would require to know that the applicant can meet the licence obligations. The licensing procedure is quite extensive but thanks to the professionalism of the persons involved, this procedure should not take more than 5 to 6 weeks.
The application for a gaming licence requires the following documentation:

1. Detailed profile of the promoting company

2. A copy of the last audited accounts of the promoting company, where applicable

3. A business plan indicating the economic activity – including job creation if any – which will be carried out from Malta

4. A plan of the premises earmarked for adoption as a call centre.

5. Personal details of all shareholders having more than 5% interest in the local operations.

Basic Requirements

• Both hardware and software involved in the operations must be located in Malta, and there exist companies that can provide this service without the need for the licensee to obtain its own premises.

• The activities of the International Trading Company are limited to those carried outside Malta. No Maltese resident is permitted to place bets with such a company.

Licence Fees

On submission of application form – Lm1,000 (US$2,700) for any class of remote gaming licence.
On Issue of any Remote Gaming Licence – Lm3,000 (US$8100) per annum. Such a licence is normally issued for a 5 year period.
On application for renewal of any Remote Gaming Licence – Lm500 (US$1,350)

Taxation

On online gaming – Lm2,000(US$5400) per month for first six months and Lm3000(US$8100) per month for the entire duration of the licence period.
On Class 4 Licences – Lm0.0 (NIL) per month for first six months and Lm1,000(US$2700) per month for the next six months and Lm2000(US$5400) per month for the remaining period of the licence.
Online betting operations – one half of one per centum (0.5%) on the gross amounts of bets accepted
Online betting exchanges – one half of one per centum (0.5%) on the sum of all net winnings calculated per player per betting market.
Online pool betting – one half of one per centum (0.5%) on the aggregate of stakes paid.
Provided that in no case will the maximum of tax payable per annum by any licensee in respect of any one licence, exceed Lm200,000.

COMPANY REGISTRATION

A Malta based gaming operation must be carried out by a Malta registered company as specified in Regulation 4 of the Remote Gaming Regulations (LN176/2004). Gaming companies are not subject to any special tax regime. In fact, online gaming operations may be carried out through a normal limited liability company registered in Malta under the Companies' Act.

TAXATION OF ONLINE GAMING COMPANIES

Companies registered on or after 1st January 2007 are taxable at the rate of 35% however, shareholders are entitled to claim back a 6/7ths refund of the Malta tax upon distributions of profits. Alternatively, shareholders may claim a 2/3rds refund of the tax payable in Malta.
In addition, Malta does not levy withholding tax on any outbound distributions of dividends. The refund system and the absence of a dividend withholding tax ensures that profits derived by gaming companies are taxed and repatriated outside Malta in the most efficient manner.

ORDINANCE ON THE SUPERVISION OF INVESTMENT INSTITUTIONS AND ADMINISTRATORS

considering:
that it is desirable to lay down rules concerning investment institutions and administrators and to put them under the supervision of the Bank of the Netherlands Antilles;
after consultation with the Advisory Council and in concert with Parliament has laid down the following Act:

CHAPTER I DEFINITIONS

Article 1

In this Act and the provisions based thereupon:
a) investment company shall mean:
the body corporate that raises or has obtained pecuniary means or other property to be used for collective investment with the objective of allowing the participants to benefit from the revenues of the investments;
b) investment fund shall mean:
non-incorporated capital comprising pecuniary means or other property raised or obtained for collective investment with the objective of allowing the participants to benefit from the revenues of the investments;
c) investment institution shall mean:
an investment company or investment fund;
For the written consultation of Parliament see the documents of sessions 2002-2003-2710
d) participant shall mean:
the shareholder in an investment company or the beneficiary in an investment fund;
e) management company shall mean:
either the investment company or any other person fully or partially entrusted with the management of the investment fund;
f) depositary shall mean:
the person to whom the investment institution's assets are entrusted for safe-keeping;
g) administrative services shall mean:
the provision of services for investment institutions, whether for compensation or for free, in any event including:
1. managing investment institutions, in any event including the provision of natural or legal persons as directors, representatives or other executive officers of investment institutions whose responsibilities shall include decision-taking;
2. performing administration operations, including in any event, keeping the accounts and obtaining, recording, processing and providing information for purposes of the management or operation of an investment institution;
3. providing an address for service and office facilities for investment institutions;
h) administrator shall mean: a legal person whose objective is to provide administrative services;
i) the Bank shall mean: the Bank of the Netherlands Antilles;
j) the Court shall mean: the Court of First Instance;
k) the Minister shall mean: the Minister of Finance.

CHAPTER II GENERAL PROVISION

Article 2
The provisions of this National Ordinance and the provisions made pursuant to it concerning an investment institution that qualifies as an investment fund shall be directed at the management company.

CHAPTER III LICENSING OF INVESTMENT INSTITUTIONS

§1 Licensing

Article 3

1. It shall be a punishable offence to raise or obtain pecuniary means or other property for purposes of participating in an investment institution which has not been licensed by the Bank or to offer participating interests in such an investment institution in or from the Netherlands Antilles.

2. The prohibition laid down in the first paragraph shall not apply to the offering of participating interests by natural persons other than in the exercise of their business or profession.

§2 Licensing requirements

Article 4

1. The Bank shall grant a license to an investment institution if the person applying for the license demonstrates that the investment institution and the depositary, if employed by the investment institution, satisfy the requirements laid down in the Bank's instructions concerning:

a) competence and integrity;

b) financial securities;

c) conduct of business; and

d) the provision of information to the participants in the investment institution and the general public.

Such instructions shall also specify that the daily policy of the investment institution must be determined by no fewer than two natural persons and that if there is a Supervisory Board, such Board must comprise of at least three members.

2. The person applying for the license of an investment fund shall also demonstrate that:

a) the management company is a legal person with full competence;

b) the investment fund's assets are entrusted for safe-keeping with a depositary independent of the management company; and

c) the investment fund's assets are separated from the capital of the management company, the depositary and any natural or other legal persons.

3. The Bank shall decide on the application within 60 days of receiving the complete application and shall inform the person applying for the license of its decision by registered letter.

4. The Bank may grant a license to any person applying to it if such person demonstrates that it cannot be reasonably expected to fully satisfy certain requirements laid down by or pursuant to the first and

the second paragraphs, and it demonstrates that the objectives intended by this National Ordinance are sufficiently realised otherwise.

5. The Bank shall ensure that the instructions referred to in the first paragraph are made public.

Article 5

The Bank may at all times impose restrictions and conditions on the license in the interest of an adequate operation of the financial markets and the position of investors in such markets, if this is called for by the facts and conditions relating to the person to whom the license applies.

Article 6

The function of depositary shall only be taken by a corporate body whose business is to a significant degree the safe-holding and provision of administrative services for investment objectives on behalf of third parties.

Article 7

If the Bank is of the opinion that the name used or to be used for the investment institution in the Dutch Caribbeanmay lead to confusion, it may direct the investment institution to add an explanatory statement to such name.

§3 Reporting to the Bank / Instructions for investment institutions

Article 8

1. Every investment institution shall submit, on an annual basis, annual accounts including at least a balance sheet and a profit and loss account with explanatory notes on the past financial year in a form to be laid down by the Bank and within a time to be laid down by the Bank. An auditor's report and the management letters shall also be enclosed with the annual accounts.

2. Every investment institution shall submit periodical statements concerning its business to the Bank within the times laid down for this purpose.

3. The form in which the statements referred to in the second paragraph shall be drawn up, the successive points in time which they relate to, and the times within which they are to be submitted, shall be laid down by the Bank after consultation with the representative organisations, provided that they have been appointed in accordance with the provisions of article 31.

4. If the Bank deems it necessary for the purposes of efficient supervision, it may direct an investment institution:

a) to furnish it with statements as referred to in the second paragraph, concerning points of time with a shorter interval or concerning shorter times than laid down pursuant to the second paragraph;

b) to submit an external auditor's report concerning the statements referred to in the second paragraph.

5. A licensed investment institution shall not be allowed to amend its articles of association or its rules without prior permission of the Bank.

6. Any amendment of the articles of association or rules, in violation of the prohibition as referred to in the fifth paragraph, shall be null and void. At the request of the Bank the Court shall appoint an administrator with the power to reverse such invalid act.

7. When reversing the invalid act the administrator shall also act in the interest of the participants in the investment institution.

Article 9

1. A licensed investment institution and the depositary, if employed by the investment institution, shall be obliged to observe the instructions laid down by the Bank as regards competence, integrity, financial securities, conduct of business and the provision of information.

2. Without prior permission of the Bank the investment institution shall not be allowed to appoint persons who determine the daily policy of the investment institution, nor to appoint the members of the Supervisory Board if it has such a Board.

3. At the request of the investment institution the Bank may decide that the investment institution or the depositary, if employed by the institution, does not have to satisfy all rules referred to in the first paragraph if it demonstrates that it cannot be reasonably expected to fully satisfy such rules and that the objectives intended by this National Ordinance are sufficiently realised otherwise. The Bank may amend or revoke a decision referred to above if it is of the opinion that the conditions under which the decision was made have changed to such extent that the objectives intended by this ordinance are no longer fulfilled.

4. The auditor who has to furnish a report with an investment institution's annual accounts pursuant to the rules referred to in the first paragraph, shall notify the Bank as soon as possible of any circumstance discovered during the execution of the relevant activities that:

a) has breached the requirements set in respect of obtaining the license;

b) has breached the obligations laid down by or pursuant to this National Ordinance;

c) threatens the continuity of the investment institution; or

d) might threaten the granting of an approving report concerning the fairness, consistency and clarity of the accounts.

5. The auditor referred to in the fourth paragraph shall immediately send the Bank copies of the audit report, of the management letter and of such correspondence as directly concerns the auditor's report with the annual accounts and/or of any periodical statements to be submitted to the Bank, if and to the extent that the Bank shall require an auditor's report with such statements. If required by the Bank, the auditor shall give the Bank an oral explanation of the annual accounts and the documents referred to above.

6. The notification obligation referred to in the fourth paragraph shall also apply mutatis mutandis to the auditor, referred to in the fourth paragraph, who, in addition to carrying out work for the investment institution, also carries out work for another company or institution, if the investment institution is a

subsidiary of such other company or institution, or if such other company or institution is a subsidiary of the investment institution.

7. The auditor who has notified the Bank pursuant to the fourth or the sixth paragraph shall not be liable for damage or loss incurred by a third party as a result of such notification, unless it is demonstrated that, considering all facts and circumstances, in all reasonableness the notification should not have been submitted.

§4 Exemption

Article 10

1. The Bank may grant exemption from the prohibition laid down in article 3.

2. An exemption referred to in the first paragraph can be subject to restrictions and regulations in the interest of an adequate operation of the financial markets and the position of the investors in such markets. Restrictions shall only be set with respect to the scope of the exemption.

§5 Revoking the license

Article 11

1. The Bank shall only be allowed to revoke a license:

a) at the licensed institution's request;

b) if the information or documents furnished to obtain licensing prove to be incorrect or incomplete to such an extent that a different decision would have been taken if the correct and complete information and documents had been available at the time of taking the decision to grant the license;

c) if any new facts are discovered or circumstances take place on the grounds of which licensing would have been refused if they had been known or taken place prior to the time of granting the license;

d) if the licensed institution or the depositary employed by the investment institution has apparently ceased carrying out the activities referred to in article 3;

e) if the investment institution or the depositary employed by it no longer satisfies the requirements, rules, restrictions or instructions laid down by or pursuant to this National Ordinance or any other statutory obligations;

f) if the investment institution or the depositary employed by it has not or insufficiently performed an instruction or notification from the Bank as referred to in article 33 or article 34, or

g) if the investment institution has not actually commenced its business within a time to be laid down by the Bank.

2. If the Bank decides to revoke a license it shall do so by serving a bailiff's writ on the licensed institution concerned.

Article 12

1. The Bank may apply to the Court to have an investment company wound up if its license has been revoked. The Court shall appoint one or several liquidators.

2. The assets of an investment fund whose license has been revoked shall be liquidated within a time to be laid down by the Bank. The court shall appoint one or several liquidators on the Bank's request.

3. In respect of an investment fund which has been licensed pursuant to article 4, the Bank may grant dispensation concerning the provisions of the second paragraph, if the fund's activities are continued outside the public domain. In the interest of the participants such dispensation may be subject to restrictions and instructions.

4. The Bank shall immediately report to the Minister concerning an investment institution whose license has been revoked.

Article 13

If an investment institution suspends the acquisition of its participating interests, it shall immediately inform the Bank accordingly.

CHAPTER IV LICENSING OF ADMINISTRATORS

§1 Licensing

Article 14

No person shall be allowed to exercise the business of administrator in or from the Dutch Caribbeanwithout prior licensing from the Bank.

§2 Licensing requirements

Article 15

1. The Bank shall grant a license to an administrator applying to it on condition that the applicant satisfies the requirements specified by the Bank concerning:

a) competence and integrity; and

b) conduct of business.

Such instructions shall also specify that the daily policy of the administrator must be determined by no fewer than two persons and that if there is a Supervisory Board, such Board must comprise of at least three members.

2. The Bank shall grant the license by means of a registered letter within 60 days of receiving the complete application.

3. The Bank may grant a license to any administrator applying for a license if such administrator demonstrates that it cannot be reasonably expected to fully satisfy certain requirements laid down by or pursuant to the first paragraph, and it demonstrates that the objectives intended by this National Ordinance are sufficiently realised otherwise.

Article 16

The Bank may at all times impose restrictions and conditions on the license in the interest of an adequate operation of the financial markets and the position of investors in such markets, if this is called for by the facts and conditions relating to the administrator to whom the license applies.

§3 Reporting to the Bank / Instructions for administrators

Article 17

1. Every administrator shall submit, on an annual basis, annual accounts including at least a balance sheet and a profit and loss account with explanatory notes on the past financial year in a form to be laid down by the Bank and within a time to be laid down by the Bank. An auditor's report and the management letters shall also be enclosed with the annual accounts.

2. Every administrator shall submit periodical written compliance reports concerning its business to the Bank within the times laid down for this purpose.

3. The form in which the reports referred to in the second paragraph shall be drawn up, the successive points in time which they relate to, and the times within which they are to be submitted, shall be laid down by the Bank after consultation with the representative organisations.

4. If the Bank deems it necessary for the purposes of efficient supervision, it may direct an administrator to furnish it with the written reports referred to in the second paragraph at points of time with a shorter interval or within shorter times than laid down pursuant to the second paragraph.

5. A licensed administrator shall not be allowed to amend its articles of association or its rules without prior permission of the Bank.

6. Any amendment of the articles of association or rules as referred to in the fifth paragraph shall be null and void. At the request of the Bank the Court shall appoint an administrator with the power to reverse such invalid act.

7. When reversing the invalid act the administrator shall also act in the interest of the parties concerned.

Article 18

1. A licensed administrator shall undertake to continue to observe the instructions laid down by the Bank with regard to expertise, integrity and business conduct.

2 Without the prior permission of the Bank the administrator shall not be allowed to appoint the persons who decide on the daily course of action of the administrator and, if there is a Supervisory Board, the members of the Board.

3. At the request of the administrator the Bank may decide that the administrator does not have to satisfy all rules referred to in the first paragraph if it demonstrates that it cannot be reasonably expected to fully satisfy such rules and that the objectives intended by this National Ordinance are sufficiently realised otherwise. The Bank may amend or revoke a decision referred to above if it is of the opinion that the conditions under which the decision was made have changed to such extent that the objectives intended by this ordinance are no longer fulfilled.

4. The auditor who has to furnish a report with an administrator's annual accounts pursuant to the rules referred to in the first paragraph, shall notify the Bank as soon as possible of any circumstance that he has discovered during the execution of the relevant activities and that:

a) has breached the requirements set in respect of obtaining the license;

b) has breached the obligations laid down by or pursuant to this National Ordinance;

c) threatens the continuity of the administrator; or

d) might threaten the granting of an approving report concerning the fairness, consistency and clarity of the accounts.

5. The auditor referred to in the fourth paragraph shall immediately send the Bank copies of the audit report, of the management letter and of such correspondence as directly concerns the auditor's report with the annual accounts and/or of any periodical statements to be submitted to the Bank, if and to the extent that the Bank shall require an auditor's report with such statements. If required by the Bank, the auditor shall give the Bank an oral explanation of the annual accounts and the documents referred to above.

6 The notification obligation referred to in the fourth paragraph shall also apply mutatis mutandis to the auditor, referred to in the fourth paragraph, who, in addition to carrying out work for the administrator, also carries out work for another company or institution, if the administrator is a subsidiary of the other company or institution, or if the other company or institution is a subsidiary of the administrator.

7. The auditor who has notified the Bank pursuant to the fourth or the sixth paragraph shall not be liable for damage or loss incurred by a third party as a result of such

notification, unless it is demonstrated that, considering all facts and circumstances, in all reasonableness the notification should not have been submitted.

Article 19

An administrator shall ensure at all times that sufficient competence is available within the investment institutions for which it performs administrative services and that the integrity of the directors who represent the investment institutions or who decide on the policy of the investment institutions, and of others who co-decide on the policy, satisfies the Bank's instructions. The administrator shall also ensure that in all reasonableness the investment institutions for which it performs administrative services are not in breach of the statutory obligations that apply to them.

Article 20

An administrator shall inform the Bank immediately if it is of the opinion or has reason to suspect that an investment institution for which it carries out administrative services:

a) is or will not be capable of meeting its obligations;

b) does not comply with instructions pursuant to this National Ordinance or other legislation or regulations that apply to such investment institution; or carries out its business in a manner that does or may harm the interests of its participants or other beneficiaries.

§4 Exemption

Article 21

1. The Bank may grant exemption from the prohibition laid down in article 14.

2. An exemption referred to in the first paragraph can be subject to restrictions and regulations in the interest of an adequate operation of the financial markets and the position of the investors in such markets. Restrictions shall only be set with respect to the scope of the exemption.

§5 Revoking the license

Article 22

1. The Bank shall only be allowed to revoke a license:

a) at the request of the licensed administrator;

b) if the information or documents furnished to obtain a license prove to be incorrect or incomplete to such an extent that a different decision would have been taken if the correct and complete information and documents had been available at the time of taking the decision to grant the license;

c) if any new facts are discovered or circumstances take place on the grounds of which a license would have been refused if they had been known or taken place prior to the time of granting the license;

d) if the administrator has apparently ceased to satisfy the definition stipulated in article 1, h;

e) if the administrator no longer satisfies the requirements, rules, restrictions or instructions laid down by or pursuant to this National Ordinance or any other statutory obligations;

f) if the administrator has not or insufficiently performed an instruction or notification from the Bank as referred to in article 33 or article 34; or

g) if the administrator has not actually commenced its business within a time to be laid down by the Bank.

2. If the Bank decides to revoke a license it shall do so by serving a bailiff's writ on the licensed administrator concerned.

Article 23

1. The Bank may apply to the Court to have an administrator wound up if its license has been revoked. The Court shall appoint one or several liquidators.

2. If requested the Bank shall report to the Minister concerning an administrator whose license has been revoked.

CHAPTER V THE REGISTER OF INVESTMENT INSTITUTIONS AND ADMINISTRATORS

Article 24

1. The Bank shall keep a register of investment institutions and administrators divided into two main sections as follows:

- Section I - Investment institutions

- Section II - Administrators

The Bank may subdivide the main sections into sub-sections for further categories of investment institutions and administrators to be specified by the Bank.

An investment institution or administrator licensed pursuant to article 3 or article 14 shall be entered in the register by the Bank on the very date of granting the license. Such registration shall not be made in more than one main category or sub-category.

2. An investment institution or administrator whose license has been revoked shall be removed from the register.

3. The registration of an investment institution or an administrator as well as the removal from the register shall be published in De Curaçaosche Courant within two weeks of the day on which it was effected.

4. The Bank may decide to delay the publication of a removal referred to in the third paragraph until a time to be decided by the Bank if such publication could seriously harm the interests of the participants or the parties concerned.

5. In the month of January of every year a list of registered investment institutions and administrators as per 31 December of the preceding year shall be published in De Curaçaosche Courant.

6. The Bank shall keep a copy of the register open to public inspection free of charge.

CHAPTER VI NON-DISCLOSURE AND THE EXCHANGE OF DATA OR INFORMATION CONCERNING INVESTMENT INSTITUTIONS AND ADMINISTRATORS

Article 25

1. No data or information furnished pursuant to this National Ordinance or obtained from an institution as referred to in article 28 or obtained during the examination of accounts, documents or other information shall be made further use of or disclosed in any further or other manner than as required for the performance of tasks pursuant to the application of this National Ordinance or decisions taken pursuant to this National Ordinance.

2. Notwithstanding the provisions of the first paragraph the Bank shall be authorised to report a suspected offence in order to maintain a healthy financial industry. In cases where the Bank has reported a suspected offence, or in cases where the Bank is called on to act as a witness or an expert, the Bank shall be authorised to furnish information as part of the investigation, the preliminary judicial investigation or the court hearing.

Article 26

In the interest of an adequate operation of the financial markets and the position of the investors in such markets the Bank may, where necessary, in deviation of article 25 make public:

a) its refusal to grant a license if such refusal can no longer be appealed against; or

b) the fact that an investment institution or administrator to whom, in the opinion of the Bank, the prohibition outlined in article 3 or article 14 applies, does not have a license.

Article 27

The Bank may, notwithstanding article 25, periodically publish the most important data derived from data or information gained during the execution of the task assigned to it pursuant to this National Ordinance, provided that such data is not traced back to individual investment institutions or individual administrators. After permission in writing of the investment institution or the administrator concerned, data with regard to individual investment institutions or administrators may be published.

Article 28

Notwithstanding article 25 the Bank may furnish data or information obtained during the performance of the task assigned to it pursuant to this National Ordinance to governmental institutions on the Dutch Caribbeanor abroad or to institutions appointed by the government of the Dutch Caribbeanor foreign countries charged with the supervision of financial markets or of natural persons and legal persons active in those markets, unless:

a) the objective for which such data or information is going to be used is insufficiently specified;

b) the intended use of the data or information is not compatible with the supervision of financial markets or natural persons and legal persons active in such markets;

c) the furnishing of the data or information would not be in keeping with the laws of the Dutch Caribbeanor with public order or the data or information relates to individual investors;

d) the non-disclosure of the data or information is not sufficiently guaranteed;

e) it is reasonable to assume that the furnishing of the data or information will or could conflict with the interest that this ordinance attempts to protect; or

f) there is insufficient guarantee that the data or information will not be used for any other objective than the one for which it is furnished.

Article 29

In the framework of supervision the Bank has the power to allow examinations by foreign bodies responsible for the supervision of investment institutions or administrators with investment institutions or administrators in this country that are under the consolidated supervision of such supervisory institutions. In such event the Bank shall set conditions to or provide instructions for the implementation of the supervisory activities in advance. The officers of the foreign bodies responsible for the supervision of investment institutions or administrators shall be obliged to strictly observe the Bank's instructions.

CHAPTER VII SPECIAL PROVISIONS CONCERNING INVESTMENT INSTITUTIONS AND ADMINISTRATORS

Article 30

The Bank may grant or revoke a license pursuant to this National Ordinance, or set restrictions and conditions to such license , or amend restrictions and conditions previously laid down, if:

a) the investment institution or its management company or the administrator has its registered office in a state where financial institutions from the Dutch Caribbeanare not allowed or are subjected to unreasonable restrictions; or

b) a natural person or corporate body with the nationality of a state referred to under a) above can directly or indirectly exercise dominant control of the investment institution or the administrator.

Article 31

1. By national decree an association of investment institutions and depositaries and/or administrators may be appointed as a representative association.

2. As regards the policy concerning the supervision of investment institutions and administrators the Bank shall consult the representative associations at least once a year and at all other times when the Bank deems such consultation necessary.

Article 32

The cost associated with the implementation of the provisions laid down by or pursuant to this National Ordinance shall be charged to the investment institutions and administrators. By national decree containing general measures further rules shall be laid down concerning the passing on of such cost.

CHAPTER VIII IMPLEMENTATION, SUPERVISION AND DETECTION

Article 33

If the licensed investment institution or the depositary, if employed by the investment institution, or the administrator is found not to satisfy the requirements, rules, restrictions or instructions laid down by or pursuant to this National Ordinance, the Bank may issue an instruction to the investment institution, the depositary or the administrator specifying that it should satisfy such requirements, rules, restrictions or instructions within a time to be specified to the bank.

Article 34

1. If special circumstances threaten an adequate functioning of the investment institution, the depositary or the administrator as a result of which the Bank is of the opinion that reinforcement of the bodies of the investment institution, the depositary or the administrator has become desirable, the Bank may send a written notification of the fact that from a certain point in time all or certain bodies of the investment institution, the depositary or the administrator shall only be allowed to exercise their powers after the approval of one or several persons appointed by the Bank and duly observing the instructions by such persons.

2. If the Bank is of the opinion that special circumstances make immediate action necessary it may, contrary to the provisions of the first paragraph, immediately send a substantiated notification with immediate effect to the investment institution, the depositary or the administrator.

3. As regards the notification referred to in the first and second paragraphs, the following shall apply:

a) the bodies must fully cooperate with the persons appointed by the Bank;

b) the Bank may allow the bodies to perform certain acts without approval;

c) the Bank may replace the appointed persons at all times;

d) if any damage or loss has resulted from acts performed in violation of a notification as referred to in the first paragraph those persons who have performed such acts in their capacities of bodies of the investment institution, the depositary or the administrator, shall be personally liable towards the investment institution, the depositary or the administrator. The investment institution, the depositary or the administrator may invoke the invalidity of these acts if the other party knew or should have known that the required approval had not been granted; and

e) the notification shall remain effective until the circumstances referred to in the first paragraph no longer apply, however it shall be limited to a maximum of two years.

Article 35

1. If an investment institution or administrator fails to satisfy its obligations resulting from this National Ordinance or fails to satisfy such obligations in time, the Bank may impose a fine on the investment institution or administrator for every day that it has been negligent as regards the performance of its obligations.

2. The amount of the fine for the various offences shall be laid down by a national decree containing general measures.

3. Prior to imposing a fine, the Bank shall send the investment institution or administrator concerned written notification of its intent to impose a fine and shall allow it to remedy its failure within a reasonable period.

Article 36

1. The Bank officials appointed by the President of the Bank shall be responsible for the supervision of the observance of the provisions laid down in or by virtue of this Act.

2. Only to the extent that the following is reasonably required for the performance of their duties, the persons appointed by virtue of the first paragraph shall have the power to:

a. ask any information;

b. demand access to all financial accounts, documents and other information carriers and to make copies of such or to take such with them temporarily.

3. By national decree constituting general measures, rules can be laid down regarding the way in which the persons appointed pursuant to the first paragraph carry out their tasks.

4. The persons appointed pursuant to the first paragraph shall always be given all cooperation that is required on the grounds of the second paragraph.

Article 37

1 In addition to the officials referred to in article 184 of the Code on Criminal Procedure the Bank officials appointed for this purpose by national decree shall be responsible for the detection of the offences made punishable by this Act. Such appointment shall be published in De Curaçaosche Courant.

2. By national decree constituting general measures, rules can be laid down regarding the requirements which the officials appointed by virtue of the first paragraph should comply with.

CHAPTER IX PENAL PROVISIONS

Article 38

1. Any breach of article 3, first paragraph; article 6; article 8, first paragraph; article 8, second paragraph; article 8, fifth paragraph; article 9, first paragraph; article 9, second paragraph; article 9, fifth paragraph; article 14; article 17, first paragraph; article 17, second paragraph; article 17, fifth paragraph; article 18, first paragraph; article 18, second paragraph; article 18, fifth paragraph; article 20; article 25, first paragraph; or article 36, fourth paragraph shall be punishable by confinement for up to one year and a fine of up to two hundred and fifty thousand guilders or by one of these punishments.

2. Any intentional breach of any of the provisions referred to in the first paragraph shall be punishable by up to four years' imprisonment and a fine of up to five hundred thousand guilders or by one of these punishments.

3. The acts made punishable by the first paragraph shall be considered misdemeanours (overtredingen). The acts made punishable by the second paragraph shall be considered felonies (misdrijven).

CHAPTER X AMENDMENT OF OTHER NATIONAL ORDINANCE

Article 39

The following new paragraph shall be added to article 11 of the Central Bank Statute 1985 (O.G. 1985 no. 183):

5. The Bank shall carry out the supervision of investment institutions and administrators as laid down in the National Ordinance on the Supervision of investment institutions and

CHAPTER XI FINAL AND TRANSITIONAL PROVISIONS

Article 40

1. The prohibitions laid down in articles 3 and 14 shall not apply until three months after this National Ordinance has taken effect.

2. In respect of investment institutions or administrators that have applied for a license from the Bank within three months of this National Ordinance taking effect, the prohibitions laid down in articles 3 and 14 shall not apply until on the second day after the Bank has dispatched its decision concerning the application.

Article 41

This National Ordinance shall take effect on 1 January 2003.

Article 42

This National Ordinance may be cited as: National Ordinance on the Supervision of Investment Institutions and Administrators.

ECONOMY AND ECONOMIC DEVELOPMENT STRATEGY

DEPARTMENT OF AGRICULTURE AND BUSINESS OPPORTUNITIES

Telephone
International dialing code + 297-8-58102/56372/56473
FAX
International dialing code + 297-8-55639

Postal address
Department of Agriculture, Husbandry, and Fisheries
Piedra Plat 114A
Aruba Dutch Caribbean
Electronic mail
General Information: dirlvvm@toaruba.com
Webmaster: webmaster@toaruba.com

In 1997, the Department of Agriculture established the new Section of Nature Management. This section will focus on the management of natural and rural areas on Aruba, including conservation issues, research and monitoring.

LOCAL PLANTS

The Department of Agriculture, Santa Rosa, offers the service for locals to acquire local plants which are adapted to the dry and harsh climatic conditions on Aruba. This to encourage people to use Aruba's plant species in their landscaping and to promote revegetation in residential and rural areas. Local flora expert and section employee Mercedes Petrocchi explains: "One of the focal activities in this field is to create a stock of local plants for landscaping and revegetation projects. For example, in the Arikok National Park project lots of trees will be planted for upgrading of this nature area, and to safeguard and improve the endangered plant and tree populations. In our nursery we grow a wide variety of local plants, such as Lignum Vitae (*Guaiacum officinale*) and the famous Watapana tree (*Caesalpinia coriaria*). Recently, we expanded our activities by growing rare and endangered trees from seed and cuttings".

SANTA ROSA HERBARIUM

In 1996 we started to collect specimens of local plants in order to build a collection of dried plants prepared for study. In less than two years we created a unique store of most of the local species, about 300 known at this time. Pressed plant species are mounted, labeled and filed under their proper family, genus and species and different growth forms. Besides leaves, roots, seedlings and flowers, we also started to collect seeds of the plants. Even under the arid circumstances of Aruba, where the longest period of the year the trees are leafless and herbs are not present, the herbarium can show examples of most of these plant parts. Also considering the fact that numerous trees are extremely rare and almost extinct, samples of these plants can be of high interpretive and conservational value. The plant collection is accompanied by a slide collection and a database.

[drawing 1: specimen arranged in fold of paper]

PARKE NACIONAL ARIKOK

Nature Management also supports the new initiatives of the Parke Nacional Arikok (Arikok National Park): a wilderness area of about 18% of the land surface that will be declared, designed and managed as a nature preserve. More information about the Parke Nacional Arikok initiatives can be found on **http://www.arubanationalparks.com/**

RESEARCH: THE PUDRENA PROJECT

The Pudrena Project is a government initiative, started in 1994 by the Department of Agriculture and the Wageningen Agricultural University (WAU), the Netherlands, with the aim to map out Aruba's natural resources and put forward plans for sustainable use. Since then, a series of studies have been conducted by students and faculty members of the WAU together with local experts of governmental and non-governmental organizations.

The following list represents the main topics the project has focused on so far:

1. *Effects of grazing by goats on regeneration of trees in the Arikok/Jamanota region*, a M.Sc.-thesis by Marc A.J. Hoogeslag (1995).
2. *Ecological and agricultural assessment of aloe fields on Aruba*. Post-M.Sc.-study by Lidy E. van der Straten-Rouwkema M.Sc. (1995)
3. *Vegetation survey in the Arikok region*. A field study by Henk Roest (1995)
4. *Watershed management, erosion control and land restoration*. A field study by Marten H. Schut (1995)
5. *Natural resource assessment, zoning and concept plans for the Arikok National Park*, by Fedde Boersma (1996).
6. *Natural resource assessment and zoning plans for the Colony coastal area*, by Byron G. Boekhoudt M.Sc. and André H. van Schaik M.Sc.

7. *The Bubali Bird Sanctuary*, a concept plan for the Bubali pond by Dana Kamphorst (1996)
8. *Sea turtle nestling on Aruba in 1996*, a field report by Dana Kamphorst (1996)
9. *The Spanish Lagoon - Balashi Natural Monument*, Concept plan by Bart Hingst M.Sc., René G. Geelhoed M.Sc., Veron H. Haandrikman and André H. van Schaik M.Sc.
10. *Recreation and tourism in Aruba's natural areas*, by Bart Hingst M.Sc.
11. *Vegetation survey, flora inventory and herbarium building*, in cooperation with the CARMABI-institute, Curaçao (1997).
12. *Endangered tree species ecology and conservation*, a M.Sc. graduate project by Johan van der Perk (1997).
13. *Protected landscapes, buffer zones and rural development*, a M.Sc. graduate project by Joost J.C. van der Linden (1997).
14. *Erosion surveys, soil and water conservation*, a post-M.Sc. study by René G. Geelhoed M.Sc. (1997).

The project was officially completed in august 1997, but the research program will continue as a part of the new section of nature management of the Department of Agriculture.

PILOT PROJECTS

PARKE NATURAL CUNUCU ABAO

Mercedes Petrocchi, together with co-workers and the department of Public Works, is currently engaged in a park project in a residential area in Cunucu Abao. "A wooded area is being developed into a small park, with preservation of the existing flora as a starting point. Trails are laid out and play facilities for children are being installed as well as an artwork", Mercedes explains. The first stage of this project will finish in the end of 1997. In the future, more parks in residential and rural areas are planned. The Cunucu Abao project now shows us how to build and manage the natural areas in residential zones.

CUNUCU DI ALOE

Aloe fields are an important part of Aruba's history, considering aloe plantations once covered roughly one third of the island's area. Aruba was one of the world's main suppliers of aloin, a substance found in aloe sap and an essential natural ingredient in laxative preparations. An estimated one sixth of the aloe fields remain, but most of the fields have been overgrown by other plants in recent years, while their existence is threatened by land clearing for industrial and housing projects.

[picture 1: Men at work, constructing an interpretive sign at the restored aloe cunucu.]

[picture 1: Men at work, constructing an interpretive sign at the restored aloe cunucu.]

One aloe field near the Spanish Lagoon Wetland Preserve is currently being restored to its former glory by the Agriculture department, and is expected to be opened for the public in 1997. "An aloe field such as this, surrounded by a dry stone wall was once a typical sort of Aruban landscape", André van Schaik stresses. The original stone wall and the aloe oven are restored and drip barrows are placed in the field. The aloe field is being made more accessible for the public with pathways, and its vicinity to the wetland preserve and the ruins of the Balashi gold mill give added historical and environmental interest. Van Schaik: "This can be regarded as a pilot project to see how it appeals to the public. It shows a part of Aruban agricultural history. Aruba is famous for aloe and this is a good project to start off with".

Aloe vera research report

"Growing Aloe vera for gel production; report on four years of agricultural research on Aruba" by André H. van Schaik. Department of Agronomy, Wageningen Agricultural University, The Netherlands; Department of Agriculture and Fisheries, Aruba (1994). 58pp + annexes.

ISBN 90-6754-360-8.

Aloe vera L. (*Aloe barbadensis Mill.*) is an interesting plant: its chemical components have many different applications, and most of them are known and practiced for millennia. Since the introduction of the plant on Aruba, about 150 years ago, the succulent Aloe vera played an important role in the history and culture of this Caribbean island. It was grown for the production of the brownish-yellow leaf exudate. This product was exported and processed for pharmaceutical purposes. Almost one-third of Aruba's land surface was covered with aloe plantations, and several generations of Aruban were economically dependent on this culture. After World War II the cultivation of aloe on Aruba decreased, which was mainly due to the increase of job opportunities in the local oil industry. Also, the introduction of synthetic substitutes reduced the demand for aloe products. Since then, most of the Aruban aloe plantations have been abandoned and neglected, which induced degeneration of the aloe fields. The increasing urbanization and expansion of tourism and recreation have put pressure on the remaining aloe fields in the past decades.

About 20 years ago, great interest aroused for another product of the aloe plant: the aloe gel. This gel, a clear liquid substance from the central part of the leaf, is well known for its healing properties for surface wounds and burned skin, and has excellent qualities as an ingredient for skin and hair care products. In contract to the increase of aloe acreage in the United States, large scale cultures for aloe gel production have never taken place on Aruba.

[*picture 2: a typical aloe field with a dry stone boundary*]

The history of aloe culture on Aruba, the new use of aloe pulp and the increasing market for aloe gel gave rise to the commence of an agricultural research project on Aruba in 1989, which lasted until 1993. The research was conducted by the Department of Agriculture and Fisheries (Santa

Rosa), the Wageningen Agricultural University (the Netherlands) and the local cosmetic company Aruba Aloe Balm. The main objective of this program was to investigate the prospects for aloe gel production on Aruba. Emphasis was put on the growth and development of the plan under the specific conditions on Aruba, and on the cropping system for gel production. This information can initiate new agriculture activities on Aruba and diversify the economy of the island.

The report "Growing Aloe for Gel Production" by André H. van Schaik illustrates the most important research findings from this project. General characteristics of growth and development of Aloe vera are described, with special reference to the growth of aloe under the specific conditions of Aruba. Cultural practices to optimize plant growth and cultivation of aloe are mentioned, mainly based on the results from field experiments of the Aloe vera research project. Prospects and constrains of aloe culture on Aruba are also described.

To order this report (US$20), please contact André van Schaik, Department of Agriculture and Fisheries: postal address: Piedra Plat 114-a, Aruba. Tel: +297.858102, Fax: +297.855639, E-mail: dirlvvm@setarnet.aw

RECLAMATION OF ARABLE LAND FOR AGRICULTURAL PURPOSES

Many formerly cultivated area's were abandoned when the oil-industry developed in the third decade of this century. It then became easier for most people to earn an income year round with less effort than in agriculture and with increased certainty. Many people left the cunucu (countryside) for a more comfortable life in town with electricity and a running water system. Densely populated residential areas and the developing economy, together with the availability of motorcars were the cause for people to return to the countryside after the second world war had ended. From then on agriculture became an additional source of income for the people who once used to be completely dependent on the primary sector.

Many of them were the inheritors of property-land and others hired their land from the government. Family-pride and need of money caused them to work their fields which had laid fallow for years in a row. Shrubs and secondary plantgrowth had to be rooted up and lots of debris had to be removed before the land could be cultivated again. For most smallholders this was much of an effort, and adequate machinery was not available for hire on a commercial basis.

When the Department of Agriculture was installed, one of the first tasks was to buy tractors and shovels and make these available to the small farmers at an affordable rate. Reclaiming land for agriculture is still one of the tasks for the Section Rain-dependent Agriculture today.

Land preparation for rain-dependent crops, i.e. clearing, ploughing and/or disk-harrowing

Especially at the beginning of the rainy season our section gets many requests for preparation of the fields for the next crop. For this purpose we use several heavy tractors carrying disk-ploughs and disk-harrows.

To be certain that all arable land is prepared at the beginning of the rainy season we do recommend that all applications are made in time. By working complete communities at a time little time and energy is wasted with transport and planning.

Once the rains have started many a piece of land is inaccessible for heavy machinery due to the high contents of lutum which makes the soil weak and slippery under wet conditions.

PRECISION-DRILLING OF ROWCROPS

For graincrops such as Sorghum and maize seed-drilling equipment is available at special request. This machinery is especially useful when ploughing has been done along the contour-lines. When the seed is drilled in rows perpendicular at the direction of the slope the plants form after germination a natural barrier which prevents precipitation from running-off , thus storing the water where it belongs.

RETENTION OF PRECIPITATION IN RESERVOIRS (DAMS OR TANKI'S)

Rainfall on Aruba is poor (an average of 425 mm/year) and badly divided. Most precipitation occurs during the months of September through January. It pours down in a few heavy showers. This causes the majority to run off through the wadi's, causing damage and flooding in residential areas on its way to the sea. To prevent the damage and flooding as much as possible several large tanki's have been dug out in the recent past for storage of the majority of the run-off water. The tanki's of Tanki Leendert and Tanki Flip which both serve the purpose of protecting the lower parts of Oranjestad from flooding have a storage-capacity of 40.000 to 50.000 m^3 each with a depht of more than 10 meters.

Dams and tanki's (there are altogether 250 of these on Aruba, among which a 40 are public dams and tanki's) are mostly constructed and maintained under supervision of the Department of Agriculture. Although they serve the same purpose - to collect and store run-off precipitation - dams and tanki's are quite different constructions.

Dams are constructed mostly in wider parts of wadi's which have sufficient depth of soil to be scraped of and shoveled toward the lower end, where a dam of ample height is set up with it. On top of it a concrete runway is laid out for redundant water. The primary causes of dams are to retain water for agricultural purposes and to control erosion further down the wadi's.

Tanki's may or may not be constructed in wadi's. They are usually dug out in the lower parts of a catchment area. The outcoming material is usually transported to elsewhere and used for road-building and the like.

Both types of reservoirs need maintenance whenever possible, i.e. when the reservoirs are empty and dry. All debris is then removed and the clay and organic particles are used as enrichment of arable land or filling elsewhere.

To avoid the development of large amounts of mosquitos in the reservoirs an ample number of fish (Tilapia spp.) are released in the reservoirs as soon as there is sufficient water in it.

Dams and tanki's have most of the times a sub-optimal shape, due to boundaries of property-land and/or other restrictions, e.g. bedrock or important roads. Due to evaporation and high winds the daily loss of water measures up to 8 mm of surface water. An unsolved problem is how to reduce these enormous losses without spoiling the remaining water for general purposes.

Beside their functions mentioned above, the water reservoirs are very important as drinking places for wild fowl, goats, sheep, donkeys, iguanas etc.

DELIVERY OF WATER FROM THE RESERVOIRS TO SMALLHOLDERS/FARMERS

Santa Rosa offers the service to smallholders to transport water from the reservoirs (dams and tanki's) to their plantations as long as the conditions hereunder are met with; he/she should tend at least 400 m^2 of fruit and/or vegetable crops, watering these crops should be done with a drip-irrigation system, he/she should have a storage-capacity of at least one truckload of water (10 m^3).

The price of one truckload of water is at present AWG 25,-

EXTENSIONWORK

Extension-work is, as far as rain-dependent agriculture is concerned, part of our task. Free advice is given to anyone who is planning agricultural activities or wants to make improvements and/or investments. If need be, we can assist with feasibility-studies. For this purpose we keep a keen interest in new and/or better developments, methods and (seed)varieties by means of literature, demonstrations, (inter)national meetings etc.

EROSION-CONTROL

It is important that ploughing etc. is done along the contour (altitude) lines of the fields instead of along the slopes, primarily to restrict erosion, but to avoid the running-off of water as well. Planting or sowing crops in rows along the contours may help as well to prevent running-off of scarce water. In stony fields the rocks etc. should be reaped and laid in contour-ridges by hand. These ridges are commonly known as faha's. In the long run these may serve very well as erosion-control barriers.

ADVICE AND FEASIBILITY-ASSESSMENT OF PROJECTS

Since it became necessary to invest heavily in land and fencing, technology and equipment to make a project profitable, hardly anyone can do without a bankloan. Therefore a well designed businessplan is a prerequisite. Section Rain-dependent Agriculture may be helpful with the technical part of your businessplan , with basic figures, with applications for permits and/or dispensations or with a second opinion. For the smallholder we can do a free feasibility-assessment or we might help with alternatives.

CONSTRUCTIONS

Constructions. Section Rain-dependent Agriculture is charged with constructions in general, both on behalf of the Dept. of Agriculture itself and on behalf of third parties, such as fisherman's-piers and fisherman's shelters, with the exception of immobilaria.

CITES ADVISORY WORK

CITES-advisory work. In accordance with the 'Landsverordening van 13 februari 1995 (AB-1995 no.2)' and 'Landsbesluit ontheffing beschermde niet-inheemse flora en fauna van 22 december 1995, (AB 1996 no.1)' the Dept. of Agriculture advises the Minister of Public Health concerning exempts for im/export and trade of endangered plant-species. Applications for such exempts should be made at the Section of Rain-dependent Agriculture at least two weeks before the planned im- or (re)export.

PHYTO-SANITARY SERVICE (PLANT-QUARANTAINE SERVICE)

Presently the Dept. of Agriculture is preparing the Plant-Quarantaine Service of Aruba. In cooperation with the Plantenziektenkundige Dienst of the Netherlands jurisdiction is being stated and training of plant-quarantaine inspectors is on its way. Installment of this new service is planned for early in 1998. In the future this new service will be detached from the section of Rain-dependent Agriculture.

WELL SURVEYING

At present no new wells are drilled in Aruba for agricultural purposes as the subterranean water in general is much too high in soluble salts for plants or for animal drinking water. Most of the wells in existence are no longer in use, and to avoid accidents with animals or humans sliding in, many of the open wells are being filled up or covered with a concrete lid. Only a few wells may still produce water of an acceptable quality. If the total of soluble salts is below 1500 ppm it can be used for all agricultural applications without restriction. All water containing more than 5000 ppm is useless for agricultural purposes. In case of doubt samples can be tested in our laboratory.

FISHERIES

Fisheries is a small but very dynamic section at the Department of Agriculture, Husbandry and Fisheries. It is a section that exceeds the limitations of its name and manpower capacity. Besides the traditional tasks of collecting various fisheries statistics, coordinating activities around fisheries centers and doing fisheries research, the fisheries section is also very active in various aspects of preserving the well being of the Aruban marine environment.

The fisheries section has information regarding various aspects of fisheries of Aruba. Estimates of catch rates, average catches per trip, seasonal patterns of oceanographic conditions and fish migrations are some of the data available from this section. Reports from a joint research project of FAO/UNDP are also available.

One of the conclusions from this research project, however, was that fisheries of Aruba and the fisheries resources are best served by keeping the fisheries at artisanal levels and not increase to commercial levels. This caused a shift in focus for the section. Its main objective is now to do more research about the marine environment and seek better ways to protect it.

Nowadays the fisheries sections conducts various research projects such as mapping the underwater world around Aruba. A survey of the south coast has been completed and research on the north west side is now underway. Another project the fisheries section is involved in, is the helping of the Aruba Watersports Association setting up mooring buoys, and disseminating information about the harmful effects of anchoring on reefs. Additionally, the section is involved in a continuing public awareness campaign with the Aruba Tourism Authority, called the **Aruba Reef Care Project** which consists of annual reef clean-up activities and marine life symposia. One of the medium term projects is to set up a marine reserve and management area for Aruba.

MARINE RESERVE

The main priority in setting up a marine reserve and management area is to generate public awareness regarding the fragility of the marine environment as an ecosystem, especially of the coral reefs and sea grass beds. This heightened awareness can only be reached by educating the general public. Everybody must realize the importance of this environment and related ecosystems in regard to the island economy and more importantly as a national heritage. It must become recognized by everyone that a well protected and managed marine reserve will benefit Aruba and its people in the long run.

"The best protection is to set up a marine nature reserve with an as far reaching legislation as possible for Aruba. The opportunity for this department to spearhead the marine reserve project and formalize on proposals regarding similar projects from the 70's is a great challenge", says an enthusiastic Peter-John Jonkers, the newest member of the fisheries section, who will be in charge of compiling a proposal for a marine reserve and management area.

Proving that conservation works for development and not against it is a second major challenge. It's the goal of this section and cooperating parties to put Aruba's Marine Nature Reserve right up there besides other successful marine reserves in the Caribbean.

The vision of this section is to develop into an independent marine research institute that manages marine reserve areas, coordinates research, and disseminates public education and awareness about the marine environment and the fisheries of Aruba. The institute would benefit the island by stimulating economic activities that are in harmony with the marine environment by means of Marine Protected Areas. The idea is to work closely with the tourism sector and have an integral approach for the best use of the marine resources of Aruba as a goal. To reach this goal the fisheries section will:

1. continue its close collaboration with the fishermen, aiding them as much as possible by means of information, maintenance of various fisheries centers, and regulations to preserve the resources;
2. continue research on all aspects of the marine environment of Aruba, including inventarization, surveys, monitoring, etc;

3. inform the public as much as possible, in cooperation with NGO's and other governmental departments through public awareness campaigns, brochures, exhibitions, symposia, etc;
4. take the necessary steps for the implementation of marine reserve and management. This includes doing the necessary research, contacting usergroups and international agencies for assistance, presenting proposals for management, legislation and maintenance of the marine reserves & management areas.

GOAT AND SHEEPS

The first goats and sheeps where brought to the island in 15th century by the Spaniards. They were left to roam the island and were slaughtered and salted to provide the many ships with food for their crew. Later on the Dutch introduced a more intensive husbandry system. Since than the local people kept on raising goat and sheep for their own consumption and to sell or exchange with neighbors and friends.

A goat or a sheep was slaughtered at very special events like weddings, Christenings and Holy Communions. The time of year during which most goat and sheep are slaughtered is at Christmas and New Year. The sheep and the goat are locally called 'Bestia Chikito', which means small animal. The 'Sopi di Bestia Chikito'(chevron or mutton soup) has very much become part of our tradition.

Even tough chevron and mutton forms part of the local menu, the amount of animals kept is very much reduced since the beginning of the nineteen hundreds.It was in the nineteen seventies that more attention was given to animal husbandry of setting up a more functional animal husbandry section. This section started to work on the main priority which is to improve the sheep and goat husbandry by means of upgrading the local animals. These have become, because of a very intensive inbreeding, a small animal with an adult carcass weight of 10 pounds.

UPGRADING OF LOCAL ANIMALS

To upgrade the local animals, full breed animals had to be imported from abroad. In 1977 the Barbados Black Belly sheep was imported from Barbados. Some of the ewes were sold to farmers and the rams were kept on the premises and used to mate local animals. At first not one of the farmers liked the idea of crossbreeding, but as the results were seen, the Black Belly was accepted. The crossbreeds were bigger animals.

That same year two Toggenburg bucks were imported from Holland and these were also used for crossbreeding. The farmers could bring their animals to the Department to be mated at a minimum feed cost. There is no breeding season, the animals breed all year round.

In 1980 four milk type breeds of goat were imported from the U.S.A., which are the Saanen, the Toggenburg, the Anglo Nubian and the French Alpine. These breeds not only had influence on the growth but naturally also on the milk production. Although most farmers were in meat production, these new breeds were readily accepted. A significant increase of 30 pounds in carcass weight, of 4 month old animals, was noticed after 8 years.

South African Boer

South African Boer

Due to an increase in the demand for chevron and mutton, meat type breeds like the Suffolk sheep and later on the South African Boer goat were imported.

Dorper

Dorper

The Suffolk did well, but because of the wool their acceptance did not last long. The Boer was readily accepted. We are still compiling data of this breed and its crossings with the milk breeds and the local animals.

We are in the event of ordering a new meat type Sheep, The Dorper (hair), to replace the Suffolk.

Services available to the farmers

- We sell animal feed at cost price (hay, concentrates and artificail milk). Due to the lack of rain during most of the year, there is almost no fodder.
- We sell pure bred animals. Prices are subsidized by the Government.
- We offer pure bred males for mating.
- We do spaying, hoof-trimming, shearing, dehorning and docking at no or very low cost.
- We offer extension services.
- We are in the process of establishing a market for goat milk and are currently selling goatmilk to the public.

Feel free to contact us for any information you might want about the different sections of our department.

PIG BREEDING

s to the exact date pigs were first introduced onto this island there still exist uncertainty. According to Dr. Jan Hartog, prominent historian, pigs, along with other types of livestock, were first introduced here between 1500 and 1636 by the Spanish conquistadores. The pig was of the scavenger type and in the subsequent years evolved into a very hardy and highly adapted animal to local conditions. It thrived in the wild, surviving on a diet of roots and tubers, supplemented with kitchen waste and any leftovers from the agricultural fields. Meat obtained from the slaughtered animals was either sold for some extra income or preserved in brine to be eaten later with beans. This dish still remains very popular today. Up to this day there still are wild pigs (though few in number) roaming certain parts of the island.

PIG PRODUCTION IS GETTING ORGANIZED

Due to population rise and an ever increasing demand for fresh pork, the government started to import improved breeds since the fifties. In the late seventies a more coherent strategy was put into effect, combining a more professional approach on behalf of the department of agriculture and interested pigfarmers. The ultimate goal of setting up a local meat processing plant was then also achieved. After some initial drawbacks, the local meat factory managed to break even, but after a major economic crisis affected the island severely in 1985, the government decided to shut it down. The private company which took over didn't pay the farmer a favorable price (i. e. a price lower than carcass costprice), therefor most of the pigfarmers had to close down their fattening units and a new low point was reached in local pigproduction.

DEVELOPMENTS IN THE NINETIES

In the nineties we see the rise of the independent pigfarmer(market-wise) due a booming economy and tourist trade. Several investors who tried to set up large pig projects to substitute the import of pork, coulnd't start because studies always show negative rates of return due to high operational costs and low product price.

The small farmer is very successful these days since he does get a fair price in a number of market outlets due a flourishing economy.

THE ROLE OF THE PIG HUSBANDRY SECTION

Our aim is to encourage pig production. To accomplish such we offer a number of services to the interested, pigfarmer or not. To the pigfarmer we offer good quality fatteners at a reasonable price accompanied with sound management advice concerning housing, feeding and hygiene.

We import our breeding stock from reputable breeders from the U. S. at a relatively young age to allow for acclimatization. We work with the white mother breed cross (Landrace*Yorkshire) for the female line, bred to the Duroc male to produce the commercial female line, which in turn is bred to Hampshire males to produce fatteners. We have a rather small sow herd from which we accumulate all production data, most common occurring problems and eventual solutions. The demand for fattener is so large that not many studies were made concerning performance traits.

STRATEGIC & PRACTICAL INFORMATION FOR CONDUCTING BUSINESS

INVESTMENT AND BUSINESS CLIMATE

Aruba is located about twenty miles off the northen coast of Venezuela. Aruba is approximately 19.2 miles long and 4 miles across, has a population of nearly 90.000 people and has a tropical climate with an average daily temperature of 27 degree Celsius with a cooling northern trade winds.

On January 1st 1986 Aruba became a separate entity within the Kingdom of the Netherlands. With Aruba s new status, the Kingdom of the Netherlands has three separate components: The Netherlands, The Dutch Caribbeanand Aruba. The Government of the Netherlands is responsible for the defense and foreign affairs of the Kingdom.

Based principally on a Western system of parliamentary democracy, Aruba is governed by a single house of parliament and the Council of Ministers, who are chosen by the elected parliament members. Aruba has also a Governor, appointed by her Majesty the Queen of the Netherlands, which is an independent body representing the Queen. There is a judicial system, with the highest court located in the Hague, Netherlands. The currency is the Aruban Florin, which is pegged to the United States dollar.

TOURISM

Tourism, which contributes nearly 38% of the GDP, 70% of total experts and 35 % of employment is the main economic activity in Aruba. Our tourism industry has shown impressive results as compared to other destinations in the Caribbean. The boom in our tourism industry is the result of a great effort by the Government in close cooperation with the private sector and with the support of the Aruban people. Aruba offers its white sand beaches, comfortable shopping malls, nightlives, a great hospitality of the Aruban citizens, and safety.

The positive developments in our tourism industry has been reflected in a dramatic increase in the number of tourists from higher income levels, in the number of repeat visitors as well as the cruise-tourism.

ECONOMIC DIVERSIFICATION

One of the main objectives of our economic policy is to further diversify the Aruban economy. In this context, the Government is actively promoting telecommunications, the development of our financial service industry, as well as the freezone of Aruba. With regard to the freezone the Aruban Government supports transshipment activities, light industries and high-tech industries. Another aspect of the economic diversification is the development of the primary sector of Aruba. A particularly positive aspect of the Aruban economy is that inflation remains under control at a level consistent with reasonable price stability. The latest official data indicating an average increase in consumer price inflation (CPI) of only 3.1% in 1997.

ENVIRONMENT

One of the major goals of the Government is to achieve a balance between the economic development on one hand and the protection and conservation of our natural environment on the other hand. Therefore, a project called "Parke Nacional Arikok" is being implemented. The essence of this project is that a third part of Aruba has been designated as protected natural area. This project has three targets: first to preserve our natural resources for the generations to come, second to awaken national consciousness of the importance of our natural environment and finally to stimulate eco-tourism in Aruba.

REGIONAL DEVELOPMENT

In 1994 the Government realized that the economic development in Aruba was largely concentrated in the western part of the island. In order to promote the economic development in the eastern part of Aruba, the Government started a project called "The Sasaki Development Plan". This Development Plan is an equitable growth model developed for the region of San Nicolas. It includes an ambitious investment program related mainly to infrastructure, road and housing projects. The investment needed to develop the eastern areas will be financed by private and Government funds.

ECONOMIC STABILITY

The Government has succeeded in maintaining economic growth of 5% annually, in order to prevent an overheated economy. The Government has managed to reduce the inflation in Aruba to approximately 3% annually. The level of foreign exchange reserves comply with the international requirements of three (3) months import coverage. This guarantees the stability of the local currency, the Aruban Florin is pegged to the US dollar at an exchange rate of 1.75 to one. In addition, unemployment is practically non-existent. The overall economy is supported by a good road infrastructure, excellent harbor facilities for transshipment as well as for cruise-tourism. At the moment the Government is expanding the airport to make Aruba a hub for Latin America and by next year we will have a sublime Information Technology infrastructure to offer. The outlook for the future is favorable.

After double digit growth rates during the late 1980s, the Aruban economy has settled to a more moderate pace in the 1990s. Real Gross Domestic Product grew with approximately 4.0%, the nominal GDP reached an estimated Af 2,631.1 million and the GDP per capita approximately Af 29,325 ($ 16,964), while the economy was at its full employment level in 1996. Private investment was the major engine of the rapid growth of the Aruban economy.

In order to maximize economic opportunities in the second half of the 1990s, the Government policy is primary focused on international developments. As a result, the most dynamic sectors of the economy are tourism, oil refining and transshipment, international trade and finance.

In Aruba, there is a well established legislation in force which has created an investment friendly environment through a combination of tax policies and low tariffs on imported capital goods. Attractive incentives exist with respect to manufacturing industries, free zone activities and offshore companies.

Promoting both productivity and new capital intensive investments directed towards export coupled with limited labor force requirements, that can be met locally by technically highly skilled manpower are the major thrusts of Government policy. In essence the economic policy aims to create high-level employment, transfer technology, control inflation, strengthen Aruba's financial and monetary foundation, increase productivity, distribute income equitably and substantially improve social conditions.

Moreover, large public investments are continuously taking place in order to maintain the physical infrastructure. The water and power plant has been expanded, while the telecommunication and airport facilities are being upgraded to ensure the desired levels of service and efficiency.

Finally, we look forward to your decision to become a part of our business community.

Minister of Economic Affairs, Tourism
Social Affairs, and Culture
Dr. Lili Beke-Martinez

ARUBA ECONOMIC CONDITIONS

POPULATION

Aruba's population of about 87,970 people is made up of a broad international mixture of well-educated people with a pleasant nature and a zest to work. Arubans are descendants of the Arawak Indians, the Spanish and the Dutch settlers. There are over 40 nationalities living in friendship and harmony on the island. Arubans are known for their warmth and friendly hospitality.

per year-end	**1992**	**1993**	**1994**	**1995**	**1996**
Total	71,304	77,973	80,333	83,651	87,971
Male	35,232	38,761	39,977	41,591	43,682
Female	36,072	39,212	40,356	42,060	44,289

Source: Central Bureau of Statistics (CBS)

The density of population amounts to 456 persons per square km or 1,142 persons per square mile. The birth rate per thousand is 16.5 while the death rate is 5.3 per thousand. The infant mortality rate per thousand is 3.0 (1994).

GROSS DOMESTIC PRODUCT (GDP)

	1992	**1993**	**1994**	**1995**	**1996**
Nominal GDP (Af million)	**1,871**	**2,002**	**2,249**	**2,453**	**2,631.1**

Nominal growth (%)	**9.8**	**7.0**	**12.3**	**9.1**	**7.3**
Real growth (%)	**5.8**	**1.6**	**5.9**	**5.7**	**4.0**
GDP per capita (Af)	**26,240**	**25,676**	**27,996**	**29,324**	**29,910**
GDP per capita (US$)	**14,659**	**14,344**	**15,640**	**16,382**	**16,708**

Source: DEACI Estimates

INFLATION

The rate of inflation moved more or less parallel to that of the major trading partner, the United States.

The height of the rate of inflation is partially attributable to domestic developments. The rapid economic expansion during the past eight years has resulted in supply-side constraints, particularly in the labor and housing markets, which pushed up price levels.

CONSUMER PRICE INDEX

per year-end	**1992**	**1993**	***1994**	**1995**	**1996**
CPI	137.4	146.2	100.8	103.9	107.1
Yearly change (%)	4.5	6.4	4.7	3.1	3.1

Source: Central Bureau of Statistics (CBS)

- The basis December 1984= 100 has been shifted to August 1994= 100

LABOR

LABOR MARKET

The continued growth of the economy demanded for the import of foreign laborers. This together with a higher participation of the local population, especially of females, contributed to a remarkable increase of the labor force in comparison to 1992.

per year-end	1992	1993	1994	1995	1996
Population	71,304	77,973	80,333	83,651	,
Labor Force	33,941	36,725	39,685	41,575	,
Employment	33,735	36,471	38,954	39,834	,
Unemployment	206	254	196	266	
Unemployment (%)	0.6	0.7	0.5	0.7	0.
Participation rate(%)	47.6	47.1	49.4	49.7	49.

Source: Department of Labor Estimates

MINIMUM WAGES

Statutory minimum wages are in force for workers above the age of 18 and as of January 1, 1997 the following minimum wages apply to:

- business : Af 1,060.20 (US$ 592.30);
- household personnel: Af 494.65 (US$ 276.35).

AVERAGE MONTHLY SALARIES

per year-end (Af)	1991	1992
1. Agriculture and Fishery	1,315	1,395
2. Mining and Quarrying	1,319	1,390
3. Manufacturing, excl. Oil refining	1,380	1,450
4. Utilities	1,850	1,935
5. Construction	2,560	2,730
6. Trade, Hotels and Restaurants	1,420	1,510

7. Transport, Distribution and Communications	2,310	2,430
8. Finance, Insurance and Real Estate	1,890	2,005
9. Community, Social and Personal Services	2,285	2,410

Source: Department of Labor

Excl. management and highly qualified personnel and public employees.

WORKING HOURS

A maximum of 8 2 hours daily for a 5 days' working week, not exceeding 42 2 hours is allowed, or a maximum of 8 hours daily not exceeding 45 hours for a 6 days' working week, except for enterprises such as hotels, casinos, restaurants and oil refining, for which shift work is required and a maximum of 48 hours per week is allowed.

HOLIDAYS WITH PAY

Each employee is entitled to a paid holiday of at least fifteen working days per year. Eleven days of the year are public holidays.

Overtime work per hour is compensated as follows:

- Monday through Saturday: + 50%;
- Sunday : + 100%.

Work on a public holiday is compensated 100% above the normal hourly wage.

Shift work is compensated 15% above the normal hourly wage, when mutually agreed upon or when a collective labor agreement is in force.

CESSANTIA (SEVERANCE PAY)

The employee whose employment has been terminated for reasons other than his fault is entitled to a layoff compensation, which is calculated as follows:

- - One (1) week pay per each year between 1 and 10 years of service;
- - One-and-a-quarter (1 1/4) week pay per each year between 11 and 20 years of service;
- - Two (2) weeks pay for each year of service above 20 years.

In virtue of this ordinance the employer is obliged to contribute with a premium of Af 40 per year per employee to the Cessantia Fund.

For more information, apply to:

Directie Arbeid
L.G. Smith Boulevard 15, Oranjestad
Phone: 837646
Fax : 837422

SOCIAL SECURITY

Both employer and employee contribute to a social security plan which provides the following coverage: health, accident, old age and widow and orphans benefits. The insurer is the **Social Insurance Bank**.

The social charges represent between 22.0% and 26.5% of the base salary, of which 4.0 percentage points are paid by the employee.

HEALTH INSURANCE

Each employee earning up to a yearly maximum of Af 47,970 (as per Jan. 1, 1997) must be insured by his employer. The health insurance includes coverage for medical care, specialists, medicines, hospital care and wage compensation. The premium for this insurance is 8% of the employee's salary and is paid fully by the employer.

ACCIDENT INSURANCE

Regardless of his income each employee must be insured by the employer for on-the-job accidents. The premium is not standard, but differs from industry to industry. Employers pay the premium on a basis of 0.5% to 5.0% calculated on the employee's salary up to a maximum yearly income of Af 47,970.

Some of the prevailing premiums according to industry are:

Stevedoring...........5.00%	Water sport............1.75%
Airlines..................4.25%	Hotel......................1.25%
Construction..........3.00%	Agencies.................1.00%
Sheet metal...........2.25%	Administration.........0.50%

OLD AGE AND WIDOW/ORPHANS INSURANCE

At the age of 60, every citizen is entitled to an old age pension.

The premium for the old age pension and widow and orphans pension is 13.5% of the annual income, of which the employee contributes with 4.0% and the employer with 9.5%. In case of a self-employed the premium is 13.5%. The maximum yearly premium amounts to Af 6,476.

The monthly premium has to be transferred by the employer before the 15th of the following month to the Tax Collector's Office.

For additional information, apply to:

Sociale Verzekeringsbank
L.G. Smith Boulevard z/n
Phone: 872785
Fax : 875532

EXPORT-IMPORT & TRADE

FOREIGN TRADE

The trade policy of Aruba is liberal. The Government encourages the free enterprise principle and therefore it takes no part in active business activities beyond public utilities.

In order to establish a business in Aruba a license is needed. Although there are no limitations on foreign ownership of a business, the Government policy is based on the right to reserve the ownership of businesses, in which no large investment is involved and no specific know-how is required, to local citizens.

With the exception of aspects related to public health and safety, imports are not subject to restrictions. There are no restrictions with regard to exports either.

The major trading partners are the USA, the Netherlands, Venezuela, Japan and Colombia.

PREFERENTIAL TARIFF TREATMENT

Aruba is a beneficiary country of the following trade regulations.

The **"Generalized System of Preferences"** (GSP) involves the granting of preferential tariffs for exports of primary semi-manufactured and manufactured goods of developing countries to developed nations on a non-reciprocal base. The developed countries that agreed in 1964 to provide preferential treatment to developing countries subsequently have introduced their own GSP schemes which provide either fully free entry or entry at reduced import duty rates.

NATIONS OFFERING PREFERENTIAL TARIFF TREATMENT TO ARUBA:

- USA;
- European Union (EU);
- Australia · Canada · Japan · New Zealand · Norway · Sweden

European Union

Being part of the Kingdom of the Netherlands, Aruba has been qualified as an OCT (Overseas Country and Territory) by the European Union since 1964. This qualification, laid down in the Council Decision, means that products originating in Aruba can be exported free of any import duties and quota to the common market.

Goods are considered to have originated in Aruba if they are either wholly obtained or substantially transformed from imported materials and components.

The preferential export possibilities to the European Union market are more comprehensive for Aruba as an OCT than as a beneficiary developing country in the framework of GSP.

TRANSSHIPMENT OF FOREIGN GOODS

In addition, goods originating in third countries and circulating in the domestic market, have duty-free access into the European Union market as well, provided that:

- the import duties paid in Aruba are at least equal to those applicable, according to the Common Custom Tariffs, for the same products in the European Union;
- the products are not subject to any measure in the European Union such as anti-dumping, agricultural policy restraints and quotas;
- the goods have not undergone any operations in Aruba.

DEROGATION FROM THE RULES OF ORIGIN

The Council Decision includes provisions which allow temporary derogation from the rules of origin for the following reasons:

- the development of existing industries;
- the creation of new industries.

The request for derogation has to be made by the concerned authorities of the country or territory or by the concerned Member country.

DEROGATION FROM THE DIRECT SHIPMENT RULE

In 1986 the European Commission adopted a derogation from the direct shipment rule of the GSP scheme in favor of Aruba.

This derogation allows products originating in any GSP eligible country to be transshipped through Aruba without losing their originating status, provided that:

- the goods have remained under the supervision of the customs authorities of Aruba;
- they have not undergone any operations, other than simple operations, such as sorting, changes of packing, affixing of marks, labels or other distinguishing signs on products or their packing;
- no product has been added in the course of these simple operations, except for products needed for the packing of the goods and the identification of the packages.

European Union members include:

Austria, Belgium, Denmark, Finland, France, Germany, Greece, Ireland, Italy, Luxembourg, Portugal, Spain, Sweden, The Netherlands, and United Kingdom.

THE CARIBBEAN BASIN INITIATIVE

The Caribbean Basin Economic Recovery Act of 1983, which is commonly referred to as the **Caribbean Basin Initiative (CBI)**, provides trade and tax measures to promote economic revitalization through expansion of the private sector opportunities in the Caribbean Basin region. Aruba has been designated a beneficiary country of the CBI in 1986.

The centerpiece of this program is the duty free entry into the USA for a wide range of products manufactured in CBI beneficiary countries. To be eligible for duty-free treatment, an article must be grown or manufactured in one or more CBI beneficiary countries and imported directly from a CBI country into the US customs territory. Furthermore, at least 35 percent of the article's customs value must be attributable to direct costs of processing in one or more beneficiary countries. US origin materials may account for 15 percentage points of the required 35%, while materials from Puerto Rico and from the US Virgin Islands may count toward the full 35 percent. If the article contains materials originating in a non-CBI country, the final good must be an article of commerce that is "new and different" from any foreign materials used in its manufacture. Achieving this transformation must entail a significant effort. This is called the "substantial transformation" requirement and is enforced by the US Customs Service.

Articles, not eligible for duty free treatment are textiles and apparel which are subject to textile agreement, canned tuna, petroleum products, footwear, certain leather, rubber and plastic gloves, luggage, handbags and flat goods, and certain leather wearing apparel.

The Customs and Trade Act of 1990, signed into law in August 1990, includes the Caribbean Basin Economic Recovery Expansion Act of 1990 or known as **CBI-II**. The most important provision of CBI-II is the permanent extension of the original CBI legislation passed in 1983.

The bill does not greatly expand the list of products eligible for duty-free treatment, however, it contains other benefits and provisions, such as the granting of duty-free treatment and quota exemption for imported articles, other than textile and apparel, and petroleum products, that are assembled or processed in whole of US fabricated components or US-origin materials or ingredients, other than water, in a CBI-beneficiary country.

An important aspect of this provision is that it is applicable to merchandise that historically has been excluded from CBI coverage. Products such as footwear, handbags, and luggage produced from US materials and components can now be manufactured under this provision and returned to the United States free of duty.

FREE ZONE

The free zone offers facilities to commercial and industrial enterprises in order to stimulate further development of international trade. In addition, certain services can be rendered in or from the free zone, i.e. maintenance and reparations of foreign goods.

The free zones are situated in the vicinity of the harbor of Oranjestad and Barcadera.

Only a limited liability company, founded under Aruban law and exclusively for free zone operations, is admitted to conduct a business in the free zone. Admittance to the free zone is granted if it is expected that the operation will contribute to the further development of Aruba into an international distribution and production center, or as an international center for services.

Profits of free zone enterprises earned from exports are taxed at 2%. Goods, imported into the free zone for re-export are completely free of duty. Only a minimum of administrative formalities is required since the customs system has been simplified.

Sales to the local market are allowed only with permission of the Minister of Economic Affairs and may not comprise more than 25% of total annual sales. Normal excise and import duties are applied to goods imported from the free zone into the domestic market, while profits earned from these sales are subject to the normal tax rate, according to the Profit Tax Ordinance.

The free zone activities have had a positive impact on the development of international trade, as shown in the table below.

IMPORTS AND EXPORTS TO AND FROM THE FREE ZONES

Year	Imports	Exports	Local Sales	Turnover
1992	616.7	562.8	23.4	586.2
1993	412.1	462.4	25.7	488.1
1994	499.0	482.7	14.1	496.8
1995	621.4	753.8	12.4	766.2
1996	.	.	.	.

Source: DEACI
Figures are in millions of Af

RENTAL OF SITES AND BUILDINGS IN THE FREE ZONE.

Business space can be rented in units of "300 m^2 at a yearly rental cost of Af 90 per m^2 in the free zone of Bushiri.

Parcels to accommodate the construction of own facilities are available on a long lease term, at a yearly lease of Af 3.00 per m^2 in the free zone of Barcadera.

For more information, please contact:

Free Zone Aruba (FZA) N.V.
Schotlandstraat 49

Phone: 820909
Fax : 820888

E-mail: fzanv@setarnet.aw

FINANCIAL SERVICES SECTOR

The Profit Tax Ordinance contains favorable provisions granting thereby special tax rates to investment companies.

With these provisions the Government aims at developing Aruba into an international financial services center.

Offshore companies, based on the nonresident status of their shareholders, are exempted from foreign exchange control.

OFFSHORE TRADING COMPANIES

For offshore trading companies the Profit Tax Ordinance creates the possibility of having offices of a company incorporated in Aruba to organize, invoice and administer the company's foreign transactions. If the proceeds of these companies are generated from operations taken place outside Aruba, the Inspector of Taxes may provide tax rulings leading to a profit tax rate of 2.4% for profits until Af 100,000 and 3.0% for profits exceeding that amount.

OFFSHORE BANKING COMPANIES

An offshore bank is a foreign banking institution incorporated in Aruba exclusively for offshore transactions. These companies are licensed by and under supervision of the Central Bank to conduct international banking transactions with customers who are non-residents of Aruba and with offshore companies domiciled in Aruba as well. Profits of offshore banking companies including profits from investment and interest income operations, according to the Profit Tax Ordinance will be taxed at 2.4% and 3%. Other foreign source income is taxed at the rates of 24% and 30%, unless the Inspector of Taxes rules that the lower tax rates are applicable.

INVESTMENT AND HOLDING COMPANIES

According to Article 14 of the Profit Tax Ordinance an investment company is defined as an Aruban based company, of which the objective is primarily to invest its assets in "securities", such as shares and other certificates of participation, bonds or other interest bearing claims under whatever name and form.

The term "securities" does neither include bills of exchange, promissory notes, acceptances and other claims on debts, originating from commercial or credit transactions within Aruba, nor claims on debts which are secured by mortgage rights to real property located or established in Aruba.

The profits of the Aruban based company are taxed according to a special regime, which compared with the one applied to ordinary business companies is advantageous.

The net proceeds from such securities, except the benefits resulting from an increase in value or the alienation of assets, are taxed at 1/10 of the prevailing guaranteed rates of 24 and 30%.

The benefits resulting from an increase in value or alienation of assets are exempted from taxation.

FINANCE COMPANIES

Finance companies are taxed in the same manner as investment companies. However, interest paid by a finance company will be deductible from the taxable profits under the provisions of Article 14, if the interest is paid to a bank or similar finance company.

Interest paid to third parties can also be deducted if it is established that this is paid conform the arms-length-principles. In such cases it is advisable to obtain a ruling from the Inspector of Taxes.

ROYALTY COMPANIES

The Profit Tax Ordinance defines a royalty company as a company based in Aruba, of which the objective is primarily to derive:

- income from the alienation of licensing of copyrights, patent rights, designs, secret processes or formulas, trademarks and analogous property;
- income from royalties, including rental income from motion pictures and from the use of industrial, commercial or scientific equipment, as well as from the operation of mines and quarries, any other natural resources and from other real estate properties;
- considerations paid for technical assistance outside Aruba.

The net proceeds of royalty companies, as far as they are derived from operations outside Aruba and not resulting from a change in value or the alienation of the corresponding assets, are subject to 1/10 of the prevailing guaranteed tax rates of 24 and 30%.

Capital gains resulting from a change in value or alienation of the assets are exempted from taxation.

SHIPPING AND AVIATION COMPANIES

The Profit Tax Ordinance contains special provisions for the taxation of shipping and aviation companies aiming thereby to promote the establishment of these companies by offering an attractive fiscal regime.

Eligible companies will be taxed for profits not exceeding Af 100,000:

- 80% of the profits at a rate of 2.76%, and
- the remaining 20% at a full tariff of 27.6%.

The effective profit tax rate averages 7.73%.

Profits exceeding Af 100,000:

- 80% of the profits at a rate of 3.45%, and
- the remaining 20% at a full tariff of 34.5%.

The effective profit tax rate averages 9.66%.

In addition, there are provisions for:

- Accelerated depreciation of 1/3 of the cost of acquisition;
- Investment allowance of 8% of the amount invested, which may be deducted from the taxable profits of the year of investment and of the subsequent year;
- Survey and replacement reserve;
- Compensation of losses which can be carried forward for six years instead of five years, while in addition losses incurred during the first six years can be carried forward indefinitely.

ARUBAANSE VRIJGESTELDE VENNOOTSCHAP (A.V.V.) OR ARUBA EXEMPT COMPANY (A.E.C.)

In addition to the existing possibilities for foreign investors to use the Limited Liability Company ("Naamloze Vennootschap" or- abbreviated "N.V.") as an offshore company, a new legal entity with a very flexible structure has been introduced in 1988. This new legal entity is called "Aruba Vrijgestelde Vennootschap" (A.V.V.) - translated into English "Aruba Exempt Company" (A.E.C.).

There are many similarities between the offshore N.V. and the A.E.C., but also some fundamental differences. In general, it can be said that the A.E.C. has a more flexible corporate structure than the N.V.

The A.E.C. can be used as - for example - an investment, a finance, a trading or a holding company and is at the same time meant to be a vehicle to further develop the financial services sector of Aruba.

The most outstanding features of the A.E.C. are:

Flexible structure.

- establishment by one (legal or moral) person;
- annual accounts are not mandatory;
- shares may be issued at par value or without previously fixed nominal value;
- minimum authorized capital amounts to Af 10,000 of which at least one voting share must at all times be issued to a third party;
- incorporator(s) need(s) not to participate in the issued share capital;
- shareholders' meetings may be held in places other than Aruba, provided that those places are stated in the articles of incorporation;
- minutes of shareholders' meetings are not mandatory;
- easy liquidation procedure;
- files and records may be held anywhere in the world;
- no business and director's licenses are required.

Financial liabilities.

- the A.E.C. is not subject to Aruban Profit Tax;
- the annual government fee amounts to Af 500;
- minimum annual registration fee payable to the Chamber of Commerce is Af 60.

Conditions for operating an A.E.C.:

- the A.E.C. may only exercise its activities outside Aruba, except for those activities which are necessary in relation with the maintenance of its office in Aruba;
- the A.E.C. cannot conduct any banking or life insurance activities or other activities which would qualify the A.E.C. as a credit institution or credit association;
- the A.E.C. does not qualify for the advantages of the existing tax treaty between The Netherlands and Aruba;
- the A.E.C. should have at all times a legal representative in Aruba, which:
  - must be an onshore N.V. incorporated according to Aruban law;
  - and must have as its object clause, among others, to act as legal representative of A.E.C.s.

Differences between Offshore N.V. and A.E.C:

The main differences between the Offshore N.V. (the low tax company) and the A.E.C. (the zero tax company) are:

	A.E.C.	Offshore N.V.
• annual accounts	optional	yes
• shareholders' meetings in Aruba	optional	yes
• Subject to Aruba Profit Tax	no	2.4 and 3.0%
• annual Government Fee	US$285	$0.00
• minutes of meetings	optional	yes
• shares without previously fixed nominal value	optional	no
• banking or life insurance activities	no	yes
• Government retribution at incorporation and for amendments of articles of incorporation	no	US$ 170

For more information, please contact:

The High Commissioner of the Aruba Financial Center
Schotlandstraat 49
Phone: 297 834611
Fax : 297 8834665

INTELLECTUAL PROPERTY

Aruba is a party to the Paris Union (1883) for the Protection of Industrial Property, to other Unions related to patents, trademarks and industrial designs, and is also a party to the Bern Convention (1886) for the Protection of Literary and Artistic Works.

The tasks in these fields are entrusted to a specialized Government agency: the Bureau of Intellectual Property.

PATENTS

Aruba has its own Patent Act and grants patents for the Aruban jurisdiction via the Patent Section of the Bureau of Intellectual Property.

Two types of patents are available: small patents through a registration procedure with a protection period of 6 years, and normal patents subject to newness search based on world-documentation granted for 20 years, both as of date of filing.

A patent may be transferred or licensed, having effect to third parties only after annotations thereof at the Bureau.

Compulsory licensing is possible if the patent after three years of its grant is not properly used in Aruba.

Inventions made by an employee within the scope of his employment normally belong to his employer.

TRADEMARKS

Trade and Service Marks can be registered in all classes of the International Classification established by the Nice Union, to which Aruba is a party. Registered trademarks are effective as of the date of filing.

Trademark owners, not domiciled in Aruba are required to submit their application through a Trademark Agent authorized by the Bureau.

Although protection of a trademark or commercial name might be derived by first use in Aruba, it is strongly recommended to have same registered for protection.

The new Trademark Act grants exclusive rights to solely registered trademarks, with a transition period of one year for domestic trademark-owners (by right of first use) to duly register their trade or service marks to ensure continuation of exclusive rights.

International Registration is not possible at the moment because of granted temporary postponement of the applicability of the Madrid Arrangement by the International Bureau in Geneva, in order to have adequate executing rules established. The new Act will provide for said rules.

INDUSTRIAL DESIGNS

There is no special law governing protection of industrial designs besides those of the Copyright Act and the Bern Convention.

However, in accordance with our obligation as a party to The Hague Union concerning the International Deposit of Industrial Designs, an Industrial Designs Act has been drafted.

In the meantime deposits are accepted and official proofs thereof are granted as artistic works of applied art protected by the Copyright Act and the Bern Convention.

COPYRIGHT

The Copyright Act gives protection to literary, musical, artistic, photographic and audiovisual works till 70 years after the decease of the author with regards to author's economic rights and forever with respect to his moral rights.

According to the Bern Convention for the Protection of Literary and Artistic Works, to which Aruba is a party, protection is not conditional upon compliance with any formality (principle of "automatic" protection). However, to assist copyright owners in establishing first date of a work, deposits are accepted and official proofs thereof are granted upon request.

Works originating in one of the contracting states of the Bern Union is given the same protection as granted to the works of nationals.

A Copyright Association for Music Composers is awaiting official recognition by the Government. This Association represents composers-members in their economic rights and establishes royalties and other remuneration due to the same authors.

It also acts as the collecting agent of foreign composers and music writers, members of other similar organizations in the world, on a reciprocal basis for its own members in same countries.

For more information, please contact:

Bureau Intellectuele Eigendom
Adriaan Lacle Boulevard 3
Oranjestad
Aruba

Phone: 823200
Fax : 838773

TRANSPORTATION

AIR TRANSPORTATION

The "Aeropuerto Internacional Reina Beatrix" is located at 4.0 km (2.5 miles) east of Oranjestad and is served by 12 scheduled airlines to 27 destinations, and is also frequented by an increasing number of charters.

The airport offers a 9,000 foot Category I Precision Approach runway, operating under ILS system. Since February of 1996, Aruba has entered into a new era in aviation with the set up of a state-of-the-art air traffic control system. It made Aruba independent of other countries, which thus far have been controlling the airspace of Aruba. An extended range primary surveillance radar, a Mode-S secondary radar and an automation system for approach control and tower operations have been supplied. The airport traffic control tower has also been renovated. The radar system complimented the face-lifting program of the Queen Beatrix Airport deemed necessary to make Aruba's economy stronger. Not only will it serve the tourism industry purposes better, but it will also enhance Aruba's service position for all sorts of industries, especially the export and import of goods.

The passenger accommodation facilities will also undergo further renovation and expansion in order to meet the latest requirements for the steadily increasing passenger traffic. There are plans for a major expansion starting in July 1997.

Beside the increase in passenger traffic, there is also a consistent development in air cargo. The handling of air freight is concentrated in a modern cargo building encompassing approximately 3,000 m^2 of storage space.

The airport also has a world-class catering facility, serving local and long haul aircraft.

AIR TRAFFIC AND PASSENGER TRANSPORT

Year	Aircraft movement	Arriving	Departing	Transit
1992	33,457	703,616	698,128	232,175
1993	32,850	750,732	745,227	139,792
1994	32,558	778,012	769,447	133,853
1995	33,091	817,956	810,675	127,659
1996	32,223	814,283	798,479	128,203

Source: Aruba Airport Authority

SCHEDULED AIRLINE COMPANIES PRIVATE CHARTERS

Air Aruba (National Carrier) Avia Air

ALM (Dutch Antillean Airlines) Oduber Aviation

American Airlines

Aserca (Aeroservicios Carabobo)

Avensa (Aerovias Venezolana S.A.)

Avianca (Aerovias Nacionales de Colombia S.A.)

KLM (Royal Dutch Airlines)

SAM (Sociedad Aeronautica de Medellin Consolidada S.A.)

Servivensa

VASP

Freight Service

Air Aruba ALM American Airlines

KLM Las Americas

Freight Agent

American Airlines Cargo Service Center

Amsterdam	Caracas	Maracaibo	San Juan
Atlanta	Curacao	Miami	Sao Paulo
Bogota	Houston	Newark	Sint Maarten
Bonaire	New York	Lima	Tampa
Boston	Panama City	Manaus	

SEA PORTS

Aruba has three sea ports of which the port of Oranjestad and Barcadera are administered by the Aruba Ports Authority.

The Port of **Oranjestad,** Aruba's container port and cruise ship terminal, is accessible to all types of vessels. It has a depth of 38 feet MLW and 4,070 feet of docking space. The container terminal has a 50 ton gantry crane with a maximum capacity of 60,000 TEUs containers per year and a 140 ton mobile crane. There are also two roll-on roll-off ramps and facilities for 36 reefer connections are available.

Barcadera is the industrial port with a depth of 36 feet and 1,148 feet of docking space.

The Port of **San Nicolas** has the oil terminals and one reef berth administered by the Coastal Aruba Refining Company. The other reef berth for transshipment is administered by Wickland Oil Company.

MARITIME TRAFFIC

Year	Total Calls	Tankers	Cruise ships	Gross Registered Tonnage (x 1,000)
1992	2,358	603	321	33,111
1993	2,237	591	352	34,376
1994	2,661	723	345	42,196
1995			311	
1996			273	

Source: Aruba Ports Authority

PRINCIPAL CARGO LINES

Caboven	CGM - Compagnie Generale Maritime
Crowley Line Europe	West Indies Line (EWL)
Flota Mercante Colombiana	Fritz Maritime
Genesis Continental Line	Hapag Lloyd AG Company
Harrison Line	King Ocean Line
Laser Line	Nedlloyd Lines
Sea freight Agency, Inc.	Sealand, Inc.
Super Shipcare Services (SSS)	

CONNECTIONS WORLD WIDE

From Aruba direct shipping connections on a frequent basis are available to the European and some Latin American countries by the major shipping lines.

Also, regional shipping connections are available, either direct or via transshipment.

OCEAN FREIGHT COSTS

Information on the various container ocean freight costs can be obtained from the Aruba Stevedoring Company.

Other charges, among others, are:

the local handling cost of US$ 335 and US$ 528 per container for a 20' and a 40' container respectively.

the Port Authority charges such as :

a Terminal Utilization Charge (T.U.C.) of US$ 25 and US$ 50 per container for a 20' and 40' container respectively;

35% Surcharge amounting to US$ 126 and US$ 203 per container for a 20' and 40' container respectively.

The handling cost for a transshipment container is limited to US$ 79 and a 35 percent Port Authority Surcharge which amounts to US$ 27.

A special handling rate is also applied to industries which are established in the Aruba Free zone and re-export full loaded containers with transshipment cargo destined to foreign final destinations. However, certain conditions or restrictions apply.

For more information, please contact:

Aruba Stevedoring Company (ASTEC) N.V.
Port Administration Building
L.G. Smith Boulevard 23
Oranjestad, Aruba
Phone: 822558
Fax : 834570

UTILITIES

ELECTRICITY

Electricity is produced by the "Water- en Energiebedrijf Aruba (WEB) N.V.". The total power generating capacity of the steam turbines amounts to 114 Megawatt. There is also a 20-Megawatt standby Diesel Gas turbine. The WEB N.V. produced an average of 63 MW, which together with a contracted supply from the refining company, was sufficient to comply with the average demand of 80 MW in 1994.

The WEB N.V. is continuously investing in the power production facilities in order to maintain its constant and reliable supply.

The WEB N.V. delivers electricity to the distribution company "N.V. Electriciteit-Maatschappij Aruba (Elmar)".

Power is supplied at a 60-Hertz frequency and at 127 and 220 Volts.

Consumption of electricity rose strongly during the last ten years from 219,000 MWh in 1986 to 499,900 MWh in 1995. This increase has been properly managed by a comprehensive and adequate power distribution network which is continuously upgraded. Provisions are being made to guarantee Elmar's ability to realize any future increment in demand.

Both the "Water- en Energiebedrijf (WEB) N.V." and the "N.V. Electriciteit-Maatschappij Aruba (Elmar)" are independently managed companies residing under the government owned holding company "Utilities Aruba N.V.".

The following tariffs in Af are applicable and are based on the monthly consumption:

TARIFF A: DOMESTIC PURPOSES

0 - 250 kWh :	18.5 ct/kWh
251 - 500 kWh :	14.5 ct/kWh
over 500 kWh :	14.0 ct/kWh

Minimum charge: Af 5.50 monthly

TARIFF B: BUSINESS PURPOSES

0 - 250 kWh :	18.5 ct/kWh
251 - 10,000 kWh :	17.5 ct/kWh
10,001 - 20,000 kWh :	16.5 ct/kWh
over 20,000 kWh :	15.0 ct/kWh

Minimum charge: Af 16.50 monthly

Tariff Air conditioning business purposes: 13.7 ct/kWh

Minimum charge: Af 8.00 per AC-Connection monthly

A fuel surcharge of Af 0.0661 per consumed kWh must be added to all tariffs.

INDUSTRIAL PURPOSES

The cost of power charged to industries differs for companies considered as small industries and for those considered as other industries.

Small industrial activities with a consumption of over 10 kW but not exceeding 50 kW, are charged Af 8.00 per kW peak load and a consumption charge of Af 0.126 per kWh supplemented by a fuel surcharge of Af 0.0661 per consumed kWh.

Minimum charge: Af 75.00 monthly

For other industries, consuming more than 50 kVA, the monthly cost of power is based on three components: the peakload, the consumption and the fuel surcharge.

For calculating the peak load cost a distinction is made between three peak load ranges: 50 - 500 kVA, 500 - 1,500 kVA and that exceeding 1,500 kVA.

No distinction is made in the consumption cost and fuel surcharge.

The peak load cost for the three ranges is calculated as follows:

Cost peak load : 50 - 500 kVA

- first 50 kVA : Af 1,750
- additional kVA: Af 28.50 per kVA

Minimum charge: 0.6 x kVA* x Af 28.50 monthly

Cost peak load : 500 - 1,500 kVA

- first 500 kVA : Af 14,250
- additional kVA: Af 23,50 per kVA

Minimum charge: 0.6 x kVA* x Af 23.50 monthly

Cost peak load : exceeding 1,500 kVA

- first 1,500 kVA: Af 35,250
- additional kVA : Af 21.00 per kVA

Minimum charge: 0.6 x kVA* x Af 21.00 monthly

* Depends on installed transformer capacity.

The consumption cost is calculated as the monthly consumption based on Af 0.085 per kWh. The fuel surcharge amounts to Af 0.0661 per consumed kWh.

WATER

All the industrial and potable water produced by the "Water- en Energiebedrijf Aruba (WEB) N.V.", the world's second largest desalination plant, is from the seawater. The drinking water is pure and refreshing.

The total installed desalination capacity of the Multi Stage Flash (MSF) units is 36,000 metric tons per day. Average daily consumption in 1994 was about 28,000 metric tons. The total storage capacity in reserve and the mains amounts to approximately 176,000 metric tons, which is equivalent to 6 days of consumption. A significant investment program for updating the water distribution network is in progress, because of the expanded economic activities.

TARIFFS:

- Af 5.25 per metric ton for business and industrial use;

- Af 5.15 per metric ton for domestic use.

GAS

Gas is supplied by the Aruba Gas Supply Company Ltd (ARUGAS). Propane is delivered on site in cylinders of 100 lbs, which remain the property of the ARUGAS. A deposit of Af 100 per cylinder is required.

Tariff: Af 71.15 per cylinder for commercial purposes;

Af 38.00 per cylinder for domestic purposes.

Instead of having gas delivered in cylinders of 100 lbs, tanks of 60, 120, 250, 500, 900 or 1000 gallons can be purchased or leased. These tanks are refilled regularly by a tank truck.

Tariff: Af 0.797 per liter for commercial use;

Af 0.43 per liter for domestic use.

TELECOMMUNICATIONS

Telecommunication services are provided by SETAR (Servicio di Telecomunicacion di Aruba), a Government owned company. The local telecommunication infrastructure, considered as advanced and sophisticated, consists of 5ESS/PRX digital and PRX-A electronic exchanges. These exchanges have the combined capacity to connect about 33,500 subscribers and can easily be expanded due to the modular design of the digital exchange switches. The exchanges are interconnected by means of fiber optic and by a digital microwave network to guarantee route diversity, high availability and reliability.

The penetration rate of services is one of the highest in the region.

A digitalization project, consisting of the installation of switching and transmission equipment in order to comply with the growth until the year 2000, is in progress. The digital exchange switches have the capacity to provide all new telephone services. An Integrated Services Digital Network (ISDN) is also available.

For international telecommunication, SETAR has a network consisting of a 5ESS Gateway Switch, Telex Exchange, Standard A and Standard B earth stations, and Digital Microwave.

With the available infrastructure SETAR can provide its clients with IDR and IBS satellite services. The earth stations are furthermore equipped for video up and down linking.

SETAR is expected to be connected with the world fiber optic network by the America's One Submarine Fiber Optic cable via extension to Camuri Venezuela in the near future.

International Direct Dialing is possible with all countries in the world, and in addition SETAR has the possibility to complete all calls via international operators service.

SETAR is installing a packet switching node for credit card validation purposes and additional data communication services. In addition to above-mentioned services, SETAR is developing the mobile communications infrastructure. A new city-paging system with tone, voice (mail), numeric and alphanumeric option has been installed.

Cellular telephony is available, while a trunking system (Public Mobile Radio System) will be available soon.

TAXES

CORPORATE TAX

Corporate or Profit tax is levied on:

the profits of locally established limited liability companies, limited partnerships, other companies or societies, of which the capital is wholly or partly divided into shares, cooperative societies and mutual insurance companies;

the profits of locally established societies, of which the capital is not divided into shares, and foundations other than those exclusively for the protection of a general social interest;

the profits of institutions established outside Aruba, including all companies and societies, of which the capital is wholly or partly divided into shares, and as far the profits are derived from a permanent establishment in Aruba, from locally located immovable (real estate properties), from noncommercial claims secured by a mortgage on real estate properties located in Aruba.

TAXABLE CORPORATE PROFIT

Profits are understood as the sum of realizations which by any name and in any form are derived purely from business operations and from capital employed outside business operations. No profit tax is levied on the profits (dividends income) made by an Aruban company as a shareholder in other Aruban companies. However, profits and losses resulting from the alienation of such participation are taken into account when calculating the company's taxable income.

All dividend income received by an Aruban company from a non-Aruban company will be taxed at a rate of one tenth of the normally applicable rates between 31.05% and 39.1%, provided the foreign company is subject to some sort of profit tax and the participation of the Aruban company is at least 10%.

For profits realized with the sale of assets, there is the possibility of creating a so-called **"replacement reserve".** Replacement, however, must take place within four years.

Losses in any fiscal year may be carried forward to be offset against profits of the following five years.

ACCELERATED DEPRECIATION

Accelerated depreciation for 1/3 of the initial cost of the investment can be applied for business assets such as premise and machinery.

INVESTMENT ALLOWANCE

For investment exceeding Af 5,000 an investment deduction of 12% on new buildings and 8% on other assets is allowed annually for the first two fiscal years. However, business assets such as land, houses, cars and yachts, are excluded.

TAXATION PROCEDURES

All companies must file annually their financial statements comprising a balance sheet and a profit and loss account with their return profit tax with the Inspector of Taxes. The tax is levied over the financial book year, which normally is the calendar year.

CORPORATE TAX RATES

Taxable Profits		**Tax Payable**	
Minimum	Maximum	Minimum	Plus for every Af 100 in excess of amount in first column
100	40,000	31	31.05
40,000	50,000	12,420	34.50
50,000	60,000	15,870	37.95
60,000	70,000	19,665	41.40
70,000	80,000	23,805	44.85
80,000	90,000	28,290	47.15
90,000	100,000	33,005	49.45
100,000	1,000,000	37,950	37.95
1,000,000		379,500	39.10

AVOIDANCE OF DOUBLE TAXATION

With exception of a limited double taxation treaty with the United States of America, Aruba has no tax treaties. However, within the Kingdom of the Netherlands a Kingdom Act, "Belastingregeling voor het Koninkrijk", is in force. It prevents double taxation within the Kingdom. The Government has as policy the conclusion of double taxation treaty with other countries.

As of January 1, 1988, the tax treaty with the United States of America has been terminated by the US Government, with the exception of Article VIII and its ancillary provisions, regulating interest income from the United States.

On the basis thereof interest received by an Aruban company from US sources is exempted from US withholding tax if certain conditions are met. Exemption is allowed if the company elects to be taxed on its interest income at the rates of 24 to 30% and in a situation that the shares of the company are held by a Dutch company.

Matters of taxation between the Netherlands, Aruba and the Dutch Caribbeanare regulated in the "Belastingregeling voor het Koninkrijk (BRK)". The principal benefit derived by Aruban offshore companies from the BRK relates to the tax treatment of dividends received from the Netherlands. Withholding tax on dividends paid by a Dutch company to a resident of Aruba is 15%. If an Aruban company holds at least 25% of the capital of a Dutch company, then the withholding tax is further reduced as follows:

- to 7.5%, or;

- to 5.0% if the Aruban company elects to be taxed in Aruba at the rate of 5.5%.

PERSONAL INCOME TAX

Residents: Individuals residing in Aruba are taxable according to their net income from any source per calendar year (the world wide criterion). There are deductions for personal obligations such as pension premium, life insurance premium, interests paid on debts, certain gifts, and extraordinary expenses such as sickness-, invalidity-, subsistence costs for certain relatives and next of kin and the burial costs of relatives. Tax allowance for children is granted to residents by allowing a deduction from their net income.

Nonresidents: Under the provision of the Income Tax Ordinance, a nonresident is subject to tax for income derived from certain sources including gains from the alienation of shares from a so called substantial participation in an Aruban onshore company (the territorial source criterion).

A substantial participation is defined as a participation of 25% or more of the nominal paid-up capital either alone or together with certain relatives during the last five years.

A nonresident shareholder of an Aruban offshore company is specifically exempted from the substantial participation provision and therefore will not be subject to any form of personal income tax on dividends, interest, liquidation distributions or other payments received from the company, nor will such a shareholder be subject to income tax on capital gains on the disposal of his participation in the company. There is no withholding tax on such payments by an offshore company to its nonresident shareholder.

INCOME TAX TABLE

Effective January 1, 1997 the following rates are applicable:

Taxable Income	Payable Tax	
	Group I	Group II
10,700	-	322
12,100	328	452
20,000	1,125	1,314
30,000	2,557	2,925
50,000	7,140	8,046
75,000	15,805	17,571
100,000	26,614	29,142
150,000	50,804	55,091
200,000	77,892	83,794

Tariff group I is applicable to:

the married employee whose spouse, with whom he or she is conducting a marital household, does not have an income from business or labor activity;

the employee who is permanently separated from his or her spouse and who has been part of a marital household for at least five years;

the divorced employee who has been part of a marital household for at least five years;

the unmarried employee who has the right on tax allowance for children.

Tariff group II is applicable in all other cases not mentioned under points 1-4.

WAGE TAX (PAYE)

The Wage or Pay As You Earn (PAYE) tax is an advance levy on the personal income tax. This tax is levied as an estimate of the taxable income and is a fixed percentage of employee's wage or salary according to the table stipulated by ministerial decree.

The employer is liable for the withholding of wage taxes and has to transfer it before the 15th of the following month to the Tax Collector's Office.

CAPITAL TAX

There is no Aruban withholding tax on capital, and no obligation as to the declaration of capital.

DIVIDEND TAX

There is no levying of taxes on dividends or on interest.

REAL ESTATE PROPERTY TAX (GRONDBELASTING)

Yearly, this tax is levied on the value of the real estate. The tax rate amounts to 0.4% of the value of both unimproved property and improved land with structure, and is charged to the owner of the properties.

PROPERTY TRANSFER TAX (OVERDRACHTSBELASTING)

This tax is levied on the acquisition of title to immovable property. The tax rate is 3 % of the real estate value and is payable by the purchaser.

INHERITANCE, ESTATE AND GIFT TAX

Under the Inheritance Tax Ordinance:

- an inheritance tax (Successierecht) is levied on the increase in net wealth obtained as heir or legatee from a resident of Aruba;
- a gift tax (Schenkingsrecht) is levied on the increase in net wealth obtained as a gift from a resident of Aruba.
- an estate tax at the rate of 8% is levied as an heir, a legatee or as a gift from a nonresident of Aruba.

The rate of inheritance and gift tax ranges between 2% and 24%, depending on the degree of kinship and the value obtained from the resident.

In case of death the maximum rate is 6% for goods left to the surviving spouse, children, grandchildren and parents of the deceased.

IMPORT DUTIES

The standard tariff of the import duty is 7.5%. Primary foodstuffs are in general taxed at 0%, while higher tariffs are applicable for other goods, depending on their luxury.

EXCISE TAX

Excise taxes are levied on alcoholic beverages, cigarettes and fuel products.

TRANSIT AND EXPORT DUTIES

No duties are levied on exports, except on irregular transit. In the latter case a low levy is applicable.

GAMBLING LICENSES

Fixed gambling license rights of Af 5,000 monthly together with a 3% levy on the gross income to be paid by the casinos.

ROOM TAX

A tax payable by the guest at a rate of 5% over the cost of accommodation is levied

ADDITIONAL INFORMATION:

For additional information on taxes, apply to:

Directie der Belastingen or Gütenbergstraat 6 Oranjestad Phone: 833512 Fax : 833407	Inspectie der Belastingen Paardenbaaistraat 11 Oranjestad Phone: 831800 Fax : 836753

For information on import and excise duties, apply to:

Inspectie der Invoerrechten en Accijnzen
L.G. Smith Boulevard 84-88
Oranjestad
Phone: 821800
Fax : 837164

FISCAL INCENTIVES

To encourage investments in specific industries the government has introduced a number of tax incentives on a selective basis. These fiscal incentives are for the purpose of the broadening of the economic base and to stimulate exports.

MANUFACTURING INDUSTRIES

A non traditional manufacturing industry, with an initial investment of at least Af 100,000 is eligible for fiscal incentives.

Incentives

- Reduction of corporate tax rate to 0%;

- exemption from income tax on dividends paid out to shareholders, provided the dividends are paid within two years after the year the profit has been made;
- exemption from import duties on building supplies for the premises;
- exemption from import duties on packing materials, machinery and equipment, raw materials, semimanufactured products and components, to be used in the production process;
- exemption from real estate tax.

The incentives are granted for a maximum period of ten fiscal years.

DEVELOPMENT OF FALLOW LAND

A company, engaged in the development of fallow land in the sense of zoning the land, the construction of roads and the establishment of premises to be sold, is eligible for fiscal incentives.

To qualify for these incentives the company's investment should be at least Af 1 million, in addition to the cost of land.

Incentives

- Exemption from import duties on materials and goods needed for the construction of roads and premises;
- exemption from real estate tax on the land and the premises for the period needed for improving the land and the sale of the premises;
- exemption from the corporate tax on profits derived from the sale of the improved land and the premises;
- exemption from income tax on dividends paid out to shareholders, provided the dividends are paid within two years after the year the profit has been made.

HOTELS

Tax incentives can be obtained for the construction of hotels if the initial investment amounts to at least Af 1,000,000.

Incentives

- Reduction of corporate tax to 0 % of the net taxable profit;
- exemption from income tax on dividends paid out to shareholders, provided the dividends are paid within two years after the year the profit has been made;
- exemption from import duties on materials and goods needed for the construction, furniture and fixture of the hotel;
- exemption from real estate tax.

The incentives are granted for a maximum period of ten fiscal years.

SUMMARY OF INVCENTIVES

Nature	Conditions	Taxation

a. Manufacturing Industries	Minimum investment of Af 100,000 in non-traditional manufacturing	Reduction of: • corporate tax to 0%. Exemption from: • income tax on dividends paid out to shareholders; • import duties on machinery and equipment, raw-materials, semi-manufactured products and components, and packing materials; • import duties on building supplies for the premises; • real estate tax. Duration: maximum 10 years.
b. Free Zone Compaies		Corporate tax rate of 2% on Companies profits derived from • international sales. • Exemption from import duties on goods imported in the free zone for re-export. In force up to the year 2015.
c. Development of Fallow Land	Minimum investment of Af 1,000,000 not including cost of land, and to be committed within 5 years	Exemption from: • corporate tax; • income tax on dividend paid out to shareholders; • import duties on building supplies; • real estate tax. The tax exemption period is determined by the Government.
d. Hotels	Minimum investment of Af 1,000,000	Reduction of: • corporate tax to 0%. Exemption from: • income tax on dividends

		paid out to shareholders; • import duties on building supplies, furniture and fixture of the premise; • real estate tax. Duration: maximum 10 years.
e. Offshore Trading and Offshore Banking Companies		Corporate tax 2.4% and 3%
f. Investment and Royalty Companies		Corporate tax 2.4% and 3% No profit tax on capital gains. In force up to the year 1999.
g. Shipping and Aviation Companies		Effective corporate tax rate of 7.73% and 9.66% In force up to the year 2000.
h. Aruba Exempt Companies	Not applicable to banking or life insurance companies	Tax exempted.

MONEY, BANKING AND FINANCE

CENTRAL BANK

The "Centrale Bank van Aruba" (the Bank) started operations on January 1, 1986. At the same time, the Aruban Florin (Af) was introduced, which is pegged to the US dollar at Af 1.79 per US$ 1.00.

The principal functions of the Bank, as stipulated in the Central Bank Ordinance are:

- to maintain the stability of the value of the Aruban currency and to determine monetary policy towards that end;
- to supervise and promote a sound development of the banking and credit system;
- to issue bank notes;
- to act as banker for the Government;
- to be the central foreign exchange bank and as such to regulate the flow of payments to and from other countries, and;
- to act as advisor to the Minister of Finance on financial matters.

Commercial banks and other non-monetary financial institutions

There are six commercial banks, providing a wide range of domestic and international financial services. Further, the onshore financial system consists mainly of ten life insurance companies, one Government and eight company pension funds, one saving fund, three finance companies, six relatively small credit unions, two mortgage banks, five other financial institutions and one investment bank. The latter provides investment banking services to both local and foreign investors.

OFFSHORE BANKING

Presently, there are three offshore banks active in Aruba. These banks are only allowed to conduct transactions with nonresidents. Until now, these banks have been subject to a very limited supervisory regime. Therefore, the Bank -until it has adequate legislative powers- has adopted a prudent admission policy for offshore banks: only applications from financially sound and reputable banks are considered for admission, provided they are subject to high quality supervision on a consolidated basis in their home country.

FOREIGN EXCHANGE TRANSACTIONS

The Bank administers the foreign exchange regulations, based on the State Ordinance on foreign exchange transactions. Merchandise import payments can be made freely. As from January 1, 1997, all foreign exchange limitations regarding payments to nonresidents related to the purchase of services, the so-called current transactions, are eliminated. Thus, a special license for these transactions is no longer necessary. Moreover, a general license is granted for local entities to make foreign investments for an amount equivalent to a maximum of Af 500,000 per calendar year. No license is required for current foreign payments related to interest and redemptions on loans and distribution of dividends (including interim-dividends), if and only when the requirements mentioned in the Notice concerning foreign exchange transactions 97/L.1 have been met:

> Payments related to interest and redemptions on loans: A license has been obtained from the Bank to conclude the loan.
>
> Payments related to distributions of dividends (including interim-dividends) and profits: A license has been obtained for the sale of the domestic share, and a written acknowledgement with respect to the amount of the (interim-)dividend or profit have been granted by the Bank.

Exports of goods and services do not require a license, but export proceeds must be generally converted into local currency within eight working days or credited to an account with a local bank or with a foreign bank, which is notified to the Bank.

A license is required for the following transactions:

- transfers of profits and dividends;
- purchases from and sales to nonresidents of domestic securities;
- foreign investments by resident natural persons exceeding Af 200,000 a year;
- purchases from and sales to nonresidents of domestic real estate;
- proceeds from the liquidation of direct foreign investments and loans received from nonresidents as well as loans extended to nonresidents; and
- other short- and long-term investments by residents abroad and by nonresidents in Aruba.

A foreign exchange commission of 1.3% is levied on all payments made by residents to nonresidents, except when settled in Netherlands Antillean guilders.

ARUBAN INVESTMENT BANK

The Aruban Investment Bank N.V. (AIB) is a private corporation.

The total subscribed capital of the AIB amounts to Af 11,867,000 while the Government granted the AIB a subordinated loan of Af 20 million to increase its financial resources. The objectives of the AIB are to support long-term investments and the expansion of the private sector through the mobilization of domestic and international financial and technical resources and the provision of investment banking services.

Specifically, the AIB is involved in the following activities:

- the promotion of new projects;
- the provision of medium and long-term loans;
- equity participation;
- management of funds;
- issuance of guarantees;
- mergers and acquisitions;
- financial advisory and investment banking services including underwriting, brokerage, mergers, acquisition and refinancing;
- economic advisory services including but not limited to: feasibility studies, market surveys, statistics and trade legislation.

TOURISM

Tourism has contributed positively to the economic growth and continues to be the main economic activity. Further more, tourism is the main employer and the main foreign exchange earner.

Since 1987 stay-over tourism experienced an average annual growth of 13.7%, which can be qualified as one of the highest in the Caribbean Region. The number of tourist arrivals increased in 1996 with 3.5%.

The United States continue to be the major tourist market, accounting for 57.8% of the total stay-over visitors in 1996, followed by Venezuela with 11.7% and the Netherlands with 5.6% of the market respectively.

During 1996, visitors stay-over was 4,713.728 nights, with an average of 7.4 nights per tourist.

At the end of 1996 the hotel room capacity totaled 6,687 rooms, of which 3,739 rooms in the high rise and 2,948 in the low rise hotels. In 1996, the amount of cruise ship passengers experienced an increase of 6.1% after a growth of 15.4% in 1995. The number of cruise ship calls decreased to a total of 273 in 1996.

Year	Hotel rooms	Stay-over visitors	Visitor nights	Cruise ship passengers	Receipt (Af million)
1992	5,680	541,714	3,902,293	216,587	796.3
1993	6,089	562,034	4,027,754	251,104	835,4
1994	6,189	582,136	4,233,740	257,138	837.9
1995	6,666	618,917	4,473,072	296,712	931.8
1996	6,687	640,832	4,713,728	314,917	1,084.4

Source: Aruba Tourism Authority

In order to meet the growing demand for skills in the tourism sector, a training center for the hotel trade and tourism, the Aruba Hotel School has been established in 1982. This center consists of teaching facilities for 250 students, and a 154 room hotel, the Bushiri Beach Hotel. The programs provide basic and advanced hospitality trade education, leading to an Associate Degree.

Aruba's magnificent stretch of white sand beaches that continues for miles along the west coast are among the finest in the world.

Most of the resorts and casinos are located along this beach.

Tourists can spend the evening in exotic restaurants and nightclubs, discos or casinos. Restaurants serve a wide range of cuisines.

MAJOR HOTELS

Hotel	Room	Phone	Fax
La Cabana Beach Resort	803	879000	875474
Holiday Inn Aruba Beach Resort	600	863600	865165
Wyndham Aruba Hotel & Casino	479	864466	868217
Americana Aruba Beach Resort	419	864500	863191
Marriott Aruba Resort & Casino	413	869000	860649
Radisson Aruba Caribbean Resort	386	866555	863260
Hyatt Regency Aruba Resort & Casino	360	861234	861682
Costa Linda Beach Resort	326	838000	836040
Aruba Sonesta Hotel	298	836000	834389

Casa del Mar/Aruba Beach Club Resort	278	823000	826557
Aruba Sonesta Suites	247	835600	825317
Tamarijn Aruba Beach Resort	236	824150	834002
Aruba Palm Beach Hotel	202	863900	861941
Divi Aruba Beach Resort	202	823300	834002
Playa Linda Beach Resort	194	861000	865210
Caribbean Palm Village	171	862700	862380
Bushiri Beach Resort	154	825216	826789
Divi Village Resort	132	824150	
The Dutch Village	123	832300	835217
Aruba Stauffer Hotel	100	860855	860856
The Mill Condominium Resort	99	867700	867271
Paradise Beach Villas	80	874000	870071
Manchebo Beach Resort	71	823444	833667
Amsterdam Manor Beach Hotel	70	871492	871463
Talk of the Town Resort	64	823380	820327
Bucuti Beach Resort	63	836141	825272
La Quinta Beach Hotel	54	875010	876263
Sunset Villas Resort	22	861120	862506

For additional information visit our web site at http://www.aruba.com/

ESTABLISHING A COMPANY (N.V.)

In Aruba a limited liability company ("N.V.") is a legal entity, established by at least two persons (legal or moral), who are by law designated as its founders. A Deed of Incorporation, which includes the bylaws of the N.V., is drawn up and executed before a civil law notary. This Deed must be in the Dutch language.

FOUNDERS

The founders are the initial shareholders, but there can be more shareholders/non-founders who participate in the issued capital at incorporation. There is no legal requirement as to nationality or residency of the founders and or shareholders. Representation can take place by proxy. If a non-resident wishes to establish a N.V., an existing trust or management company can take care of the incorporation process and may also provide for representation.

DEED OF INCORPORATION

The Deed of Incorporation should in any case contain the following:

Name of the N.V., which may be in any language, provided that it is composed of Latin characters. The name should either start or end with the words "Naamloze Vennootschap" or the abbreviation thereof: "N.V.". In principle one is free to choose the name of the N.V., but prior to incorporation a name search has to be requested;

Statutory **Seat**, which must be situated in Aruba;

Object clause of the N.V.;

Authorized capital, which must be at least Af 50,000;

Issued capital must be at least Af 10,000 and at all times at least one fifth of the authorized capital;

Par value of shares;

Number of shares for which each of the founders (and eventual third parties) participate in the issued share capital as well as the amount paid-up on those shares at incorporation;

Name(s), date(s)/place(s) of birth and address(es) of initial **managing director(s).**

CAPITAL REQUIREMENTS

There are no other legal requirements as to the debt/equity ratio than the requirement that participation of the founders in the issued share capital equals to at least one fifth of the authorized capital. The guidelines have fixed the one fifth of the authorized capital at Af 10,000 , the so-called minimum issued capital. Furthermore, it is stated in the guidelines that the issued share capital of a mortgage bank must be at least Af 40,000 and that the issued share capital of a bank or an insurance company must be at least Af 200,000.

PROCEDURE

The Deed of Incorporation is filed with the Minister of Justice, together with a request for obtaining the ministerial Certificate of No-Objections. The N.V. exists as a legal entity from the date it meets the following two constitutive requirements:

the Certificate of No-Objections has been granted by the Minister of Justice; and

the Deed of Incorporation has been executed before a civil law notary.

The civil law notary who has been in charge with the execution of the Deed of Incorporation must place an announcement as to the incorporation of the N.V. in the Official Gazette of Aruba. Furthermore, the managing director(s) of the N.V. must register the N.V. in the Commercial Register, which is supervised by the Chamber of Commerce, and deposit a true copy of the Deed of Incorporation at said Chamber.

LICENSES

Before starting its operations, the N.V. must apply for the following licenses:

a **business license** allowing the N.V. to establish a business. An application thereto must be directed to the Minister of Economic Affairs;

a **director's license** for each of the N.V.'s foreign managing directors. An application thereto must be directed to the Minister of Economic Affairs;

a **residence and work license** for any non-resident, who intends to take up residence in Aruba, to be employed by the N.V. An application thereto must be directed to the Minister of Justice.

CHAMBER OF COMMERCE

The Aruba Chamber of Commerce and Industry was instituted by law in 1930. Its main objective is to promote the collective interests of commerce and industry in its territory. This is pursued through its advisory activities and the administration of the Commercial and Foundations Registers, which have been entrusted by law to the Chamber. The Board of the Chamber consists of 9 members. To become eligible for membership one must have the age of 25 years, the Dutch nationality and must have been a resident of Aruba for the last two years.

The Chamber can:

Provide the government upon request or at its own initiative with information, advice and recommendations on any matter concerning the business community in general.

Assist you when registering a business in the Commercial Register, and when making any amendments thereon. According to the Commercial Register Ordinance all businesses operating in Aruba must be registered in the Commercial Register of Aruba, and all changes in the registered data must be submitted to this Register.

Provide you with an extract of the registration of a business. An extract is a document issued by the Commercial Register, containing the most important and essential details of a registered enterprise. Details as, name of the enterprise, trade name if any, registration number, objectives, date of establishment, owner or management and proxies, and capital in the case of companies.

Legalize certificates of origin. These are document certifying the origin of the goods to be exported under a special regime upon request of importing countries.

Legalize EUR-1 certificates. These are document certifying the origin of the goods, and which are required for export to countries of the European Common Market.

Provide you with declarations or letters of recommendation.

Upon request these letters can be issued in Dutch, English, or Spanish, to be used by businessmen related to their business contacts abroad.

Supply you with information and guide you with regard to business community in Aruba.

Conduct company and trade name checks.

Provide you with all other information from its data bank and library, such as addresses and business information on international commerce, foreign industries, products, international exhibitions, etc.

COMMERCIAL REGISTER

Registration in the Commercial Register is mandatory for all enterprises carrying on a business in Aruba. The Commercial Register is under the supervision of the Chamber of Commerce and Industry and is open to public. The Register contains detailed information on the name of the company, objectives, date of establishment, authorized capital, directors, etc. Registration in the Commercial Register is subject to an initial fee and a subsequent yearly contribution. The initial fee is based on the paid-up capital and the yearly contribution is collected on the company's invested capital.

Initial fee or yearly contribution due to the paid-up capital or invested capital in Aruban florin (Af).

Paid-up or Invested capital		Fee or Contribution	
Minimum	Maximum	Initial Fee	Yearly Contribution
-	25,000	60	60
25,000	50,000	75	75
50,000	100,000	125	100

100,000	200,000	150	125
200,000	500,000	250	175
500,000	1,000,000	500	200
1,000,000	2,000,000	1,000	400
2,000,000	3,000,000	1,000	500
3,000,000	4,000,000	1,000	600
4,000,000	5,000,000	1,000	750
5,000,000	upwards	1,000	850

Limited liability companies with an authorized capital of more than Af 50,000 in bearer shares and companies with bearer bonds or limited liability companies operating as financial institutions or insurance companies are required to file their annual financial statements with the Commercial Register.

The Commercial Register carried at the end of 1994 approximately 10,000 registered companies. Of this total roughly 53% are locally operating companies and the other 47% are so-called offshore companies. The vast majority of the offshore companies are incorporated as Aruba Exempt Companies.

COST OF INCORPORATION

The main expenses incurred in forming a company are:

1. **Civil law notary's fee**: depending on the authorized capital and the work involved;
2. **Stamp duty** on Ministerial Certificate of Nihil Obstat on the Deed of Incorporation and the registration of the Deed: approximately Af 300;
3. **Initial registration in the Commercial Register** payable to the Chamber of Commerce: depending on the paid-up capital;
4. Publication in the Official Gazette: approximately Af 40;
5. A **business license**: depending on the authorized capital, a minimum of Af 100 and a maximum of Af 500;

   Each **director's license**: Af 50.

ENTRY REQUIREMENTS

TOURIST

Visitors to Aruba need proof of identity and are allowed to stay up to 14 days. For citizens of countries having a visa abolition agreement with the Netherlands, the length of stay may be up to 3 months. Citizens of the Netherlands or the Dutch Caribbeanmay stay up to 6 months.

Citizens of the following countries must have a visa to enter Aruba:

Afghanistan, Burma, Cambodia, Cuba, Dominican Republic, Haiti, Iran, Iraq, Libya, Mauritania, North Korea, Peru, Republic of China, Syria and Vietnam.

On arrival US tourists may submit:

- a valid passport;
- a valid "laissez passer" of the United Nations;
- a genuine (original-official state issued) birth certificate with a raised seal and a photo ID for citizens born in the USA;
- a genuine (original) US certificate of naturalization with a raised seal and a photo ID for citizens born outside the USA; or
- a re-entry permit or an Alien Registration Card (Green Card) for non-US citizens residing in the USA.

On arrival, Canadian visitors must have one of the following:

- a valid Canadian passport;
- a miniature birth certificate, a miniature baptismal certificate or a miniature certificate of proof of Canadian citizenship for Canadian citizens born in Canada;
- either an original certificate of naturalization or a miniature certificate of proof of Canadian citizenship for Canadian citizens born outside of Canada; or
- a national passport together with Canadian Immigration Identification with a landing stamp in the national passport or a certificate of identity for Canadian residents.

Visitors from European Union members countries must have in their possession on arrival:

- A valid passport; or
- A European Union Travel Card.

Furthermore, tourists should have a return or an onward ticket and adequate subsistence to be self-supporting during their stay and must prove this, if requested by local competent authorities.

Tourists are not allowed to engage in any business or work activity during their stay in Aruba.

Except tourists, everyone should have a permit to prove their legal presence in the island. This means that everyone should not travel to or be in the island pending the process for a permit for residence and/or work.

WORK PERMIT

Any foreigner who desires to exercise a profession must have a work and residence permit. The work permit will normally be granted only if there are no qualified persons locally available for the specific job or profession. Applications for work permits will only be taken into consideration if filed through the prospective employer, who has to accept full responsibility for any possible expenses to be made by the Government with regard to the employee.

The first step to be taken by the employer is the placing of the vacancies with the job classifications at the Job Center of the Department of Labor, followed by the placement of ads in the newspapers during one to two weeks. If no qualified applicants have responded to the ads, the request for a work permit can be made.

The key to a successful and quick response to any request for a work permit is to submit all the required documents at the same time, completely and accurately filled out.

Applications should be submitted on official Government paper or on paper with official Government stamps of Af 4.

The application must contain the following information:

- name, given names, birth date, place of birth and nationality of the employee;
- the job or profession to be engaged in;
- name and address of the employer/enterprise, which must be provided with a stamp of the Wage Tax Division of the Inspectorate of Taxes;
- the address of the employee in Aruba;
- a birth certificate of the employee;
- 2 passport photos;
- certificate of good conduct "police record" from the country of origin or from the country where the applicant had his home address for the last ten years, not older than 2 months;
- diplomas or certificates related to the job/profession and position to be occupied by the employee;
- a medical certificate not older than one month certifying that the employee is not suffering from any contagious disease, HIV, VDRL, TBC or mental illness (the HIV certificate is not compulsory for children under the age of ten, and for Dutch nationals);
- a proof of guarantee of the financial capabilities of the employer;
- draft of the working agreement concluded or to be concluded between employer and employee, which should be in accordance with the Aruban labor laws;
- copies of job vacancy posting, newspaper ads and recap of these results;
- a proof of payment of the required legal fee of Af 350;
- a copy of the entry in the Commercial Register at the Chamber of Commerce and Industry in case one is to set up a business of his own;
- a copy of the director's license from the Minister of Economic Affairs in case it concerns a person to be employed as a director of a company.

Before the permit is granted a deposit must be paid. The amount of this deposit varies from country to country.

One may request a **residence permit without a work permit**, then applicant must submit:

1. bank references indicating that applicant is financially self-supporting or any other proof that he will not become a financial burden to the Government or the community;
2. his home and business addresses for the last ten years;
3. the reasons why to immigrate to Aruba;
4. certificate of good conduct "police record" from the country of origin or from the country where he had his home address for the last ten years, not older than 2 months;
5. a valid passport and identity documents;
6. three (3) passport photographs;
7. a medical certificate not older than one month, certifying that applicant does not suffer from any contagious disease or mental illness, HIV, VDRL, TBC (the HIV certificate is not compulsory for children under the age of ten, and for Dutch nationals);
8. a proof that applicant has a permanent address in Aruba;
9. a proof of payment of the required legal fee.

Before the permit is granted a deposit must be paid, which varies from country to country.

APPLICATION FOR RESIDENCE AND WORK PERMITS

Applications for residence and work permits should be addressed to the Minister of Justice, through the Director of the Department of Public Order and Security.

Additional information can be obtained at:

Directie Openbare Orde en Veiligheid
Caya Dick Cooper 11
San Nicolas
Phone 297 843322
Fax 297 843258.

MANUFACTURING INDUSTRIES

Company	Product
Building Materials: **Arubaanse Verffabriek** **Caribbean Paint Factory** **Barcadera Cement Aruba** **ACM & Industries**	**Paints, fillers** **Paints, fillers** **Cement** **Cultured Marble Sanitary items**
Petroleum Products:	**Petroleum Refining**

Coastal Aruba Refining Company	
Chemicals: **Aruba Candle Company** **AllSCO N.V. Industrial** **R.J. van der Sar N.V.**	**Candles, disinfectants** **Detergents** **Disinfectants, soaps, detergents**
Paper and Plastic Products: **Carex Paper Products Toilet** **Hoori N.V.**	**Paper, kitchen towels** **Disposable plastic**
Cosmetics and Pharmaceutical Products: **Aruba Aloe Balm N.V.**	**Aloe-based skin care products**
Food and Beverages: **Compack N.V.** **Palmera Quality Product** **Playa Liquor and Bottling**	**Meat Products** **Alcoholic Beverages** **Alcoholic Beverages**
Miscellaneous **Sleep Comfort Mattress Co.** **Matrassenfabriek Baroud**	**Mattresses** **Aruba Mattresses**

INDUSTRIAL AND COMMERCIAL SITES

In Aruba most of the land is owned by the Government, which land cannot be purchased but can be obtained on a long lease term.

Duration of the long lease agreement is 60 years and can be renewed for another 60 years when expired. The fee is 6% of the value of the land per year. In order to obtain a parcel of land in long lease, the interested party must secure an option contract. Option is granted for a period up to 6 months and the fee due per year amounts to 50 percent of the costs of a long lease. Extension of the option period is possible up to a maximum of 5 years, dependent on the size of the project.

A formal application must be submitted to the Minister of Public Works to obtain a specific parcel of land. This petition should contain data of the applicant and a description of the project. Of utmost importance is specific information on financing of the investment involved. Applicants should consider waiting time, due to the amount of requests.

SITES

The government offers different sites located in Bushiri, Wayaca, Barcadera and Balashi for industrial and commercial purposes.

ORANJESTAD

The Bushiri area is available for commercial activities. This site is located in the vicinity of the Port of Oranjestad. The site rental is Af 3.00/m^2/yr (US$ 0.16/sq ft/yr).

WAYACA

The Wayaca site is located just opposite the airport. This site area is very limited and is intended for commercial activities. The rental amounts to Af 2.10/m^2/yr (US$ 0.11/sq ft/yr).

BARCADERA

The Barcadera site, located in the industrial port area, covers 43 ha (106.3 acres) and allows for industrial activities.

The site is located at 3.5 km distance from the airport and 8.0 km from the port of Oranjestad. The site rental is Af 3.00/m^2/yr.

The Government policy is to move all free zone activities to the Barcadera area.

BALASHI

The Balashi site covers 8.6 ha and allows for light industrial activities. This site is located at 1.5 km from the industrial port. The rental amounts to Af 2.10/m^2/yr.

BEACH SITES

Practically all land along the beaches is owned by the Government. In areas along the hotels, sites have been designated for tourism auxiliary projects, such as recreational projects.

For further information on lease land, please contact:

Dienst Domeinbeheer
Sabana Blanco 71
Aruba
Tel: 833000
Fax: 838078

BUILDING COSTS

The indicative unit construction costs, expressed in Af per m^2 (US$/sq ft) are illustrated hereafter.

In these costs a distinction is made between standard and high standard facilities.(*)

	Standard		High Standard	
	Af/m^2	US$/sq ft	Af/m^2	US$/sq ft

Warehouse	650	33.75	1,100	57.10
Production	900	46.75	1,300	67.50
Office	1,500	77.85	2,000	103.80
Laboratory	1,900	98.60	2,400	124.60
Housing	900	46.75	1,300	67.50

* Standard facility being a complete metal, not applicable for housing or concrete prefab construction, while high standard being in bricks with extra insulation.

INVESTING IN ARUBA

ARUBA FOREIGN INVESTMENT AGENCY

The Aruba Foreign Investment Agency (AFIA), on behalf of its partners, informs foreign companies and investors about the investment climate in Aruba.

The AFIA is a combination of an investment and export consultancy and technical assistance.

The AFIA is a division of the Aruban Ministry of Economic Affairs and Tourism.

The Director and staff of The AFIA will kindly advise and assist you with any information and or inquiries.

The AFIA has access to addresses, economic and financial information, and statistical and technical data. The AFIA can answer any question you might have about government incentive policies

The AFIA maintains close contact with the financial community; the service industry; the Customs body; and government bodies.

Once a company has decide to establish an operation in Aruba or abroad (for local companies) the AFIA continues to be available for general consultation.

The AFIA s services are completely confidential and free of charge. AFIA only office is on the island of Aruba, but soon will be opening offices in the U.S.A., Europe and South America

Carlyle A. De Coteau
Director Aruba Foreign Investment Agency
Royal Plaza Mall, Suite 228
P.O.Box 5186 Royal Plaza

L.G. Smith Blvd. Z/N
Oranjestad, Aruba D.W.I.

E-mail afia@toaruba.com

SERVICE

The AFIA analyses and develops classifications of potential companies which are or are going to internationalize, regionalize or restructure operations and for which Aruba, as an outstanding platform, has something to offer.

It is of essential that the AFIA is able to pave the way to and from Aruba through insights into the strategic developments and require a feel for the decision making process of the potential customer.

The opinion and experience of customers, in turn, are valuable input for policy making by the AFIA.

The AFIA presents itself as a port of entry and departure to the network in Aruba. It offers its clients (foreign and local) know-how regarding the business possibilities in Aruba and in the region and have access to organizations and parties (including the rest of the government) that can possibly contribute to the client success.

One way of achieving this is by organizing fact-finding missions, which are visits to Aruba (and for the local companies a trip abroad) by decision makers, managers or advisors who must prepare the choice of location for a company.

DEVELOPING TRENDS

In this changing world we are currently experiencing a trend called; globalization of the world economy. We are seeing more and more companies decentralizing and expanding operation abroad especially to the South American continent.

Because of an open international attitude, Aruba is easily accepted by other nations in the Caribbean, Latin America and South America. Aruba have numerous practical assets (primarily its people) that can serve foreign business interest, especially headquarters operations, coordinating of activities and agent networks. Particularly now that so many companies are changing from an individual national to a worldwide strategy.

AFIA will do everything possible to assist you to implement and process your Caribbean, Latin / South American headquarters plans.

AFIA can surely play a role in achieving your business objectives.

PHYSICAL INFRASTRUCTURE

The island s physical infrastructure is a prime example of its investment in facilities. Evidence of the planning, vision, efforts and determination of its people and government.

The redesigning, remodeling and expansion of the international airport Queen Beatrix, will undoubtedly propel the airport into a higher atmospheric status. User-friendliness, efficiency and service is the main priority and goal. Over two hundred weekly flights to and from South America and daily connecting flights from North America. Remarkably flexible Customs, taxation, banking, service and support provide reliable and rapid handling.

CURASAO -INVESTMENT AND BUSINESS OPPORTUNITIES

BASIC INFORMATION

Curaçao is the largest of the five islands that together make up the Netherlands Antilles. The other four islands are Bonaire, St. Marten, St. Eustatius and Saba. Curaçao is located in the southwestern Caribbean, 44 miles off the coast of South America and rather close to its sister islands of the ABC group, Aruba and Bonaire. It is approximately 38 miles long and from 2 to 7.5 miles wide depending on where on the island you are.

The average temperature is in the mid 80s all year round and the island has relatively little rain throughout the year making Curaçao a perfect vacation destination especially with the added perk of it being outside the hurricane belt. Curaçao is known to have a minimum of 30 beautiful yet intimate beaches scattered along its coast. The well known Seaquarium Beach is home to the Sea Aquarium as well as the Sea Aquarium Beach Resort. The waters are calm and excellent for swimming and diving. In fact Curaçao is like a hidden treasure chest to the Scuba diving world. The waters surrounding this tranquil island are full of the most colorful and exciting reefs, marine life and shipwrecks. A must stop for diving enthusiasts.

ECONOMY

The Curaçao economy relies heavily on tourism, petroleum transshipment, and offshore banking all of which are closely tied to the United States, Europe and South America and almost all consumer and capital goods are imported, with the US and Venezuela being the major suppliers.

The oil refinery earnings represent more than 90% of all exports. About 200 cruise ships come annually, and nearly 240,000 tourists, most from Europe and specifically the Netherlands, visit each year.

GOVERNMENT

Curaçao's government is based on a parliamentary democracy, and Parliament comprises a council of ministers and a prime minister. A governor general, is appointed by the queen of the Netherlands to be the crown's representative in the Netherlands Antilles. Curaçao falls under the Dutch legal system.

CLIMATE

Curaçao is warm and sunny year round with an average temperature about mid 80s (27°C). The rainy season occurs between October and February with short, occasional showers, mostly at night, with sunny weather during the day. Total annual rainfall averages only 22 inches (570 mm).

HISTORY

Curaçao has a very rich and unique history. It is the largest of the Dutch Caribbean islands and was first settled by the Spanish in 1527. The Dutch gained power in 1634 and have primarily retained possession of the island well into this century. Curaçao was at the center of the slave trade in the Caribbean and once slavery ended in 1863 petroleum became vital to their economy well into the 21 st century, along with tourism. Rather than ignore it's dark history, Curaçao has chosen through its' museums on the island to to educate those that visit, through very sophisticated exhibits depicting the black holocaust. The museum located at Hotel Kura Hulanda is in the capital Willemstad, as are all the museums and has probably the largest collection of African artifacts in the Caribbean.

Punda, which means the point, is the oldest part of Willemstad. Otrabanda, which means the other side, is where the first buildings were actually constructed. Curaçao's "Floating Lady" official name the Queen Emma Bridge was built in 1888 and still functions as a major connection between the east and west sides of Willemstad and swings open several times throughout the day to admit ships to the harbor.

Today Curaçao is known as the gem of the scuba diving world and is often compared with Grand Cayman as a diver's paradise. The capital Willemstad has fantastic shopping and a very technologically advanced business districts. When in Curaçao the Floating Market is a must a spot known throughout the Caribbean, where islanders from surrounding islands come in boats to sell almost everything from fresh fruit to art and crafts.

CURRENCY

The local currency is the Netherlands Antillean guilder also known as the florin and abbreviated as NAf or ANG. The stable rate is US$ 1 = NAf 1.77 for cash. The exchange rate can vary very slightly from stores and hotels. There is no black market and no restrictions on the amount of money one chooses to bring into the country. International credit cards are accepted at most major commercial establishments.

ENTRY REQUIREMENTS:

US and Canadian citizens need either a valid passport, or proof of citizenship in the form of an original birth certificate accompanied by photo ID, and an onward or return ticket. Most other nationals need only a passport. Visitors from the Dominican Republic, Colombia and Haiti require a visa.

ECONOMIC GROWTH

Curaçao is committed to economic growth and to leveraging and nurturing its unique comparative advantages. At the core of economic policies are the interests of investors which are reflected in the underlying principles of the investment upgrade program, economic development strategy, privatization program, and legislative reform. Curaçao recognizes that essential to its economic growth is the need to create an environment that is attractive, open, and friendly to foreign investment. This guide is designed to provide investors an overview of Curaçao's economy and links and referrals to more detailed information and assistance.

LOCATION

Curaçao is located in the southwestern Caribbean, at'altitude 12' north and longitude 68' west. The island is just 44 miles (70 km) north of South America. It is 2.5 hours by air from Miami. See Map

SIZE

444 square kilometers (182 square miles);

61 km long: 5-14 km wide.

POPULATION

Curaçao has 150,000 inhabitants; 40 to 50 different nationalities live on the island.The nationalities are mainly from Europe, South America, Africa and the native Indians that once inhabited the island before the Europeans came.

TIME ZONE

Curaçao is on Atlantic Standard Time: one hour later than US Standard Time (the same time as Daylight Savings Time) and four hours earlier than Greenwich Mean Time.

LANGUAGE

Dutch is the official language but Curacoans are multilingual and speak English and Spanish very well along with Papiamento, the local Creole language with it's heritage taken from Spanish, Portuguese, English, French, Dutch and West African.

INVESTMENT AND BUSINESS CLIMATE

ACCESS TO EU MARKET

Curaçao's Economy is based on shipping, tourism and oil refining. The total population is 150,000 and speak at least four languages including Dutch as the official language, but Papiamento, English, Spanish are also spoken.

Telephone Codes: 599, Netherlands Antilles' code; 9, island code

Time Zone: 4 hours behind Greenwich Mean Time (-4 GMT). Daylight Saving Time is not observed

Tipping: 10%-15% in restaurants, unless a service charge or gratuity has already been added to your bill.

Curaçao is known as a world class financial center. However, Curaçao also has the ability and knowledge to provide advanced business services in the fields of Business Training, Business Tourism, and Electronic Commerce. Curaçao's geographical position, sophisticated financial services, reliable infrastructure, multi-lingual workforce, political stability and favorable tax regime make it an attractive location from which to set up a regional headquarters, operate a business, and realize the inherent benefits.

The Government of Curaçao, as well as the leading companies, are aiming to make Curaçao a center of e-Business excellence, through investments in all areas of the Island's technology infrastructure. They are committed to the introduction of policies ensuring the growth of information-based business within the favorable tax environment of the Island.

In so far as the Netherlands Antilles applies the common import tariff of the EU single market, it can freely export products into the EU which it has sourced externally, without additional processing. Products originating in the Netherlands Antilles, or which have undergone "substantial economic transformation" there, have EU origin. This provides Curaçao direct access to the European Union (EU), which currently consists of approximately 360 million consumers. This indeed is a privileged trade relationship with the EU and investors to the island will also have access to these potential consumers. Curaçao's special access to the EU is a result of the Overseas Countries and Territories (OCT) arrangement.

the world Curaçao was once a haven for international trade throughout the history of the Caribbean; the island's location makes it a perfect air-and-sea hub for the Latin American and Caribbean markets, which has a combined population of more than 460 million people. Globalization today puts Curaçao once again in a position to be a major trading center for most products destined for the South, Central and Caribbean markets.

Furthermore, Curaçao is also able to take advantage of a favored relationship with the United States market, which consists of over 300 million inhabitants. This trade relationship is a direct payoff resulting from the 1990 Caribbean Basin Initiative (CBI II), the CBI allows most exports to enter the United States duty free.

These trends, in combination with the various international trade relationships, gives Curaçao the unique ability to trade with over one billion potential customers while avoiding high tariffs.

GOVERNMENT SYSTEM

The legal, financial and regulatory systems in Curaçao are based on Dutch civil law system, with some English common law influence.

Curaçao is a constituent island of the Netherlands Antilles ; the others being Bonaire, Saba, St Eustatius and St Marten. The Netherlands Antilles, Aruba and The Netherlands each have equal status within the Kingdom of the Netherlands, as regions autonomous in internal affairs. The Dutch monarch is locally represented by a Governor, while the Netherlands Antilles are represented in the Government of the Kingdom by a Minister Plenipotentiary. Foreign policy and defense matters are decided by a Council of Ministers of the Kingdom, including the Plenipotentiary, and executed under the authority of the Governor. The internal affairs of the islands are administered by the Central Government of the Netherlands Antilles, which is based in Willemstad, Curaçao, and responsible to the Staten, or legislative assembly. Curaçao may elect by non-compulsory adult suffrage 14 out of 22 members to the Staten. Routine local affairs on each island group (Bonaire, Curaçao and the Windward Islands) are managed by an elected Island Council presided over by a Lieutenant Governor.

The island is proud of its political stability which is based on a parliamentary democracy and is a part of the Kingdom of The Netherlands and has a seat on The Netherlands Antilles Government. Curaçao has close juridical and political ties with The Netherlands. The island has a politically stable parliamentary democracy with special access to markets in both the European Union and The United States

Local professional service companies and their employees are among the best in the entire Caribbean when it comes to education and skills.

INVESTMENT INCENTIVES

The Curaçao Government encourages and welcomes foreign investments and investors and provides a range of incentives aimed at developing the island and promoting it as a business center.

Companies operating in certain industries may qualify for the following incentives:

Exemption of import duties and economic levies on materials, on goods required for construction, on initial equipment- including expansion- of the enterprise' premises, and on packaging materials, on machinery, raw materials, semi-manufactured articles and accessory means, necessary for the industrial purposes.

Exemption of land and occupancy tax for a period of 10 years

2% corporate income tax- including all charges- on all profits induced by export.

Exemption of personal income tax on income earned from dividends and other distributions of export profits, provided that the profit is distributed two years after termination of the financial year in which the profit is realized.

Acceleration of depreciation of 1/3 of the purchase value of the business assets in the first fiscal year.

Deduction of 8% of the total investment (new building: 12%) annually for the first two fiscal years.

Indefinite carry-forward of losses incurred during the first four years of the business.

Counseling, marketing and financial assistance in the development of export markets.

Companies that establish in the Industrial Park can receive a rent reduction of 40% during the first year of the tenancy.

In addition to the tax exemptions, industries can qualify for the following incentives upon request:

2% corporate income tax- including all charges- on all profits induced by export.

Exemption of import duties on materials and economic levies on materials, on goods required for construction, on initial equipment- including expansion- of the enterprise' premises, and on packaging materials, on machinery, raw materials, semi-manufactured articles and accessory means, necessary for the industrial purposes

Exemption of land and occupancy tax for a period of 10 years.

Export Oriented Industries

Antillean limited liability companies that export at least 90% of their total finished products can obtain the tax exemptions.

FINANCING

The Development Bank of the Netherlands Antilles and the Curaçao Development Corporation can provide loans with terms ranging from 5 to 15 years at rates of 9 to 11%. A grace period of 6 to 12 months can be negotiated.

TAX STRUCTURE

TAX STRUCTURE AND SOCIAL SECURITY SYSTEM

The 5 islands of the Netherlands Antilles have in principle the same tax laws, although the sales tax on Curaçao and Bonaire is different from the sales tax on St Maarten, Saba and St. Eustatius or Statia.

The income/profit tax of residents is levied on the income/profit generated world-wide, while foreign residents are subject to Netherlands Antilles tax if they generate income or profit from Netherlands Antilles sources. The tax system is a so called classical system, which means that a corporation must pay tax on its profit while the shareholder of such corporation must (again) pay tax on dividends received from the corporation. There are however certain facilities that reduce or eliminate this economic double tax effect.

Although Aruba and The Netherlands are part of the same Dutch Kingdom and the tax laws have been the same up to the period around the second world war, the tax laws of these three parts of the Kingdom have changed in different directions. The fact that the tax laws originate from the same system makes it possible to have the same judges decide on the tax law disputes. The judges from the Netherlands fly in at least twice a year to settle tax cases.

Each part of the Dutch Kingdom has its own right to tax which means that there is also the possibility of double taxation. Already in 1964 the Dutch Kingdom has one Tax Arrangement that solves double taxation issues and arranges for the possibilities to exchange information. This TAK (Tax Arrangement for the Dutch Kingdom) has been amended several times and is at this moment (June 2006) again in discussion on the subject of the dividends paid from the Netherlands to the Netherlands Antilles.

The social security system covers on the national level old age (AOV), widows and orphans (AWW) and exceptional medical expenses (AVBZ) and on the employer-level sickness (ZV) and accident insurance (OV).

The collection of the taxes and social security contributions is being divided between the Island Collector (EO), the Land Collector (LO) and the Social Security Bank (SVB).

INCOME TAX

Capital gains generated through the sale of the source of income is in general not taxable unless it is generated in the course of a business or stems from the sale of shares in a company that form a so called substantial interest.

Residents are taxed on their income generated world-wide from the following sources:

Income from a business or profession as entrepreneur; the rules that apply here are in principle the same as the rules that apply to a corporation to calculate the profit generated;

Income from employment;

Income from property (real estate);

Income from capital;

Certain periodic receipts.

Residents are entitled to various deductions, up to specified limits, including:

Business expenses, such as moving and travel expenses;

Medical expenses;

Life insurance and pension plan contributions;

Charitable contributions;

Mortgage interest for the private home;

Interest up to ANG 2,500 annually

Alimony;

Social security contributions for the old age and widows and orphans (AOV/AWW)

Non-residents have to pay income tax as far as they generate income from Netherlands Antilles sources such as:

Income from property (real estate) situated within the Netherlands Antilles, including mortgage interest;

Income from a profession or business as far as it is personally exercised within the Netherlands Antilles or through a permanent representative or authorized agent;

Income of a managing or supervisory director(s) of a company established within the Netherlands Antilles also in the case of restriction of powers to parts of the enterprise of such entity situated outside the Netherlands Antilles;

Income from shares (including sale of shares) in a company established within the Netherlands Antilles as far as they represent a substantial participation (e.g in case 5% or more of the issued capital is held; the so called substantial participation holder);

Income from offices paid from the National or Island treasury, while the activities attaching to such offices were performed outside the Netherlands Antilles;

Non-residents can also claim certain deductions as far as they are related to the income sources in the Netherlands Antilles or they are, up to certain limits, charitable contributions and mortgage interest.

TAX RATES

The income tax rate is progressive and starts in 2006 in Curaçao with 13% and runs up to 49.4%. There is a basic deduction in 2006 of ANG 1,548.30 and if applicable a sole earner allowance, pensioner's allowance and child allowance.

The substantial interest income is taxed at 19.5% while certain special amounts are taxed at a rate between 13% and 26%.

SPECIAL INCOME TAX FACILITIES

Penshonado

Expatriates

Penshonado

The income tax offers a favorable pensioners ("penshonado") tax regime. This regime is available on the following conditions:

The "penshonado" should be at least 50 years old on the date that he registers himself as a resident;

The pensioner should not have lived in the Netherlands Antilles in the five years before making the application for the "penshonado" status;

The pensioner must own a house in the Netherlands Antilles with a value of at least ANG 450,000 (US$ 253,000) for his personal use within 18 months after his registration as a resident;

The "penshonado" must have requested the penshonado status from the tax inspector within two months after registration in the municipality register;

The penshonado must be a legally admitted resident;

The "penshonado" and his wife may in general not generate income from activities within the Netherlands Antilles unless this income is generated from a company established in the Netherlands Antilles and in which the "penshonado" has a participation of at least 40% or the income is generated from being a supervisory director of a company.

The income tax rate applicable on the income of the "penshonado" is 10% and is solely applicable to income from foreign sources (or which is considered to be income from foreign sources according to the income tax law such as interest on bank accounts kept within the Netherlands Antilles). It is also possible to report a fixed income of ANG 500,000 (USD 281,000) at the progressive income tax rate as mentioned above.

ECONOMIC FREE ZONES

Curaçao plays an integral role in international business. A special Association Agreement with the European Union allows companies that do business in and via Curaçao to export many products to European markets free of import duties and quotas. Curaçao is also a beneficiary of the U.S. Caribbean Basin Initiative (CBI), which allows most exports to enter the United States duty free.

The Curaçao Government is serious about en economic development and offers two free trade zones: the Harbor Economic Zone and the Airport Free Zone. Most of the companies located in the Harbor Economic Zone are trading firms that distribute products from the United States, Europe, and Asia to the Caribbean and Latin America. In a Curaçao Economic Zone, goods for export can be stored, manufactured, processed, assembled, packed, exhibited, and released from bond, free from all duties. In addition, services, for instance via Internet, may also be provided.

PRIVATIZATION

Curaçao launched an ambitious scheme to privatize State Owned Enterprises (SOEs). These SOEs are active in a wide variety of sectors, like telecommunications, infrastructure (harbors, airports, etc.), oil, finance and more.

Privatization is seen by the Government of Curaçao as one of the major pillars in the attracting foreign investments to the island. For the actual implementation of the privatization process, the Island Government of Curaçao established the Commissie Implementatie Privatisering' (CIP) in December 1999.

Privatization is not an end in itself. It is a means to an end, the end being economic development and social welfare of Curaçao. In the government's endeavor to rationalize its functioning, it intends to concentrate on governing and let the economy be guided by the market forces as far as possible. Herewith the government of Curaçao follows the current global trend towards privatization. Besides aforementioned objective, the government aims to enhance overall efficiency on macro- as well as micro-level. Through privatization the government strives to strengthen the forces of national economic development in general and in particular to increase the competitiveness of the State Owned Enterprises (SOEs), especially those that are exposed to global competition.

One of the main objectives is to enhance efficiency. Curaçao is a small island economy, characterized by (i) small-sized markets served by small-sized enterprises, (ii) competition from the other Caribbean islands, and (iii) a relatively high dependence on imports. It is, therefore, essential to introduce policy reforms that encourage reductions in production costs. These will flow from the emergence of competition in the market, along with the inflow of technical know-how and capital from abroad, which acts as a spur for the new owners of enterprises to operate more efficiently. In this way the economic efficiency of Curaçao will improve and will add to its competitive position in the Caribbean.

TARIFFS

Curaçao has tax treaties with the Netherlands, Norway and the U.S.

Food and beverage products imported into Curaçao are subject to four types of tariff: import duties (calculated over c.i.f. value), excise duties (on beer and spirits), economic levy (on products that are already locally manufactured), and expenditure tax (also called "sales tax").

Most imported food items, including most fruits and vegetables, cereal, soup, spaghetti, tea, and spices, receive a 10.5 percent import tax. Many products can be imported duty-free, such as: beef, chicken, some baby foods, potatoes, dried peas and beans, some grains, olive and sesame oils, milk (powdered milk duty-free only in containers less than 2.5 kg), cream, and cheese. Other import duty rates include the following: citrus fruits, 5 percent; sugar, 4.5 percent; fish, 4.5 percent; fruit juice, ground coffee, yogurt, and bread, 5.5 percent; non-chicken poultry, 17 percent; oyster, 17 percent; prepared fish or poultry, 18.5 percent; rice, 25 percent; beer, 28¢ per liter; and margarine, at about 3¢ per kilogram. Import duties on margarine, butter, sugar, beverages and alcohol are not based on c.i.f. value, but on weight or quantity.

Special excise duties are applied to imports of alcoholic beverages in addition to other taxes. Beer receives about 67¢ per liter in excise tax (in addition to 28¢/liter import duty, 50¢/liter levy tax, and a 6 percent sales tax). Duties on stronger spirits vary depending on the alcohol content of the product. For a spirit that is 50 percent alcohol content, there will be about $16.80 per liter in excise tax, plus import duties, sales tax, and levy tax.

Some products also are protected by economic levy (resulting in an additional tariff rate), such as: bacon ($1.11/kg), ham ($1.12/kg), powdered milk in containers larger than 2.5 kg ($1.00/kg), ice cream ($1.28/liter), yogurt (39¢/liter), wheat flour (14¢/kg), cornmeal flour (19¢/kg), rice (25 percent), margarine (50¢/kg), edible oils except olive and sesame (33¢/liter), bread (4.5 percent), bread dough (24.5 percent), sweetened fruit juices (33¢/liter), malt (42¢/liter), beverages without alcohol (50¢/liter), beer (53¢/liter).

Most food items, those in particular that are considered primary necessities of life, such as meat, poultry, grains, and rice, receive no expenditure tax, while most beverages are subject to a 6 percent sales tax.

BUSINESS AND INVESTMETN CONTACTS

ECONOMIC DEVELOPMENT AGENCIES

The following Agencies are available to assist you with your investment:

The Curaçao Chamber of Commerce

www.curacao-chamber.an

The Curaçao Chamber of Commerce and Industry is the voice of private enterprise. The Chamber represents the general interests of the business community, keeps a complete roster of Curaçao businesses, and provides services to local and international companies and individuals with an interest in doing business in, from or through Curaçao.

The Curaçao Tourist Board

www.curacao.com

The Curaçao Tourist Board promotes the Curaçao tourism brand around the world and provides support services to tourists and investors in the tourism sector.

The Curaçao Ports Authority & Curaçao Port Services, Inc.

www.curports.com

CPA: The harbor authority in Curaçao is the Curaçao Ports Authority (CPA) N.V.

Since 1982, the CPA, a limited liability company whose main shareholder is the island government of Curaçao, has managed Curaçao's ports. CPA is a landlord port authority, owning infrastructure and most of the superstructure of the ports. The facilities are leased out to private operators

CPS: The Curaçao Port Services Inc. (CPS) N.V. manages the Willemstad Container Terminal and other cargo facilities in Port of Willemstad based on a concession agreement with CPA, since 1983. The Port of Willemstad's strategic geographical location with respect to the United States, South America and Europe is one of the major factors that has contributed in making Curaçao such an important regional transshipment hub for container shipping

Curinde

www.curinde.com

Curinde N.V. is an abbreviation of Curaçao Industrial & International Trade Development Co. N.V. Curinde is the managing company of the Harbor Free Zone, the Airport Economic Zone and the Industrial Parks. Curinde provides professional support to parties interested in establishing a presence in one of these parks.

GOVERMENT OFFICES

Government and General Information

- Consulate General of the Netherlands in Miami:
  www.cgmiami.org
- Central Bank of the Netherlands Antilles:
  www.centralbank.an
- National Archives of the Netherlands Antilles (Dutch):
  www.nationalarchives.an/
- National Archaeological Anthropological Museum of the Neth. Ant.:
  www.curaçao.com/naam/
- Meteorological Service of the N.A.:
  www.meteo.an
- Postal services:
  www.meteo.an
- Economic Zone:
  www.curinde.com

Curacao - Government and General Information

- The Official Web Site of the Government of Curaçao (Dutch)
  www.curaçao-gov.an
- Map of Curaçao
  www.caribline.com/islands/cr/crmap.shtml
- Curaçao Tourism Bureau
  www.Curaçao-tourism.com
- Curaçao Telephone Directory
  www.white pages.an
- Curaçao Yellow Pages
  www.yellowpages.an
- Information on the local language: Papiamentu
  www.narin.com
- Curaçao Society for the Protection of Animals
  www.cura.net/dierenbescherming
- US Consulate General in Curaçao
  www.amcongencuraçao.an

GOVERNMENT AGENCIES

- Central Bank of the Netherlands Antilles (BNA)

Simon Bolivarplein 1
Tel: (+599-9) 434-5500
Fax: (+599-9) 461-5004
E-mail: **info@centralbank.an**
Website:**www.centralbank.an**

Central Bureau of Statistics (CBS)
Fort Amsterdam
Tel: (+599-9) 463-0153
Fax: (+599-9) 461-1696

Department of Economic Affairs (DEZ)
Molenplein
Tel: (+599-9) 462-1444
Fax: (+599-9) 462-7590

Department of Environmental Affairs (Milieudienst)
Groot Davelaar K22-23
Tel: (+599-9) 736-9022
Fax: (+599-9) 736-9195

Department of Labor (DAZ)
Bellisimaweg 17
Tel: (+599-9) 737-1200
Fax: (+599-9) 736-5711

Department of Public Works (DOW)
Landhuis Parera, PO Box 3227
Tel: (+599-9) 433-4444
Fax: (+599-9) 461-7969

Department of Urban and Regional Development Planning and Housing (DROV)
Plasa Horacio Hoyer 19
Tel: (+599-9) 461-2199
Fax: (+599-9) 461-2697

Development Bank of the Netherlands Antilles (OBNA)
Schottegatweg Oost 3-C
PO Box 267
Tel: (+599-9) 747-3000
Fax: (+599-9) 747-3320

Directorate of Economic Affaires
Gomez Plein
Tel: (+599-9) 465-6236
Fax: (+599-9) 465-6316

Directorate of Fiscal Affairs
Regentesselaan z/n
Tel: (+599-9) 734-2001
Fax: (+599-9) 737-2390

Directorate of Foreign Relations
Fort Amsterdam 4
Tel: (+599-9) 461-3933
Fax: (+599-9) 461-7123

Immigration Service
Waaigat
Tel: (+599-9) 866-6400
Fax: (+599-9) 465-7176
▪ Public Health Department (GGD)
Piscaderaweg 49
Tel: (+599-9) 462-5800
Fax: (+599-9) 462-7175

Social Security Bank (SVB)
Pater Eeuwensweg 9
Tel: (+599-9) 434-4000
Fax: (+599-9) 462-6536

Tax Inspectorate
Regentesselaan z/n
Tel: (+599-9) 734-2680
Fax: (+599-9) 736-7800

FOREIGN GOVERMENT OFFICES

US Consulate General in Curaçao
www.amcongencuracao.an

Consulate of Belgium
Habaai z/n
Tel: (+599-9) 461-3650
Fax: (+599-9) 461-6569

Consulate of Bolivia
Wolkstraat 16, kamer 11
Tel: (+599-9) 461-4800

Consulate of Brazil
Schottegatweg Oost 58
Tel: (+599-9) 736-6933

Consulate of Canada
Plaza Jojo-Correa 2-4
Tel: (+599-9) 466-1115

Consulate of Chili
Sta. Rosaweg 66
Tel: (+599-9) 737-5875
Fax: (+599-9) 736-4266

Consulate of Colombia
Wilhelminaplein 25
Tel: (+599-9) 461-4663 / 465-0008
(+599-9)

Consulate-General of Costa Rica
Gomezplein 10
Tel: (+599-9) 465-8611 / 465-6846
Fax: (+599-9) 465-6846

Consulate of Denmark
Bonam Kaya D 135
Tel: (+599-9) 736-6686
Fax: (+599-9) 736-6686

Consulate-General of the Dominican Republic
Kaya Papa Godett (Pietermaai) 45
Tel: (+599-9) 465-9777
Fax: (+599-9) 465-9666

Consulate of Germany
Kaya Kooyman 48
Tel: (+599-9) 461-3870

Consulate of Finland
Mensings Caminada
Schottegatweg Oost z/n
Tel: (+599-9) 737-0222

Consulate of France
Dr. M.L. King Blvd. 24
Tel: (+599-9) 465-7177
Fax: (+599-9) 465-7149

Consulate of Gambia
"Beau Rivage" Apt. 11 , Penstraat 254
Tel: (+599-9) 461-5467
Fax: (+599-9) 461-5467

Consulate of Guatemala
Alablancaweg 26
Tel: (+599-9) 767-2429
Fax: (+599-9) 736-9875

Consulate of Great Britain & Northern Ireland
Jan Sofat 38
Tel: (+599-9) 747-3322
Fax: (+599-9) 747-3330

Consulate of Haiti
Grebbelinieweg 18
Tel: (+599-9) 465-3434

Consulate of Hungary
Pietermaaiplein 15
Tel: (+599-9) 461-6744/461-6878

Consulate of India
Heerenstraat 4-B
Tel: (+599-9) 461-2262
Fax: (+599-9) 461-4345

Consulate of Israel
Blauwduifweg 5
Tel: (+599-9) 736-5068

Consulate of Italy
Bellisimaweg 10
Tel: (+599-9) 737-5973
Fax: (+599-9) 737-5973

Consulate of Jamaica
Habaaiweg 68
Tel: (+599-9) 462-6561

Consulate of Japan
Plaza Jojo Correa 2-4
Tel: (+599-9) 466-1114

Consulate of Lebanon
Winston Churchillweg 159
Tel: (+599-9) 868-4779
Fax: (+599-9) 869-0692

Consulate of Liberia
Residence Piscadera 11
Tel: (+599-9) 462-6982

Consulate of Mexico
Breedestraat 46 (P)
Tel: (+599-9) 465-0240

Consulate of Norway
Plaza Jojo Correa 2-4
Tel: (+599-9) 461-1117

Consulate of Panama
Maduro Plaza

Dokweg 19
Tel: (+599-9) 737-1566

Consulate of Poland
Postal address Snipweg 49
Tel: (+599-9) 737-8735

Consulate of Portugal
Residence Pos Kabai, Apt. 2-B
Tel: (+599-9) 738-3223

Consulate of Spain
Pimpiriweg 29
Tel: (+599-9) 736-9532
Fax: (+599-9) 736-9072

Consulate of Surinam
Kaya Jacob Posner 11, Expo Center, Unit 108, Zeelandia, P.O.B. 6072
Tel: (+599-9) 465-0099/560-5498
Fax: (+599-9) 461-8455

Consulate of Trinidad & Tobago
Kaya Papilon 1
Tel: 767-9158

Consulate of Uruguay
Kaya W.F.G.(Jombi) Mensing 41
Tel: (+599-9) 461-1760
Fax: (+599-9) 461-8335

Consulate of Venezuela
Handelskade 12
Tel: (+599-9) 461-3100 / 461-4140
Fax: (+599-9) 461-3179

Consulate of the United States of America
J.B. Gorsiraweg 1
Tel: (+599-9) 461-3066
Fax: (+599-9) 461-6489

Consulate of Sweden
Santa Anna Blvd. 16 / Infotrans Caribbean
Tel: (+599-9) 465-6345
Fax: (+599-9) 465-6017

Consulate of Switzerland
Julianaplein 26
Tel: (+599-9) 461-3550
Fax: (+599-9) 461-2732

PRIVATE DEVELOPMENT

Private Economic Development Partnership

It is in the interest of all private companies in Curaçao to promote and attract trade and investment to develop and grow the economy. While the government of Curaçao has a number of quality development programs in place, these programs are enhanced by an engaged and active private sector. The private sector initiative led by the Aqualectra - Marubeni Economic Development Partnership believes it has a role to play in helping to develop Curaçao 's economic future. In close cooperation with the Curaçao Chamber of Commerce, this partnership will strive to help make investors aware of the opportunities in Curaçao and facilitate their investment efforts whenever possible. Accordingly, this web site has been created to promote and position Curaçao properly in the minds of investors, provide them the information and resources they require, and keep them abreast of investment opportunities as they arise.

This web site is sponsored by the Aqualectra - Marubeni economic development partnership.

The Aqualectra - Marubeni Economic Development Partnership is a community development initiative of Marubeni's Curaçao Utilities Operating Company, "CUOC," and Aqualectra. As part of these two utilities companies' corporate policy, an economic development program has been undertaken which is deemed to be in the interest of their stakeholders for three reasons:

It grows the industrial base increasing the demand for their services
It benefits the co mm unities in which they operate
It is part of being a corporate good citizen

Marubeni's and Aqualectra's Economic Development Team is available to assist you with your investment activities in Curaçao. We offer a private company perspective as well as that of a foreign investor. We look forward to supporting and facilitating your investment-related activities in Curaçao by providing advice, making introductions to key government and business leaders, providing guidance with respect to local business practices, and providing private professional support through our economic development contractors.

For additional information and support from the Marubeni- Aqualectra Partnership, see the following contacts:

Marubeni
www.marubeni.com
email: info@investcuraçao.com
Aqualectra
www.aqualectra.com
email: info@investcuraçao.com
For trade and investment inquiries in the U.S., contact Marubeni & Aqualectra's Trade and Investment Consultant:
Geo Strategy Partners
Mark Towery
Managing Director
7840 Roswell Road
Building 300, Suite 350
Atlanta, GA 30350
T: 770-650-8495

C: 404-372-3686
F: 678-441-9417
mt@geostrategypartners.com
www.geostrategypartners.com

Curaçao Hospitality and Tourism Association

"CHATA" is a private sector organization that advances the hospitality and tourism sector by enhancing its business environment for the benefit of its members and the economic growth of Curaçao. CHATA's purpose is to:

Provide a tourism forum for its members
Promote cooperation among its members
Assist in promoting business for its members

Foster goodwill towards the tourism industry

Curacao Trade & Investment
Geo Strategy Partners

NEWSPAPERS/RADIO STATIONS

Algemeen Dagblad Caribbean Edition (Dutch)
www.adcaribbean.com
Amigoe (Dutch and English)
www.amigoe.com
La Prensa (Papiamentu)
www.laprensacur.com
Extra (Papiamentu)
www.extra.an
Radio Korsou
www.korsou.com
Radio Hoyer (livestream broadcast)
www.radiohoyer.com
Radio Notisia 107.9 FM
www.radionotisia1079.com
Vigilante
www.vigilante.an

UNIVERSITIES & SCHOOLS

University of the Netherlands Antilles
www.una.net
Caribbean International University (Spanish)
www.ciuna.com
Radulphus College (Dutch)
www.rc.an
St. Martinus University (Medical school)
www.martinus.edu

Language, Culture, Architecture and Museums

Info on the local language: Papiamentu
www.papiamentu.com
Papiamentu Learning Web Site
www.papiamentu.net
Translations: English-Papiamentu-English
www.donamaro.nl/papiamentu/
Curaçao Art Festival
www.curacaoartfestival.com
Herman van Bergen - artist
www.hermanvanbergen.com
Hortence Brouwn – sculptress
www.brouwn.com
Jean Girigori – artist
www.jeangirigori.com
Nena Sanchez - artist
www.nenasanchez.com
Hans Hoonings – artist
www.coraltreasures.com
Stadsherstel N.V.
www.stadsherstel.com
Historical Monuments
www.iseeyou.com/monuments/fr-b-gat.html
Kura Hulanda Museum
www.kurahulanda.com
Curaçao Maritime Museum
www.curacaomaritime.com

PRIVATE SECTOR

Curaçao Chamber of Commerce
www.curaçao-chamber.an
Association of Industrialists of the Netherlands Antilles (ASINA)
www.asina.org
Curaçao International Financial Services Association
www.cifa.an
Business Curaçao
www.businesscuracao.com
World Trade Center Curaçao
www.wtccuracao.com
InnovatieCentrum Curaçao
www.innovatiecentrum.an

(SEMI)GOVERNMENT COMPANIES

CURINDE (Economic Zone Management Company)
www.curinde.com

CUROIL

www.curoil.com
Curaçao Ports Authority/Curaçao Ports Services
www.curports.com
United Telecommunications Service
www.uts.an

BANKS

ABN AMRO Bank
www.abnamro.an
Banco di Caribe
www.bancodicaribe.com
Giro Bank
www.girobank.net
Maduro & Curiel's Bank
www.mcb-bank.com
RBTT Netherlands Antilles
www.rbtt.com
SFT Bank
www.sftbank.com

TOURISM

Curaçao Tourism Bureau
www.curacao.com
Curaçao Hospitality and Tourism Association
www.chata.org
Curaçao Vacation Guide
www.curacao-guide.info
Map of Curaçao
www.caribline.com/islands/cr/crmap.shtml
Map of Willemstad
www.caribbean-on-line.com/cr/crmap.html

TOURISM - ACCOMODATIONS

Curaçao Apartment and Small Hotel Association
www.apartmentscuracao.com
Vacation Rentals
www.intac.an
Avila Beach Hotel
www.avilahotel.com
Bon Bini Sea Side Resort
www.bonbiniseasideresort.com
Breezes/Super Club
www.breezescuracao.com
Chogogo Resort Curaçao
www.chogogo.com
Floris Suite Hotel
www.florissuitehotel.com
Habitat Curaçao
www.habitatdiveresorts.com/curacao/index.html
Hilton Curaçao

www.hiltoncaribbean.com/curacao/index.htm

Howard Johnson Curaçao Plaza Hotel
www.hojo- curacao.com/welcomenf.htm

Holiday Beach Hotel & Casino
www.hol-beach. com

Kura Hulanda Hotel
www.kurahulanda.com

Limestone Water Resort
www.limestoneholiday.com

Lions Dive & Beach Resort
www.lionsdive.com

Livingstone Jan Thiel Resort
www.janthielresort.com

Marriott Beach Resort and Emerald Casino
www.marriotthotels.com/curmc

Otrobanda Hotel & Casino
www.otrobandahotel.com

Papagayo Beach Resort
www.papagayo-beach.com

Plaza Hotel Curaçao
www.plazahotelcuracao.com

San Marco Hotel & Casino
www.sanmarcocuracao.com

Sunset Waters Beach Resort
www.sunsetwaters.com

Trupial Inn Hotel & Casino
www.trupialinn.com

MEDIA LINKS

Algemeen Dagblad Caribbean Edition (Dutch)
www.adcaribbean.com

Amigoe (Dutch and English)
www.amigoe.com

La Prensa (Papiamentu)
www.laprensacur.com

Extra (Papiamentu)

www.extra.an

Radio Korsou
www.korsou.com

Radio Hoyer (livestream broadcast)
www.radiohoyer.com

Radio Notisia 107.9
www.radionotisia1079.com

Vigilante
www.vigilante.an

RESTAURANTS

Bistro le Clochard
www.bistroleclochard.com

SCUBA DIVING AND WATER SPORTS

Atlantis Diving
www.atlantisdiving.com

Caribbean Sea Sports
www.caribseasports.com

S.A.F.E. Diving Curaçao
www.safe-diving.com

Toucan Diving
www.curacao-toucandiving.com

Wederfoort Diving School
www.divewederfoort.com/maps2.htm

ENTERTAINMENT/ACTIVITIES

What's hot in Curaçao?
www.kikotakiko.com

Curaçao Sea Aquarium
www.curacao-sea-aquarium.com

Curaçao Liqueur
www.curacaoliqueur.com

Curaçao Ostrich and Game Farm
www.ostrichfarm.net

Golf information
www.bluebay-golf.com

Curaçao Triathlon Association
www.triathlon-curacao.com

Private marine for small yachts
www.geocities.com./kimakalki/

ASSOCIATIONS

Association of Antillean Contractors
(Antilliaanse Aannemers Vereniging, AAV)
Fransche Bloemweg 4
Tel: (+599-9) 737-0201
Fax: (+599-9) 737-0203

Association of Industrialists of the Netherlands Antilles(ASINA)
Kaya Junior Salas 1
Tel: (+599-9) 461-2353
Fax: (+599-9) 465-8040

Association of International Bankers N.A. (IBNA)
A.M. Chumaceiro Boulevard 3
Tel: (+599-9) 461-5367
Fax: (+599-9) 461-5369
Website: www.ibna.an

Association of Public Notaries
(Antilliaans-Arubaanse Notariele Vereniging)
Gaitoweg 2
Tel: (+599-9) 737-1111
Fax: (+599-9) 737-1133

Bar Association of Curaçao
(Orde van Advocaten)
Polarisweg 17
Tel: (+599-9) 465-3250
Fax: (+599-9) 461-7172

Curaçao Hospitality & Tourism Association (CHATA)
Kaya Junior Salas 1
Tel: (+599-9) 465-1005
Fax: (+599-9) 465-1052
E-mail: information@chata.org

Curaçao International Financial Services Association (CIFA)
A.M. Chumaceiro Boulevard 3
Tel: (+599-9) 461-5371
Fax: (+599-9) 461-5378
E-mail:info@cifa.an
Website: www.cifa.an

Curaçao Trade & Industry Association

(Vereniging Bedrijfsleven Curaçao, VBC)
Pietermaai 21
Tel: (+599-9) 461-1210
Fax: (+599-9) 461-1366

Free Zone Association of Curaçao (FREZACUR)
Koningsplein z/n
Tel: (+599-9) 465-6070
Fax: (+599-9) 465-6101 / 465-0366

Insurance Association of the Netherlands Antilles (NAVV)
JB Gorsiraweg 6
Tel: (+599-9) 434-3800
Fax: (+599-9) 434-3873

Basic Laws and Regulations for conducting business and investment activity in the countries with special offshore status

Andorra Offshore Business Law Handbook
Anguilla Offshore Business Law Handbook
Bahamas Offshore Business Law Handbook
Barbados Offshore Business Law Handbook
Belize Offshore Business Law Handbook
Bermuda Offshore Business Law Handbook
British Virgin Islands Offshore Business Law Handbook
Cayman Islands Offshore Business Law Handbook
Cook Islands Offshore Business Law Handbook
Costa Rica Offshore Business Law Handbook
Cyprus Offshore Business Law Handbook
Dubai Offshore Business Law Handbook
Gibraltar Offshore Business Law Handbook
Grenada Offshore Business Law Handbook
Guernsey Offshore Business Law Handbook
Hong Kong Offshore Business Law Handbook
Ireland Offshore Business Law Handbook
Isle of Man Offshore Business Law Handbook
Jersey Offshore Business Law Handbook
Labuan Offshore Business Law Handbook
Liechtenstein Offshore Business Law Handbook
Luxembourg Offshore Business Law Handbook
Madeira Offshore Business Law Handbook
Malta Offshore Business Law Handbook
Mauritius Offshore Business and Investment Opportunities Handbook
Mauritius Offshore Business Law Handbook
Monaco Offshore Business Law Handbook
Nauru Offshore Business Law Handbook
Netherlands Antilles Offshore Business Law Handbook
Panama Offshore Business Law Handbook
Seychelles Offshore Business Law Handbook
Switzerland Offshore Business Law Handbook
Turks & Caicos Islands Offshore Business Law Handbook
Vanuatu Offshore Business Law Handbook

www.ingramcontent.com/pod-product-compliance
Ingram Content Group UK Ltd.
Pitfield, Milton Keynes, MK11 3LW, UK
UKHW051509290926
15471UKWH00008B/1515

9 781577 518815